Praise for *Designing*  *and Teaching Undergraduate Capstone Courses*

"Hauhart and Grahe have provided a road map for how to develop the undergraduate capstone course to fully engage students."

—Nancy H. Hensel, president, New American Colleges & Universities, and former executive officer, Council on Undergraduate Research

"Any department or faculty member implementing or revising a senior capstone course will find that this book offers useful background research in student development, teaching, and learning in a single source. The authors provide a variety of valuable techniques for managing faculty workload and creating quality student outcomes using examples from institutions of varying size and type."

—Julio Rivera, past president, Council on Undergraduate Research, and professor of management and marketing & geography and earth science, Carthage College

"A unique contribution to the literature and to practice, this book provides long-needed insights and guidance on the critical components of a capstone experience. These insights will resonate with curriculum developers, faculty, and managers in universities across the world. It will be of intense interest to all those who share the challenge and exhilaration of delivering the culminating student experience that is an undergraduate capstone or final year project."

—Nicolette Lee, associate professor, Australian Government Office for Learning and Teaching National Senior Teaching Fellow, Victoria University

"In the best tradition of Boyer's scholarship of teaching, Hauhart and Grahe provide both a systematic scholarly review of capstone courses in higher education and an insightful practical guide for designing and delivering capstones in all institutional settings. Drawing on faculty and student experiences, they demonstrate the great learning possibilities of capstones and outline a well thought-out set of best practices to evoke the best from students. This will certainly be the definitive resource for capstone faculty in the years ahead."

—Theodore E. Long, president emeritus, Elizabethtown College

"This book provides readers—faculty and academic administrators alike—with a well-grounded and comprehensive treatment of one of the most under-appreciated, and at times misunderstood, courses in the undergraduate curriculum: the senior capstone. Anyone in the academy interested in helping students better understand and make meaning of their undergraduate experience should keep this rich resource close at hand."

—Mary Stuart Hunter, National Resource Center for The First-Year Experience and Students in Transition at the University of South Carolina

"*Designing and Teaching Undergraduate Capstone Courses* is the only comprehensive guide to capstone courses in the social sciences. It contains useful reviews of the literature, specific guidelines, and many examples."

—Theodore C. Wagenaar, professor of sociology, Miami University

"A comprehensive guide for improving capstone experiences and value—across disciplines—for faculty and administration and, most important, our students. This book makes a significant contribution to the increasing knowledge and pedagogy of capstone experiences in higher education."

—Jean Johnson, chair, Society for the Teaching of Psychology National Capstone Project; associate professor emeritus, Governors State University

DESIGNING AND TEACHING UNDERGRADUATE CAPSTONE COURSES

Robert C. Hauhart and Jon E. Grahe

Consulting Editor, Maryellen Weimer

A Wiley Brand

Cover design by Lauryn Tom
Cover image: © iStockphoto | ma_rish

Published by Jossey-Bass
A Wiley Brand
One Montgomery Street, Suite 1200, San Francisco, CA
94104-4594—www.josseybass.com/highereducation

Jossey-Bass books and products are available through most bookstores. To contact Jossey-Bass directly
call our Customer Care Department within the U.S. at 800-956-7739, outside the U.S. at 317-572-3986,
or fax 317-572-4002.

Wiley publishes in a variety of print and electronic formats and by print-on-demand. Some material
included with standard print versions of this book may not be included in e-books or in
print-on-demand. If this book refers to media such as a CD or DVD that is not included in the version
you purchased, you may download this material at http://booksupport.wiley.com. For more
information about Wiley products, visit www.wiley.com.

Library of Congress Cataloging-in-Publication Data
Hauhart, Robert C., date-
  Designing and teaching undergraduate capstone courses / Robert C. Hauhart, Jon E. Grahe.—1
     1 online resource.— (Designing and teaching undergraduate capstone courses)
  Includes bibliographical references and index.
  Description based on print version record and CIP data provided by publisher; resource not viewed.
  ISBN 978-1-118-76196-0 (pdf)—ISBN 978-1-118-76200-4 (epub)—ISBN 978-1-118-76187-8 (pbk.)
1. Competency-based educational tests. 2. College students—Rating of. I. Grahe, Jon E., 1970- II. Title.
  LC1034
  375′.001—dc23

                                                                                    2014041871

Printed in the United States of America
FIRST EDITION
PB Printing   10 9 8 7 6 5 4 3 2 1

CONTENTS

Preface: The Importance of Senior Capstones in Contemporary
American Higher Education   ix

The Authors   xxi

Acknowledgments   xxiii

1   Overview of the Capstone Course   1

2   The Role of the Capstone Course in the Curriculum   15

3   Characteristics of the Capstone Course   39

4   The Role and Design of Research Projects Leading to the Capstone
Experience   61

5   Research Project Impediments and Possibilities   89

6   Designing the Capstone Course   103

7   Teaching the Capstone Course   137

8 Using the Capstone Course for Assessment   167

9 Conclusion: An Ideal Capstone Course   191

Notes   201

References   215

Name Index   239

Subject Index   245

PREFACE: THE IMPORTANCE OF SENIOR CAPSTONES IN CONTEMPORARY AMERICAN HIGHER EDUCATION

Even a brief review and discussion of the contemporary importance of the capstone in American colleges and universities suggests that the senior capstone has become a common feature of many curricula across the higher education landscape. The simple fact that a course has been adopted by many programs provides a persuasive argument for the importance of the topic generally. It would be a mistake to permit any curricular innovation as widespread as the senior capstone has become to escape examination, analysis, and review. Our book is intended to contribute to the emerging interest in designing and conducting effective senior capstones across the higher education curriculum. We conclude by laying out the plan for the book.

Many of you who have selected this book are already convinced of the importance of senior seminars or capstone courses within your discipline. There are many reasons that support your view. One is the sheer number of senior seminar or capstone courses currently offered in American colleges and universities. For example, we compared various national studies of capstone courses and estimated that over 70 percent of American baccalaureate-conferring institutions offer capstone experiences for academic credit. Considering the fact that there are more than eighteen hundred higher education institutions granting bachelor's degrees in the United States alone, graduating 1.5 million students annually, we can reasonably estimate that between 930,000 and 1,030,000 students throughout the country participate in a capstone experience each year. This is an extraordinary number. While numbers alone cannot dictate the importance of the senior seminar or capstone, no discipline or institution can ignore an experience that so many graduates will share.

There are, of course, many other reasons that the senior capstone course is worthy of our time and effort. As the culminating experience for students' undergraduate careers, the capstone is intended to tie together previous courses in theory, method, and substantive knowledge within most disciplines. There are many names and titles for capstone courses, as we shall see, but a common term that educators use to distill the essence of these courses and convey this goal is *integrative* whether the word appears in the title or catalogue description of the course or not (Boysen, 2010; Ault & Multhaup, 2003; Heise, 1992). Capstone courses also provide students with a final opportunity to demonstrate their mastery of important skills before they graduate. Creating an environment in which both synthesis of prior learning and exhibition of learned skill sets can be accomplished in a single setting is a daunting task for any course, especially a one-semester course, as many capstones remain. Therefore, it behooves us to devote suitable attention to the design and implementation of the senior seminar class. Interdisciplinary capstones attempt perhaps even a more challenging task: to tie together the particular emphases within a discipline to the broader learning sought by a general education program or the liberal arts generally. In either case, the capstone experience warrants our critical examination, as the editor of *Peer Review* acknowledged by dedicating the fall 2013 (vol. 15, no. 4) issue solely to its discussion.

The senior capstone can be a scintillating and intellectually challenging summation to the undergraduate experience, and in many cases, existing capstone courses achieve this goal. Schermer and Gray (2012), in their study of four liberal arts colleges that require a senior experience, note the importance of the senior capstone in providing the setting for a "transformative [intellectual and academic] experience." While their report generally found positive support for the senior experience from all sectors of each university community, they noted a bifurcation among faculty experiences based on student readiness, engagement, and execution. Faculty reported positive experiences where working one-on-one with students produced an engaged, collaborative learning environment and resulted in a successful outcome. Faculty reported less-than-positive experiences when students were underprepared for the challenge of engaging in independent but guided research and were not motivated to invest in the opportunity and challenge that the senior experience entailed (Schermer & Gray, 2012). Our own experience has mirrored these findings, and we have seen it reflected in the student experience as well.

A student of Robert's who experienced her senior seminar as positive is representative of those students ready to engage in a transformative undergraduate capstone experience. Entering her senior year, the student possessed a 3.85 grade point average, had worked successfully with her faculty mentor in many undergraduate classes, and identified a topic of personal interest. She proceeded to develop a comprehensive research plan for her topic, largely executed on her plan, and wrote a superlative thesis. She then worked with her seminar adviser to revise her work for submission to a respected professional journal, where it was accepted for publication. In an interview for the college website, she described her capstone course experience this way: "I worked on the thesis for a semester, continued to work on it over winter break, and through the better half of spring semester. I was relieved when it was accepted for publication. [I] couldn't have done it without the support and encouragement of [Professor] Hauhart. Saint Martin's has given me the opportunity to work closely with the faculty." Clearly students who can be shown the benefit of the senior seminar through a positive experience will gain by integrating the content and skills acquired through years of learning. Later these same students will be able to use their learning to contribute to solving short- and long-term problems within their discipline and enjoy a satisfying professional career. In the course of doing so, they will begin to form a professional network that can serve as the basis for a lifelong engagement with their discipline, the ideals of higher education, their home institution, and society generally.

Unfortunately, the truth of the matter is that some students do not have positive experiences and truly despise their undergraduate capstone. There are many reasons for such a negative experience. However, the simple fact that they do occur is also a reason to examine the design and execution of capstone courses carefully. It is arguable that a better-designed, better-implemented capstone course could reduce the number of students who do not believe they benefit from the experience. A student response to an open-ended question in a course evaluation survey in Robert's criminal justice capstone course sounded this more negative tone. The response read, "I am so done with all of this; you will get no more blood from me." And this was a response to a senior seminar course that consistently receives uniformly positive commendations from the student audience!

These examples, both positive and negative, mirror our experiences with senior capstone students and seem consistent with the student feedback noted in Schermer and Gray's (2012) final report to the Teagle Foundation, the funding source for their study. Comments like these also reflect anecdotal feedback that we receive from other instructors who teach capstone courses with whom we have spoken. When students enter a senior capstone and must develop a project without sufficient preparation or less-than-enthusiastic motivation, and then face a program that suffers from poor design, limited resources, external limitations, or lackluster delivery, it is little wonder that the experience is less positive than it could be. However, if the student experiences a senior seminar course that has been thoughtfully designed, fully supported, and carefully implemented, the experience should be a positive one and memorable for decades. A capstone experience that fulfills these goals will be a fine introduction to a professional life filled with similar challenges. Our task in this book is to identify the factors that will create a learning environment for the senior capstone that will support, within the limits of the contemporary college or university setting, the potential for a successful, transformative senior experience.

Capstone courses today take many forms, with varying goals and teaching modes. The courses are influenced by the size and type of institution, as well as the academic discipline, but they most commonly share one primary purpose: to help the student integrate learning material considered the core of the intellectual discipline in which the capstone is offered. Research has shown that in the vast majority of cases, students are most likely to complete a major project as part of this course (Hauhart & Grahe, 2012; Henscheid, Breitmeyer, & Mercer, 2000; Padgett & Kilgo, 2012; Schermer & Gray, 2012). Some classes focus almost exclusively on the project, with few lectures or no class time at all. Others include more lectures and classroom discussion, with some focused on content more than a project. A further distinction is that internship and nonacademic professional experiences are sometimes defined as capstone experiences for credit as well. A final critical distinction is between courses that are discipline specific and those that are interdisciplinary. We have attempted to approach the topic of the senior seminar or capstone course comprehensively with reference to each of these variations.

Throughout the book, we focus on the best practices in designing and teaching these courses so that students can have a transformative capstone experience rather than a negative one. Our discussion of the best practices for developing and delivering senior capstone experiences is based on the best research we have been able to locate, both our own or the peer-reviewed research that others have conducted in various disciplines. While we acknowledge that high-quality culminating experiences can take the form of a lecture-based class with exams and no papers, we find that the courses that prompt students to deeply process material through the use of a research project are most successful as senior capstone courses. Thus, projects that in one way or another compel students to integrate complex material across a discipline, or between disciplines, constitute the ideal course framework in our view. This is one reason we devote more discussion to research-based capstone courses, regardless of discipline. Though we acknowledge that this bias about the ideal course is not shared by all, it is supported by the literature arising from many fields of study and reflects the original intent of the course. We hope this book makes a convincing case for the inclusion of major research projects within the senior capstone experience.

While it is important to address how we should define a capstone experience and then design a program to meet that definition, there is also the question of whether these courses actually deliver the intended benefits to students and the community of scholars. A recent report (Schermer & Gray, 2012) studying the impact of capstone courses on student learning indicated that not all students are reaping the benefits of a culminating experience. With the skyrocketing costs of education and the increasing development of online degrees, the question of whether dedicating substantial resources to a single course required of all majors across the traditional bricks-and-mortar institution is a prudent use of resources emerges as a critical one. We argue that studies questioning the value of achieving these limited impacts can be addressed, and the failures they record mitigated, with better resources for faculty and better-motivated and better-prepared undergraduates. To that end, we intend this book to serve as a resource to the instructors of capstone courses and the departments and institutions that administer them.

The critical examination that has been extended to the senior capstone experience within higher education is relatively recent. While we have gathered together what we consider to be the very best research on capstone courses to date, we anticipate that future research will elaborate, and in some instances amend, our current knowledge. Therefore, we invite you to join with us in developing capstone course design and pedagogy in the years ahead.

We began this study of capstone courses a number of years ago after we met as new faculty members at Pacific Lutheran University. When Robert moved on to accept a tenure-track position at nearby Saint Martin's University, he assumed responsibility for teaching the existing capstone course in criminal justice. When he could not find sufficient, easily accessible, quality resources to guide his first foray into teaching a capstone course, we examined the existing literature. While we found many papers offering anecdotal accounts of capstone experiences at single institutions, we found these reports were only modestly helpful since the observations they contained were limited to the context from which they arose. In response, we began the inquiry that led to our current line of research by conducting regional and national surveys to try to identify common patterns, and ultimately best practices, across many schools (Grahe & Hauhart, 2013; Hauhart & Grahe, 2010, 2012).

Our surveys revealed few structural or functional differences between the capstones offered by sociology and psychology departments' courses. Rather, we found a number of common practices that appeared to lend themselves to successful outcomes. As we explored other fields beyond our own, we found that most capstone courses were structured similarly as well. Consequently, we place a great deal of emphasis on the framework and structural design that undergirds the successful capstone experience.

Our continuing investigation of the senior capstone experience suggests to us that while there has been considerable recent interest in capstone courses, there has been little systematic study of best practices in teaching these courses across the entire range of the university curriculum to date. Contemporary writing on capstone courses by others similarly suggests that the lack of a sufficiently developed, quality capstone literature still exists, although the research has markedly improved in recent years. As recently as 2012, Padgett and Kilgo described what they characterized as a "surprising dearth" of research on capstones at the student, institutional, and programmatic levels.

To the degree that others struggle with finding their own resources for teaching capstone courses, it is little wonder that the intended benefits are not clearly evident. One consequence seems to be a hunger for better information about forming and leading a successful capstone course. In 2008, for example, we proposed a symposium on the study of social science capstones at the Pacific Sociological Association's annual conference in Portland, Oregon. We each intended to give a talk and hoped that there would be enough interest to garner two additional presenters. The response was so overwhelming that we were granted a second full session so that we could accommodate more of the proposed presentations. In the sessions, we heard a number of thoughtful summaries of how different institutions organized and delivered their capstone courses and the challenges instructors faced. The presentations did not, by and large, satisfactorily resolve our quest for better capstone designs, methods, and materials. Like much of the writing on capstones we had been reading, the presentations often remained mired in the specific circumstances and context of particular departments, disciplines, and institutions.

Consequently, one of our major goals in this book is to show that there exists broad agreement across many disciplines in the modern university regarding a number of structural features that produce more successful capstone courses than otherwise. In this regard, our book will be broadly comparative in each chapter rather than narrowly focused and discipline specific. We do, however, provide some discipline-specific resources and a more targeted discussion for major academic divisions in our online appendixes and we refer readers to that source. The appendixes may be accessed at https:/osf.io/tg6fa/. We have also tried to combine the most reliable and valid findings from both discipline-specific and interdisciplinary studies. By doing so we hope to be able to make recommendations about the best practices for capstone courses generally based on a broad range of research. Our goal throughout will be to provide the best guidance currently available based on a comprehensive review of the capstone literature over the past thirty years. While we focus our attention on the undergraduate capstone, many of the studies we relied on, and principles we have recommended, have applicability to graduate capstone seminars as well.

The Plan of This Book

Our plan for this book has grown organically out of the several decades of development and scholarly comment on the capstone course that have preceded our effort. Having immersed ourselves in the existing capstone literature, we have attempted to distill the most significant contemporary issues and questions that confront university and college teachers as they face designing and teaching an undergraduate capstone course, whether within their discipline or in some cross-disciplinary form. The chapters that follow address these issues in a logical progression that discusses them in the order that the questions will likely present themselves to practitioners engaged in planning capstone courses.

We begin in chapter 1 with a brief history of the capstone course within American higher education. We then follow with a capsule assessment of the status of the contemporary capstone course and summarize succinctly some of the more recent studies of note that we will discuss in more detail in subsequent chapters. Chapter 2 addresses the role of the capstone course within the curriculum. As our preliminary remarks have suggested, the senior capstone course does not exist in a curricular vacuum. Rather, a capstone course always rests on a curricular foundation, whether it does so unconsciously and implicitly or intentionally and explicitly. Naturally a well-designed, thoughtfully developed capstone course will grow more successfully out of intentional, explicit, and articulable decision making than otherwise would be the case. The purpose of this chapter is to review the range of considerations that should guide this planning. Among the factors to consider are the existing (or planned) curriculum the senior experience is intended to "cap," the objectives of the capstone course, the specific format identified for the course, and the outcomes, including tangible products, sought.

We follow our discussion of the role of the capstone course within American university curricula by addressing the common characteristics of capstone courses in chapter 3. A number of recent studies have collectively identified a series of core characteristics that typify senior capstone courses across the range of American higher education institutions. Taken together, these common features of the capstone course offer a portrait of the typical contemporary capstone experience. Ultimately this portrait of the forms and features of contemporary senior capstones paves the way for our assessment of the existing practices identified within the literature. Like our discussion of the role of the capstone, this discussion is foundational in the sense that it creates baseline standards that can form the basis for comparison across many institutions and several dimensions. The empirical basis for some of the best practice principles we later propose are found in the studies we summarize here.

Chapter 4 discusses undergraduate research opportunities throughout the core curriculum. Our research in sociology and psychology suggests that in these disciplines the major research project predominates (Hauhart & Grahe, 2010, 2012). Other studies suggest the same is true in history, political science, and the natural sciences, although the data do not permit us to categorically reach this conclusion for every liberal arts discipline. Here we will discuss the role and related design of core curriculum courses leading to the capstone experience that are specifically research based. Major questions include whether the research plan pursued in these prerequisite courses should be derived from existing faculty research or independently inspired by a student proposal and whether a discipline-supported database or research agenda should be created to foster undergraduate involvement in scientifically sound research studies.

Chapter 5 is devoted to a brief discussion of the impediments to undergraduate research generally, including in research capstones. We address issues related to project outcomes, project limitations, common impediments, and—on the brighter side—best practices that improve the likelihood of successful undergraduate research experiences. Generally we believe that learning to manage research projects through sequential prerequisites is the best preparation for completion of the typical capstone course that characterizes most academic disciplines. Readers who do not plan to offer a research capstone may wish to focus their attention on subsequent chapters that address capstone course design and teaching.

In chapter 6, we review the features to consider in designing a capstone course. In doing so, we discuss the limitations imposed by type and size of institution and other core variables, as well as bring in for consideration the principles that have been identified as contributing to core competencies sought through the capstone experience. Because many institutions already have senior capstones in one or more academic divisions, the discussion in this chapter lends itself equally to revising an existing capstone as it does to creating a new capstone where none previously existed. Among the various iterations for a senior capstone, we focus the bulk of the chapter on discipline-based capstones within major academic concentrations because these are the most common form of senior capstone regardless of type or size of institution. Padgett and Kilgo (2012), for example, found that the discipline-based course was by far the most common format in responses to their survey. Hauhart and Grahe (2010, 2012) found that within sociology and psychology, the disciplined-based research capstone was most common. Regardless of the data set, the results of several studies suggest that the most common culminating experience offered now is one within an academic major. Interdisciplinary capstones or capstones dedicated to accessing the values found within general education programs are in the minority. Our emphasis throughout the book is driven by this recognition.

We follow our discussion of designing the senior capstone by addressing the qualitative factors that should inform the execution and day-to-day teaching of the capstone course in chapter 7. In doing so, we use *teaching* in the broadest possible sense to include managing, supervising, guiding, and mentoring. Although capstone formats may vary widely, from preparation of a library-based senior thesis to a field research project to an internship-based senior experience, we will argue that research has identified a number of principles that support successful capstone outcomes regardless of the variations among approaches. In essence, there are better and worse ways to lend direction to the senior experience. We explore those practices.

The penultimate chapter addresses what some academicians consider the bane of contemporary higher education—assessment—and the role the capstone course has often been asked to play in evaluating academic majors or programs. In one sense, those who have urged the use of the capstone course as a primary basis for assessing a program have a number of persuasive points in their favor. At the same time, there are obvious potential pitfalls in pinning the evaluation of an entire program on a single course, however integrative and summative in nature. Moreover, there is the question of the criteria for assessment, especially given the unique nature of the capstone course. We review several approaches that have been developed for use in assessing capstone courses and comment on their suitability for both course and programmatic assessment purposes.

The final chapter succinctly summarizes the structural, organizational, and process features that we believe can produce the ideal capstone. Chapter 9 is intended to provide a point-by-point summation of the most important issues and the best practices for resolving them. In our online appendixes (https://osf.io/tg6fa/), we provide some sample capstone documents and short descriptions of published, peer-reviewed literature on capstones across common disciplines in American colleges and universities that illustrate practical application of important principles.

How to Use Our Book

While our plan for this book attempts to organize the discussion and the capstone literature in a way that makes sense, we recommend that each reader use the book as a resource in the manner that is most helpful. Thus, readers whose department or university already offers a disciplinary or interdisciplinary capstone may find more of interest in the "teaching" chapter than the "create and design" chapters. Conversely, readers who are investigating the adoption of a capstone course requirement, and thus faced with creating one, may possess more interest in the "capstone design" sections of the book. Academic administrators who wish to sponsor a campus retreat on the capstone course will find thought-provoking issues and inspiration in several chapters. Finally, readers who are more concerned about assessing their programs may benefit most from the chapter on using the capstone course for program assessment purposes. In short, for many readers, we do not believe that reading the entire book, front to back, constitutes the most beneficial approach. Rather, we view our book as a capstone resource and urge readers to use it in the manner that will be most helpful to them.

THE AUTHORS

Robert C. Hauhart is professor of criminal justice and legal studies and is social justice and prelaw advisor at Saint Martin's University, Lacey, Washington. He received the BS degree in education from Southern Illinois University and studied sociology at Washington University, St. Louis (AM), and the University of Virginia (PhD). He then studied law at the University of Baltimore School of Law and was admitted to the bar and practiced law in Maryland, Pennsylvania, New York, and the District of Columbia. From 1988 to 2001, Hauhart was a supervising attorney for the District of Columbia Public Defender Service, responsible for investigating conditions in the district's jail and prison system. Since that time, he has taught at the University of Maine at Machias, the University of New Mexico, Pacific Lutheran University, and Saint Martin's University, where he has taught the capstone course in criminal justice and legal studies each semester since 2005–2006. His scholarly work has appeared in *Teaching Sociology, Teaching of Psychology*, the *American Sociologist, Criminal Law Bulletin*, and *International Journal for the Humanities*, among other scholarly journals and reviews.

◆ ◆ ◆

Jon E. Grahe is a professor of psychology at Pacific Lutheran University, Tacoma, Washington. He received a BA degree in psychology from Shippensburg University and studied experimental social psychology at the University of Toledo. He taught at Monmouth College from 1997 to 2005, where he started teaching capstone courses both within the discipline and as an interdisciplinary general education course. Since 2005, he has taught at Pacific Lutheran University, where he primarily teaches research methods and the occasional capstone course while acting as a faculty mentor for many capstone students. He also serves as an executive editor for the *Journal of Social Psychology*; as the Western Region vice president for Psi Chi, the international psychology honor society; and as a psychology councilor for the Council for Undergraduate Research. In addition to his collaborations with Robert in teaching journals, his scholarly work has appeared in *Perspectives on Psychological Science, Journal of Social Psychology, Journal of Clinical and Social Psychology,* and *Personality and Social Psychology Bulletin* among other scholarly journals. Most recently he has been organizing collaborative research opportunities for undergraduates across institutional lines and generally advancing open science initiatives.

ACKNOWLEDGMENTS

Writing a book is an enormous task. Fortunately, all authors are blessed with support from various people who are, in a certain sense, as responsible for the sustained effort the writing entails as the authors. We are fortunate to have been supported in our effort by many people.

We thank at the outset our home institutions: Saint Martin's University, Lacey, Washington, and Pacific Lutheran University, Tacoma, Washington. Within our respective schools, we thank the collegial and supportive climate of our disciplinary homes—the Department of Society and Social Justice (for Robert) and the Department of Psychology (for Jon). The faculty and administration of both our schools have been uniformly encouraging in offering support for our efforts, and for this we are warmly appreciative.

We offer special thanks to Maryellen Weimer, who encouraged us to write this book, supported its acceptance by Jossey-Bass, and commented extensively on our work. At Jossey-Bass, we thank David Brightman for expressing interest in the project and offering us a contract; Beverly Miller for her copyediting work; Joanne Clapp Fullagar and Shauna Robinson for shepherding the book through various stages of production; and Theodore C. Wagenaar, Kathleen Jones, and one anonymous reviewer for their helpful comments.

In addition to our general thanks, we each acknowledge those whose friendship, collegiality, and intellectual contributions to this project we appreciate receiving.

◆ ◆ ◆

It seems to me particularly appropriate in a book about the senior capstone experience to acknowledge the substantial debt I owe to the more than one hundred students at Saint Martin's University who have successfully completed senior seminar under my direction since 2006–2007. Among those students, I particularly acknowledge the four former students whose projects I use to illustrate several principles in the book: Kimberly Menius, Courtney Carter Choi, Stacia Wasmundt, and Jessica Flores. Courtney Choi's project, in particular, deserves mention as she pursued it well beyond the confines of senior seminar to the point where, together, we published a revised version in a nationally recognized law journal. There is hardly any better testament to a successful capstone experience than that result. I thank all of my students for their unintended contributions to the work that became this book.

For their unfailing support, I also thank Diane Wiegand (whose assistance seems boundless), Jeff Birkenstein, Jeff Torlina, Aaron Goings, Katya Shkurkin, Carol Overdeep, David Price, Karen Jaskar, Kirsti Thomas, Serin Anderson, Julia McCord Chavez, Jill Joanis, Dr. Paul Herstein, Professor Lynn McLain, Todd Hanson, Murray Milner Jr., Rob Silzer, and, of course, my good friend, colleague, and coauthor, Jon Grahe.

Robert C. Hauhart
Lacey, Washington
Placitas, New Mexico
Petit Manan Point, Maine

◆ ◆ ◆

So many colleagues have contributed to my understanding of the capstone course that it is difficult to identify them individually. However, my colleagues at the Monmouth College psychology department who shared the capstone experience every semester for eight years certainly helped me grasp the opportunities and costs of capstone courses. At Pacific Lutheran University, though all the faculty members contribute to capstone course discussion, syllabi, and materials that we share as a program, some colleagues deserve special thanks: Teru Toyokawa, Wendy Shore, Christine

Moon, and Michelle Ceynar. I thank the dozens of students who completed research projects with me at both institutions and presented our work at conferences or submitted our work for publication. I also thank the PLU students who worked as research assistants to help us conduct the regional and national survey studies that ultimately led to this book.

I extend special thanks to Amy Stewart-Mailhot for providing research assistance and helping me navigate beyond psychology in the library. I also thank my children, Alexandra and Brady, and my wife, Lisa, who endured the Year of the Book. In the previous year, we enjoyed our "year at Mt. Rainier" by completing over forty lengthy hikes in twelve months. I can never repay them for their patience as we replaced that with a year of laptops, research, and writing. Finally, I acknowledge that my weekly research meetings with Robert Hauhart that occurred with few cancellations the past nine years on Tuesday afternoons between racquetball games were critical not only to the development of this book but also to my health and professional career generally.

Jon E. Grahe
Tacoma, Washington

DESIGNING AND TEACHING UNDERGRADUATE CAPSTONE COURSES

CHAPTER ONE

OVERVIEW OF THE CAPSTONE COURSE

In this chapter, we briefly review the introduction of the capstone to the American university curriculum and its subsequent development into a central feature of American higher education. We devote special emphasis to the centrality of the capstone course across a broad range of disciplines and an introduction of the goals often sought by educators in their capstone course. Our review focuses special attention on the nature of the senior capstone experience in the new millennium and summarizes briefly some of the recent capstone studies that we rely on throughout this book. This review supports two important points: (1) capstone courses are now offered or required at two-thirds to three-fourths of US baccalaureate institutions and (2) the disciplinary-based capstone course is far and away the most common format across these institutions. We also comment in this overview on the benefits that can be obtained by studying the negative case of the unsuccessful capstone course or practice and discuss the differences inherent in the discipline-based capstone as compared to the interdisciplinary, or general-education-based, capstone.

The History of the Capstone Course in the College Curriculum

Although the capstone course is embedded in academic disciplines that range across the entire curriculum in most US undergraduate institutions, the contemporary emergence of the senior capstone as a common academic offering did not occur until the late 1980s and early 1990s. According to some sources, capstone courses emerged first in the United States in the late eighteenth century. At that time and for many years following, it was not uncommon for college presidents to teach courses on philosophy and religion to advanced students approaching the termination of their formal undergraduate studies. These courses were broadly conceived rather than discipline specific and sought to span the liberal arts curricula of that day and time. President Mark Hopkins of Williams College in Massachusetts led such a course in the 1850s that influenced his student, James A. Garfield, who later became the twentieth president of the United States (Henscheid & Barnicoat, 2003). For the better part of the late nineteenth and early twentieth centuries, capstone courses remained idiosyncratic and occasional rather than common. New capstone courses appeared in curricula whenever a faculty member or college president wished to sponsor one, and existing capstone courses languished and disappeared whenever the sponsor lost interest. There is scant record of capstones reported from the period during the twentieth century's great wars and the worldwide depression of the 1930s.

The courses apparently began to reemerge as a feature of American higher education in the early 1970s. Still, they were far from common. In the 1970s, for example, only 3 percent of American institutions reported offering capstone courses (Levine and Carnegie Council on Policy Studies in Higher Education, 1978). In the 1980s and 1990s, the number of senior capstone courses in American higher education dramatically increased. The capstone became more widely dispersed across the curriculum as well. Scholarship regarding the course coincided with its increasing popularity. Many of the research and scholarly articles that we will discuss as foundational are from this era. Completing the historical arc, the capstone course became widely popular only toward the end of the millennium (Levine, 1998; Lucas, 2006; Thelin, 2011). In sum, the senior seminar or capstone course became a prominent feature in formal higher education in the United States only within the past few decades. Thirty years after these courses made a notable reappearance in the 1970s, over half of the institutions of higher learning in the United States offered them in one or more disciplines (Henscheid, Breitmeyer, & Mercer, 2000).

Since 2000, more frequent pedagogical studies of capstone courses have attempted to track the growth in their popularity. However, recent estimates of the prevalence of senior capstones within US higher education vary, and sometimes widely. Researchers have estimated the presence of capstones in American colleges and universities at from 40 to 98 percent. If we were to combine all the distinct samples that have estimated the proportion of institutions that offered capstones, we could reasonably conclude that approximately three-fourths of four-year higher education institutions offer capstone courses in the United States. When considering the entire history of American higher education, one is disposed to ask why capstone courses emerged across the broad range of American colleges and universities only recently. Moreover, one is inspired to wonder whether the recent trend can sustain itself or whether the capstone's popularity will wane in the future, as predicted by the authors of the "Capstone" entry in the *Higher Education Encyclopedia* (Henscheid & Barnicoat, 2003).

Sources of Modern Influence

The story of the development of the capstone in the 1980s and 1990s suggests that the emphasis was an outgrowth of a number of reports regarding higher education at that time. Moreover, there is a general history of American higher education curricular development driven by committee and foundation reports. In the 1950s, for example, the Dartmouth College political science department was stimulated to develop its capstone course as a result of a college wide report on curricular change and an earlier American Political Science Association report (Garfinkel & Tierney, 1957; American Political Science Association, 1951). These reports inspired the formation of a committee on the integration of the political science major, and that committee recommended a new "coordinating course" as a culminating experience for political science majors at Dartmouth (Garfinkel & Tierney, 1957). The surge in capstone courses during the 1980s and 1990s perhaps simply reflected the number and prestige of the several reports that supported and encouraged capstone course adoption. This influence is also easily observable within American sociology during this period. In chapter 2, we use that experience to illustrate the process of disciplinary curricular change that led to more widespread adoption of the capstone experience across many academic departments.

In 1985 the Association of American Colleges (AAC) produced an influential report, *Integrity in the College Curriculum: A Report to the Academic*

Community. The report identified a number of intellectual qualities and learning experiences that the authors believed to be missing from the higher education climate on many college campuses. These included, among others, critical analysis, writing, values, and study in depth—that is, a number of the learning objectives that could be embraced and fostered through adoption of a capstone course (Wagenaar, 1993). Wagenaar's own review of the state of the capstone in sociology at the time of his writing led him to conclude that many sociology faculty members misunderstood the nature of the capstone. He called for developing a sociology capstone that was synthetic, holistic, interdisciplinary, and required, citing the educational goals identified in the AAC's report.

Dickinson (1993), also noting the influence of national commission studies of higher education, observed that the emphasis on capstones within sociology in the early 1990s was driven in part by subsequent reports from the Association of American Colleges (1991) and the American Sociological Association (1991). Both reports emphasized the importance of critical reflection, connectedness, and diversity through a capstone that encourages students to integrate the range of coursework in the major in a focused, summative conception that provides a coherent conclusion to the undergraduate curricula. The impetus of the AAC in influencing curricular review can be found in the annals of many disciplines during the 1980s and 1990s. The biological sciences, like American sociology, undertook such a review and focused substantial attention on the capstone course as well as the undergraduate research experience generally (Carter, Heppner, Saigo, Twitty, & Walker, 1990). A few years later, Wagenaar (1993) described the emergence of the capstone course within American sociology and called for even greater adoption of the approach. The Boyer Commission report (1998) also recommended the capstone course as a critical addition to the higher education curriculum, thereby fostering the trend within sociology and other disciplines. That same year, Gardner and Van der Veer (1998) published a highly influential book on the senior experience that further focused attention on capstones within the contemporary undergraduate curriculum.

In a more recent recollection of the development of the capstone course in the history major, Jones, Barrow, Stephens, and O'Hara (2012) similarly recalled the importance of the Boyer Commission report (1998) as a reason for the renewed contemporary interest in the course. They point to this report as producing an emphasis on "liberal idealism" that led to "provid[ing] all undergraduates opportunities to 'do' real history" (p. 1096). They also note two other factors that are consistent with other reports prepared by historians: a practical motive of "outcomes assessment" and "administrative attention to undergraduate research opportunities." The capstone course provides ideal avenues to introduce both of these practical, rather than idealistic, motives because students are encouraged to complete research during the course, and research projects can be assessed in a more straightforward manner.

Where Things Stand: The Capstone Course in the New Millennium

Our short synopsis of the historical development of the modern capstone course reaches its curricular apogee today. Over the past dozen or so years, a series of foundational studies have been published that now constitute the baseline data for analysis and discussion regarding the senior capstone experience. We rely often on this group of research reports in the following chapters. These studies differ from earlier examinations of capstone courses primarily due to their more sophisticated methods and multi-institutional focus. Thus, they permit a broader comparative approach than most of the earlier anecdotal summaries of capstone courses that appeared in print. Since the data and conclusions offered by research are only as good as the methodology in place, we address the methods in each study so readers may judge for themselves the quality of the observations reported.

These studies collectively provide evidence that supports two important points. First, the data show that capstones are widely offered across many disciplines and that in most cases, those capstones are offered to students in their major fields of study and not as interdisciplinary or general education capstones. Second, these studies suggest that disciplinary capstones are most commonly research project capstones. The studies further suggest that students who participate in research-based capstones have positive experiences and develop cognitive and practical skills that students who do not engage in a research experience do not develop. These outcomes, in sum, provide persuasive evidence in our view that the capstone course makes important contributions to undergraduate education and that the research capstone, in particular, offers students the best opportunity for in-depth study leading to positive learning results. The more important studies include the following.

During summer 1999, the National Resource Center for the Study of the First Year Experience and Students in Transition at the University of South Carolina conducted a survey of capstone courses offered at American colleges and universities. Led by Jean Henscheid, with John Breitmeyer and Jessica L. Mercer, the researchers collected survey responses from 707 institutions; 549 of the responding institutions reported offering at least one capstone course. (Some respondents reported offering more than one capstone course across their curriculum.) Among the major findings, the authors reported that the courses were primarily designed and delivered by individual academic disciplines. The researchers also concluded that (1) among the least likely components of the courses were formats that took students out of the classroom; (2) capstone courses were commonly taught and administered by single instructors on behalf of academic departments; and (3) most of the courses were not at that time part of a comprehensive assessment process (Henscheid, Breitmeyer, & Mercer, 2000).

During spring 1998, Bauer and Bennett began an investigation of alumni perceptions of participation in undergraduate research as one measure of the value added by a research experience. The researchers mailed a survey to 2,444 alumni of the University of Delaware, a midsized research university with an undergraduate research program in place since 1980. The sample consisted of 865 graduates who had participated in the formal Undergraduate Research Progam (URP), each matched with two alumni who shared the same major, year of graduation, and grade point average but were not recorded in the URP database. The researchers attained a response rate of 42 percent. All respondents who reported undergraduate research experience reported high satisfaction and improved skills relating to that experience. Those who participated in the formal UR program, as compared to other research experiences, reported even greater ability to conduct research and registered more improvement in eight cognitive skills (Bauer & Bennett, 2003). This study lends support for undergraduate research both before and during the senior capstone course.

In summer 2000, researchers conducted seventy-six first-round student interviews with undergraduate students completing natural science-based capstones at one of four participating liberal arts colleges: Grinnell, Harvey Mudd, Hope, and Wellesley. In the interview, students were presented with a checklist of possible benefits derived from the literature and invited to comment. Students could also add benefits they discerned that were not on the list. Student response was overwhelmingly favorable: 91 percent of all student statements were positive. Generally, positive statements fell within one of seven areas with personal/professional (28 percent), thinking and working like a scientist (28 percent), and improved skills (19 percent) the most commonly expressed (Seymour, Hunter, Laursen, & DeAntoni, 2007).

In 2011 the National Resource Center for the First-Year Experience and Students in Transition at the University of South Carolina conducted a second national survey of senior capstone experiences. The 2011 sample yielded 276 responding institutions; 268 (97.1 percent) reported offering one or more senior capstones. Among the more important findings reported were that discipline-based courses led by a single instructor continued to be the dominant form of the capstone experience, although many institutions offered multiple types of capstones across campus. Public institutions were more likely to rely on a discipline-based traditional course, whereas private institutions were more likely to rely on a senior thesis or undergraduate research paper. Moreover, by 2011, more than half the respondents reported that capstone courses were part of the university's assessment program and that these respondents had formally evaluated the senior experience within the last three years (Padgett & Kilgo, 2012).

In November 2000, researchers studied four liberal arts colleges (Allegheny College, Augustana College, Washington College, and College of Wooster) that require each graduating senior to complete an intensive, mentored capstone experience. Data from surveys of the colleges' administrative structures, along with student and faculty mentor surveys, constituted the bulk of the first-phase data. In a second phase, data were collected from focus groups of students, faculty, and others. Survey data compiled from responses of 108 departments roughly split among the four colleges showed that two-thirds of departments have a course specifically designed to prepare students for the senior capstone experience, and 86.6 percent of departments reported "production of a senior thesis or substantial paper" as the specific course outcome sought by the department's capstone. With respect to student-faculty surveys, generally both students and mentors rated the senior capstone highly along a series of specific dimensions (Schermer & Gray, 2012).

In a study we began in 2007, we distributed an invitation to participate in an online survey to the chairperson of every department of sociology on the member list of the Pacific Sociological Association and the chairperson of every department of psychology on the member list of the Western Psychological Association. Two follow-up e-mails were sent to increase the response rate to the survey to 28 percent. We found that the overwhelming majority (75 percent) of four-year schools responding offered capstone courses, as did a slight majority (56 percent) of schools offering terminal master's degrees. PhD-granting institutions constituted the only group that did not offer an appreciable percentage of capstones (22 percent).

As a number of these studies have also found, a primary goal of the senior capstone experience within sociology and psychology programs is directed at helping students integrate material across a discipline. We also reported, as have a number of other studies, that the primary course outcome sought typically consisted of a major project leading to a field or library research paper (Hauhart & Grahe, 2010).

Another multi-institutional study within sociology (McKinney & Busher, 2011) confirmed the major findings of our regional survey. These researchers also found that the primary goal of these capstone courses was for students to engage in a major research project within sociology that would integrate their learning across the discipline and produce a final research paper. A discussion of factors in supporting, and student limitations in completing, successful capstone outcomes is also presented.

In a subsequent study, we replicated and extended our initial 2007 regional online survey by developing a national random sample of colleges and universities from the Carnegie Foundation for the Advancement of Learning institutional list and surveying the departments of sociology and psychology at those schools. From the total of 1,856 bachelor's-level or higher institutions on the Carnegie list, we selected a one-third sample from each of nine geographical regions and achieved a response rate of 25.44 percent. Like our previous regional survey and many other comparable efforts, we again found that the overwhelming majority of colleges and universities with sociology and psychology programs supported a senior capstone course—as high as 80 percent overall. Our national survey results confirmed that within sociology and psychology, and apparently like most other academic disciplines, the capstone course offered requires completion of a major project that entails research, a literature review, and an extended paper or senior thesis. Later we discuss the many other detailed findings our national survey revealed with respect to the most common practices and features of sociology and psychology capstone courses (Grahe & Hauhart, 2013; Hauhart & Grahe, 2012).

Finally, a study population of 597 undergraduate students from a single major public comprehensive university with enrollment in excess of thirty thousand was invited to complete the Undergraduate Research Questionnaire. The questionnaire consisted of thirty-two scaled items regarding the benefits derived from the undergraduate research experience: faculty support for undergraduate research methods and skills, academic benefits received, and experiences of peer support. Major findings suggested that (1) benefits derived from research participation depended on the extent of research involvement (i.e., number of hours engaged in research related activity), (2) faculty mentors play a significant role in student satisfaction and the perception that research engagement is valuable, and (3) students with high grade point averages generally invested more time in research-related activity and rated their experience more highly than those with lower averages (Taraban & Logue, 2012).

Collectively these studies map the general terrain and nature of contemporary capstone courses in US colleges and universities. The results they report form the foundation for our examination of the purposes sought by contemporary capstone courses, the form of those courses, and the structural design of capstone experiences that offer the best learning environment for students. It is apparent to us, however, that educators will continue to study and report on the evolution of the contemporary senior experience. Even as this book goes to press, the Centre for Collaborative Learning and Teaching at Victoria University in Melbourne, Australia, is engaged in organizing a network or scholars to extend capstone studies. (Interested readers may access the Capstone Curriculum Across Disciplines website at www.capstonecurriculum.com.au.) Thus, while we have gathered the best data, analyses, and recommendations regarding capstone practices currently available in the literature, we expect more extensive and refined research efforts will continue to appear. We invite readers to join us in documenting future research by visiting our website (https://osf. io/tg6fa/) and contributing to our collection of capstone materials.

The Importance of Examining the Negative Case

As we suggested very briefly in the Preface, not all reviews of the senior capstone experience reflect a positive assessment. Moreover, negative reviews are not limited to students. Upson-Saia (2013) recently reported that various pressures, including well-intentioned goals, created capstone course experiences that could not sustain the learning goals and department objectives that were added as the capstone course became the location for integration, application, and assessment. In our view, reports of negative experiences based on poor design or delivery of capstone experiences are an important starting point for analysis, reform, and revision. Therefore, we will often invite readers to join us in listening carefully to these negative assessments.

In her review of capstone courses offered in religion departments, Upson-Saia (2013) reports the overwhelming frustration she heard from her colleagues as they described their experience.[1] They noted limitations that echo other researchers, including poor motivation from students, limited faculty time, and insufficient faculty expertise. However, Upson-Saia attributed the problems to the course, not the students or the resources directly. This conclusion supports our contention that designing an effective capstone course is as, or perhaps more, important than simply "teaching" one.

Supporting the Disciplinary versus the Interdisciplinary Capstone

A capstone in architectural terms is, by definition, the coping stone that forms the top of a wall or the final stone placed in the center of an arch that will hold the entire, otherwise unstable, construction together. Thus, it is the crowning experience—within both architecture and an educational program—that is placed last and on top of the structure beneath it. In the academic setting, it is the course that integrates or knits together all the earlier educational experiences. It is the culminating experience for students.

The fact that we use the term *capstone* to refer to this final phase of an education suggests that there must be a coherent program to "cap," and this is a significant factor in developing the capstone. The fact is that a prerequisite to designing and executing a good capstone is a credible, sustained, coherent program on which the capstone may rest. In architectural terms, the "legs" of the arch or the base of the wall must be conceived well and solidly built before either will be able to support the capstone properly. With respect to a disciplinary capstone, this means the academic major must offer a solid, coherent core. The capstone course will then constitute the culminating experience that tops off the program's basic foundational courses.

The interdisciplinary or general education–related capstone presents a slightly different integrating challenge. By definition, an interdisciplinary program attempts to unite two or more orientations that may (or may not) share any substantial overlap in terms of substantive and theoretical concerns. Likewise, a capstone course that requires students to embrace broadly both their academic major and the academic values embedded in a liberal arts general education program must span many separate intellectual divisions in an effort to achieve an overarching goal. Here the architectural metaphor is less applicable since the diversity of a contemporary general education program nearly precludes finding an essential core shared by undergraduate students across an entire institution. Arguably, these differences make the interdisciplinary or general education–related capstone course even more challenging for both students and faculty than a capstone course within an academic major. This could explain why the interdisciplinary version of the capstone course has consistently been offered by a smaller number of institutions (Henscheid et al. 2000; Padgett & Kilgo, 2012).

Beyond these initial distinctions, capstones can embrace a number of different educational experiences, and throughout the subsequent chapters we remind readers of these variations at appropriate junctures. Padgett and Kilgo (2012) note, for example, senior capstones that encompass undergraduate research, a nonresearch-based thesis, a comprehensive examination, an internship experience, and a course leading to certification by an external professional body. Each of these variations on the senior capstone experience likely requires a different undergraduate preparation, envisions a different motivational script, and anticipates a different learning experience and course outcome. Schermer and Gray (2012) observe that each of the four institutions they studied has its own name for the culminating senior experience, and although each senior experience is different, they chose to subsume the four under the term *capstone* because of the several qualities that they believe all senior culminating courses share.

In short, the definition of the capstone must arise from the stated mission for a program or a specifically delineated goal or set of goals, be shaped in a way to help achieve those goals, and ultimately be judged by a set of outcomes specifically tailored to meet the objectives of the program. A capstone is therefore a creature of its context and must symbiotically respond to the educational environment in which it is enveloped in order to be considered successful. In subsequent chapters, we often emphasize the embedded nature of the capstone course in our discussions.

Conclusion

There is, as we hope to demonstrate in the balance of this book, a great deal of accumulating evidence that a properly organized capstone course can be a transformative educational experience for students and faculty alike. It is one of the high-impact practices that educators believe provide the best learning opportunities for students (Kinzie, 2012). We agree and believe that the culminating capstone experience unites faculty and students in an important shared venture that has the best opportunity to support intellectual challenge, dedication to undergraduate research, and an appreciation for scholarly activity. We do not think the capstone experience can be duplicated or achieved by any other single format currently recognized. We hope that the following chapters offer a lucid introduction to the many reasons and empirical studies that support this view. Still, we recognize that the senior capstone experience is not a self-activating one that can be installed, cookbook style, into an administrative unit of the modern academic division of labor. Sill, Harward, and Cooper (2009), in an evocative essay on the senior experience, offer an apt illustration of the slight differences that can separate the transformative educational experience from the ordinary, or mildly disappointing, one.

In the early 1990s, the senior assignment for studio art majors at Southern Illinois University's (SIU) Edwardsville campus asked seniors at year's end to collect a sample of their work that represented the skills they had acquired within various genres and mediums. Seniors were asked also to draft a short artistic statement describing their process and reflecting on the work they had accomplished. Faculty members then evaluated the miniportfolios and statements displayed, assessing both individual efforts and program success. The studio art majors did as they were instructed and installed their works throughout the art department building, and faculty dutifully reviewed all the works and rendered their judgment. Yet the results of this disciplinary effort were disappointing. Students, not fully appreciating the fact that the exercise was intended to be an integrative and reflective one, merely carried out what they viewed as their final assignment. Art faculty, facing a building full of mounted art on a Friday night late in the term, struggled to review and assess the work in a meaningful way and offer a collective evaluation. Neither the students nor the faculty experienced the deep immersion in learning and growth that a culminating experience should entail because the effort was episodic and individualized, not sustained and collectively experienced. It was, in short, not thoughtfully designed or programmatic in its execution but rather offhand, throwaway, and, in the end, alienating rather than affirming (Sill et al., 2009).

The revealing, and redemptive, lesson from Sill et al.'s (2009) account of the art studio capstone experience, however, is that the initial failed plan turned out not to be the end but rather the beginning of the art department's capstone program. Stung by the flat and disengaged nature of the student response to the assignment and equally disenchanted with the tediously uninspired demand to assess that experience, faculty collectively reorganized an existing course into a true senior culminating experience: Art 405. Rather than an experience tacked on to the senior year, Art 405 became a required, shared senior-year experience: a semester-long preparation of a representative portfolio of each student's work enlivened by a coherent program of classes devoted to integrating the senior year with earlier courses and work. Thus, a disappointing initiative was used to create a transformative educational experience for senior studio art majors and their faculty.

At our own institutions, like SIU-Edwardsville's Art Department, the onset of capstone courses also took place in the 1990s. The capstone experience became part of the expected culture for our graduating seniors. We conclude that this curricular trend was driven by the strong arguments presented by the American Association of Colleges and Universities and others who championed the traditional capstone course as a model for better-educated students. However, at some level, these changes also reflect the social normative nature of our educational system. We must recognize that the capstone course has become as integral to the curriculum of many disciplines as introductory courses. We believe, based on examining the many reports and studies we review in this book, that the senior capstone course is here to stay within American higher education for the immediately foreseeable future. Whether it will remain that way in the future is an open question.

Michael Stoloff and colleagues (2010), prominent researchers studying the scholarship of teaching psychology, may well be correct that we will see a decline in the prevalence of the capstone course. Stoloff et al. expressed their concerns regarding the sustainability of capstone programs after a noticeable difference between their sample estimate of the number of psychology departments offering capstones (40 percent) and earlier research estimates (60 percent). Contrary to Stoloff and colleagues, we find little evidence of any likely decline in interest in the capstone in our research to date. Rather, our research has confirmed that an increasing number of disciplines and institutions offer or require a senior capstone experience (Hauhart & Grahe, 2010, 2012; Grahe & Hauhart, 2013). Moreover, more professional peer-reviewed studies and publications regarding capstones are appearing, and an increasing number of educational bodies continue to call for more emphasis on the senior capstone rather than less emphasis. Ultimately only time and evidence will tell us whether there is an eventual decline in the offering of capstone courses within specific disciplines or more broadly across the liberal arts curriculum. In the meantime, we focus this book on how to best design and teach this course that is so prevalent across the majority of American four-year institutions today.

CHAPTER TWO

THE ROLE OF THE CAPSTONE COURSE IN THE CURRICULUM

There are multiple stated goals of capstone courses. These are worth exploring, both as a means of comparison for existing capstone courses and as a starting point for considering adoption of a senior capstone experience. Although there is a wide range of stated goals for various capstone courses, we found substantial consistency in our two samples of sociology and psychology departments (Hauhart & Grahe, 2010, 2012). Further review of the broad range of studies now available across the curriculum from other disciplines suggests that the goals we have identified as most common are widely shared.

We also review in this chapter the process of goal identification, disciplinary reflection, curricular examination, and capstone course development that universities and departments can expect when considering capstone course adoption. We use the experience of American academic sociology in the 1980s and 1990s to illustrate this process since it was, and remains, a bureaucratically entrenched academic specialty in American higher education and produced voluminous, and easily accessible, public records of its deliberations. Departments and schools that do not have an existing capstone course will especially benefit from this discussion. However, if your interest as a reader is limited to acquiring tips and guidance for approaches to use within an existing capstone course, you may wish to focus your attention on later chapters. Thus, readers whose interests are more instrumentally directed at the nuts-and-bolts mechanics of designing or teaching a senior capstone may wish to read further in chapters specifically dedicated to those issues.

Capstone Curricular and Learning Objectives

The purpose of capstone courses when they were developed in the late eighteenth century was to integrate concepts across the learning experience. In the two hundred years since, this remains the primary stated goal of the capstone within most universities and departments, although many other objectives have been identified as important. Since the content and approach to the capstone course are influenced significantly by the goals identified and pursued by faculty, students, and administrators, substantial time should be devoted to careful consideration of the objectives sought for the course. Often the goals sought for the capstone experience hover just below the level of articulable debate and thereby defeat collaborative examination. In our view, faculty committees designing a capstone course should voice and debate competing goals. One way of examining the range of objectives that should be considered in designing or revising capstone experiences is simply to study the goals identified by other departments and institutions over recent decades. A substantial literature is now available on capstones in American higher education; although there are serious gaps in that literature, a significant proportion is dedicated to a discussion of goal identification, formation, and selection for the capstone experience.

This chapter emphasizes the need for intentional choice in the selection of capstone objectives. We use two related discussions to guide us in this inquiry. First, we provide a capsule summary of the process pursued within academic sociology in the early 1990s, which led to the widespread adoption of capstones within that discipline. We do this as a way of illustrating representative tensions that we believe many academic disciplines face in times of curricular revision. Second, we examine broader studies of the senior experience movement in American higher education over the past two decades that sought to identify across the spectrum of disciplines the most common goals and structures developed for senior courses. Taken together, these approaches offer a number of important insights regarding the manner in which senior capstone courses are conceptualized and developed in almost any field of study. A university or department that is considering the adoption of a senior capstone experience where none has heretofore existed would be well advised, in our view, to review this chapter carefully.

Capstone Goals in Sociology: An Illustrative Case Study

Over the past twenty years, a significant proportion of the analysis of the capstone experience addressed the goals sought by those designing and managing the experience. Initially we should acknowledge that not all stakeholders in the senior capstone experience share equal influence in the formation of that experience. Administrators wield some influence by encouraging—through course development subsidies, for example—the broad outlines of curricular innovation. They do so also, to a degree, by participating as members of higher education commissions or committees that discuss the direction of higher education and lend their collective weight to decisions about educational policy. At the same time, it is faculty, by and large, who are responsible for specific changes to individual academic disciplines that are discussed and announced at the policy level of discussion. An examination of the historical process through which the senior capstone course became a focal point within an academic discipline makes it abundantly clear that it is the faculty who possess the most day-to-day interest in the shape of the senior experience. As one consequence of their teaching function, faculty members most often actively influence the design of the senior experience.

In 1993 the journal *Teaching Sociology* published a special number entitled "The Capstone Course" wholly dedicated to reviewing the senior capstone experience within American sociology departments. The articles published in this issue, which often devoted a substantial share of their discussion to the goals sought, offer both retrospect and prospect. As such, they collectively provide a window to where the discipline has been and where it believed it was headed at a particular time. The articles were exclusively written by teaching faculty since *Teaching Sociology* is a pedagogical journal edited by faculty for a faculty readership; neither administrators nor students were represented in these pages. Naturally faculty act within the broad policy initiatives in the air as one area of consideration, and administrators are often influential in creating the atmosphere in which specific curricular developments are pursued. The influence of reports issued by higher education policy committees is much in evidence in this issue of *Teaching Sociology*.

The articles from the special issue present a range of views that collectively address the goals-and-objectives question at some length. Examining academic sociology's debate is, we believe, an excellent way in which to illuminate the competing considerations that constitute this curricular terrain. It is a terrain that every program considering adoption of a new capstone course or revision of an existing capstone course must traverse.

The first two articles, by Wagenaar and Davis, put forward a consensus view of the discipline. Each represents to the reader, through citations, references, and argument, that there is one set of goals that is more or less generally accepted within academic sociology. Wagenaar (1993) seems to reach this view only after a committee representing the discipline's national association conducts a lengthy review process and adopts a set of proposed goals for study in depth. (Also see Wagenaar, 1991.) The study-in-depth theme is one that persists in discussions of the capstone within academic sociology from this time forward (Sherohman, 1997; Wagenaar, 2002). Davis (1993), writing retrospectively after the American Sociological Association (ASA) study process, simply accepts the adoption of a set of disciplinary goals as a fait accompli and resists any further examination of contradictory goals that other sociologists at the time publicly expressed.

The remaining nine authors whose views we summarize diverge from Wagenaar and Davis in ways big and small, radically and modestly. In some instances, they acknowledge the nature, extent, and direction of their deviation; in others, there is a tendency to gloss over some of the disciplinary disagreement. The result, in our view, is an illustration of the dynamic growing pains that will characterize the changes any discipline will likely experience when adopting or revising its curriculum. Disciplinary disagreements are not, in our experience, the province of any particular academic tradition. Thus, we offer our retrospective analysis of the process of curricular change in sociology as illustrative of the general nature of change that many departments and fields can expect to experience when they adopt or revise a capstone course.

Consensus Voices: Seeking Curricular Legitimacy through the Senior Capstone

Wagenaar (1993), the invited guest editor for the issue, establishes the disciplinary background for the 1993 *Teaching Sociology* articles by discussing the many departmental site evaluations, syllabus reviews, and professional conversations he conducted over the years and the impressions he gathered regarding the role of the capstone within the field. Generally he expressed concern that the capstone was misunderstood within sociology and that the course often became just another three-credit hurdle to completion of the undergraduate degree. He issued a call for a sociology capstone that was more truly integrative, interdisciplinary, and required as a means of compelling students to address the sum total of their learning within sociology. His recommendations for capstone course assignments reflected this emphasis on unifying the content of sociology through a broadly conceived engagement of in-depth study that would foster a range of educational values often proposed for the senior capstone. Wagenaar, a member of the discipline's Study in Depth Task Force, generally accepted the thirteen recommendations that the ASA adopted. His insider role within the professional association informs his approach to the capstone as an integrative experience consistent with the general tenor of educational policy recommendations at the time.

Davis's (1993) article is perhaps the most ambitious in the special issue in its attempt to delineate with specificity the various purposes the senior capstone course should pursue. Initially Davis notes that the traditional capstone "draws together the theoretical and empirical work in sociology . . . , serves as a bridge to graduate study, and helps students assume more active lives as citizens and consumers of knowledge" (p. 233). Davis (1993) then proceeds to articulate seven more specific functions that she believes should inform the sociology capstone that can be succinctly summarized:

1. Assisting students in envisioning what constitutes important sociological questions
2. Developing familiarity with the range of answers sociologists have offered in response to those questions and then developing answers of their own
3. Understanding how social theories may be subjected to empirical testing
4. Understanding the partiality of sociological questions, explanations, and empirical testing
5. Grasping how specific subfields within sociology relate to society and the discipline of sociology as a whole
6. Understanding how sociology fits into the wider liberal arts curriculum as a whole
7. Becoming aware of the choices that face us as human beings within the society and worlds within which we live

Thus, Davis's approach leaves the realm of rarefied policy discussion and subsumes itself more concretely in mapping out discrete goals for the formation and delivery of capstone courses. While her list of objectives does not solve the problem of tying policy directly to a particular general format or specific assignments, she moves one step closer by specifying a short list of identifiable outcome-directed goals.

Muddling Along: Forging a Path without a Rudder or Compass

The balance of the articles published in the special edition of *Teaching Sociology* are most useful for providing a glimpse into the manner in which an academic discipline struggles to develop the capstone in the absence of any extensive literature regarding best practices for the undertaking. The process, as the authors themselves often acknowledge, can be best characterized as "'hit or miss" or "a shot in the dark." A quick comparison of these early approaches within sociology reveals the crucial decisions that are often made on the basis of appealing rationales but a sheer absence of any comparative data regarding previously successful capstone experiences. Moreover, there is a somewhat disingenuous tendency to manufacture consensus where dissensus seems more often case.

Schmid (1993), mulling over the question of integration of the discipline, identifies a modestly different set of considerations for the senior capstone than Davis (1993), for example, did. Schmid notes that sociology education should be understood as more than a restatement of the theories, methods, and controversies that inform the discipline; it should involve some considerations of practical utility since most students will enter society rather than remain within the bubble that is academic sociology. He urges that the distinctiveness of the "sociological perspective" should be effectively conveyed to students and that this should extend beyond "just talking about" society to engagement with how one can "do sociology" in society and how that differs from, for example, direct action. Finally, he urges that the sociology capstone address the moral context within which the sociological perspective is experienced and practiced. Although Schmid acknowledges this goal can be approached in a number of ways, he favors a focus on cultural reflection that is both analytical and transformative. While it is far too glib to suggest that Schmid's and Davis's separate approaches to the appropriate goals for the sociology senior capstone have no overlap or interface, it is clear that the emphases between the two are different and diverge significantly.

Durel (1993), in his portrait of the senior capstone at Christopher Newport University, also arguably offers a significantly different conceptualization of the capstone in sociology than Davis does. Durel focuses on the role of the capstone as a required rite of passage in which graduating seniors look back at their undergraduate experience of sociology and attempt to integrate its primary lessons yet look forward to assuming new roles in society where they will be expected to deploy and exercise the lessons they learned. This suggests to Durel that a major purpose of the capstone is to foster separation from the role of student and incorporation into the role of active citizen within our participatory democracy. In this process, Durel envisions the senior capstone experience as providing a place for anticipation of and initiation into the active adult citizen role that students will inhabit for the balance of their lives. Indeed, Durel rather ambitiously suggests that the capstone course will prepare students for aggregating and then exercising their accumulated knowledge in four postgraduate areas: (1) further academic work building on their sociological studies, (2) labor market participation using their advanced analytical skills and sophisticated methodologies acquired from their studies, (3) accepting the responsibilities of family life through the formation of nurturing and supportive relationships that will enhance their own lives and the lives of others, and (4) engaging in civic and social responsibilities as active adults through informed opinion, political activism, and social compassion. Interestingly, Durel identifies virtually the same set of capstone course experiences as other sociologists as providing the vehicle for this particular transformation from student to citizen. Thus, he suggests that "presentation of research papers and critiques, active research projects and internships, cooperative learning projects, and guest speakers discussing careers and graduate programs" will do the trick (p. 224).

The explanation for Durel's position on the capstone's potential and form grows out of the underlying premise for his approach: the capstone is primarily a rite of passage, that is, an experience that one must pass through within a generational cohort. One can therefore attribute certain goals to the process, but regardless of the goals one posits or the outcomes anticipated, it is the process of going through the senior experience that matters. Whether students actually become active citizens fulfilling the multiple social roles Durel envisioned, seniors do become postgraduate adults who shared the rite of passing through the capstone together. In this view, the capstone can be defined as the transitional experience in our society that marks one as an emerging adult rather than simply a higher-order prolonged adolescent. In short, ritualized initiation into adulthood is the successful outcome sought; everything else is rigmarole—a complicated procedure erected as a means of announcing to the world that the subject has satisfactorily navigated the artificial life course constructed for his or her passage. Durel's observations are no less applicable to other academic disciplines as they emphasize the shared features of the senior transition rather than the features of a particular approach to knowledge.

Atchison (1993), somewhat to the contrary to the immediately preceding articles, argues that "remarkable consistency" exists within contemporary sociology regarding the "underlying objectives" on which departments build their programs. In this regard, Atchison also displays a consensus view of the discipline. As we have seen from this review of the *Teaching Sociology* articles so far, some commentators are proponents of capstone goals that focus almost exclusively on students acquiring, integrating, and applying this field's principles, theories, and methods. Other commentators identify a list of goals that emphasize acquisition of a liberal, humanist perspective that will, among other things, prepare students for active citizenship in a participatory democracy and entry into adulthood. In support of her contention that there is general agreement on capstone goals among sociologists, Atchison goes to great effort to repeat a list of principles Wagenaar listed in a 1991 article. However, as Wagenaar made clear—and as Atchison does not make clear in her adoption of Wagenaar's list—Wagenaar was engaging in an exercise of self-reflection and personal expression, as he quite candidly states. Wagenaar was not declaring a set of inviolable principles that others should uncritically adopt but thinking out loud about the values he would choose to guide his own pedagogy. Readers from across the American higher education curriculum can no doubt appreciate that a major hurdle in crafting a professional identity in any field of study is grappling with what is, or should be, distinctive and important for graduates within the field. As Wagenaar (1991) notes: "What follows is my attempt to put into writing what I expect of a sociology major. I started with the question: upon completion of the major, what should a sociology major know and what should she/he be able to do? . . . I pose these goals for discussion and reflection. They are preliminary and clearly not definitive. . . . These goals should not be adopted wholesale" (p. 93). Atchison, disregarding Wagenaar's caveat and caution, proceeds to examine a number of other prescriptive statements regarding the goals of sociology curricula. Seeking consensus and consistency, regardless of the differences of opinion and statement that clearly exist, Atchison finds disciplinary cohesiveness regarding the goals the capstone should embrace.

Atchison's (1993) approach, however modestly misleading by glossing over some of the disciplinary differences that existed, is highly informative with respect to the actual process through which goals for capstones are formulated. As a practical matter, the capstone is formed, by necessity, by the structure of American higher education in which the capstone experience finds itself. Then, in a rather utilitarian, if not an entirely retrospective, way, goals that can be accommodated within that structure are vouchsafed. In short, too often the capstone design process resembles the characterization applied to the legislative process—sausage making, where differences in purpose and goals are "ground together" until an unrecognizable amalgamated product results. In higher education, that product is then wrapped, labeled, distributed, sold, and consumed as "the senior capstone."

We believe this tension of institutional or departmental accommodation, high-minded abstractions, and principled curricular development ultimately must be faced. There is seldom a better place to do so than in the design of the capstone course since it is nominally and practically both the high point and the end point of the undergraduate experience. In our view, faculty members must eschew bland, artificial agreements for the sake of a fragile departmental or institutional peace and engage deeply in discussions that will produce a capstone experience of breadth, depth, and worth.

Steele's (1993) account of capstone development within his department notes one of the other common grounds for instigating change: a departmental assessment. Thus, while generic calls for a refreshed undergraduate curriculum from prestigious studies and commissions may inspire capstone design or redesign, the immediacy of a mandated assessment may also provide the context within which the disciplinary curriculum is expanded to include a capstone experience or the existing course revised. Steele's department started from the premise that "doing sociology" involved actively practicing its perspective, living it in society, and experiencing it in one's life. Operationalizing this conception led Steele and his colleagues to adopt five indicators as demonstrating that graduating seniors were "doing sociology" within their senior experience:

- Indicators of appreciation of diversity
- Indicators of familiarity with social structure and process
- Indicators of theoretical sophistication
- Indicators of methodological competence
- Indicators of personal commitment

Steele's discussion of the format he and his colleagues developed is also instructive for our work in the balance of this book. Steele observes that while a number of evaluative features were discussed and several instituted in the capstone course, "like many other departments . . . we have settled on a senior paper as the most important tool for assessment" (p. 243). As we will discuss, this is the nearly universal solution to the "assessment problem" within American higher education. Finally, Steele offers a brief precaution that will inform our discussion in a later chapter: "One cannot do everything in a capstone course; especially, the capstone course cannot correct the deficiencies in a department's curriculum or teaching" (p. 244).

Troyer's (1993) recapitulation of the trend in disciplinary restructuring and assessment that inspired widespread adoption of the capstone within sociology in the late 1980s and 1990s is significant because of its conscious recognition that this was in fact a social movement. Departments and institutions were in many cases simply swept along in the trend to adopt capstone courses and failed to intentionally design their own entry in this arena. Troyer is also perceptive with respect to the differences that exist between broad policy statements in the 1991 Association of American Colleges report, *The Challenge of Connecting Learning*, and the recommendations found in the 1991 Study in Depth report, *Liberal Learning and the Sociology Major*, prepared by the American Sociology Association's Task Force. While some commentators, such as Atchison (1993), are eager to minimize differences among the various statements of proposed goals and assert that there is substantial unanimity among the lists of objectives put forward for the capstone, denial of complexity and contradiction among the goals faculty seek for the capstone is a self-defeating strategy.

Troyer (1993), to his credit, declines to engage in this intellectual reductionism. He states clearly that in designing the capstone, faculty members need to consciously make some choices based on the various policy mandates, his or her own curriculum, and his or her view of the purpose of the major and college education more generally. Troyer intentionally chooses to emphasize a capstone design that compels students to broaden their perspective, question the existing orthodoxies (including those within social science), and focus less on synthesizing and integrating their grasp of core principles. Troyer's contribution therefore is to remind us of the need for active choice with respect to the design phase of the capstone experience, a principle that undercuts the narrowness of disciplines and applies broadly to curricular revision.

Smith's (1993) brief discussion of the capstone course at Loras College in Iowa at the time is instructive for its notable inclusion of one fact that went almost unremarked in all of the preceding articles. Smith observes that in the four semesters he taught the course, the Loras College sociology capstone had averaged five students a term. This is a fact, as we will find, that is of paramount importance in designing and conducting the capstone course. The faculty-student ratio within the senior capstone course can be a critical limitation on the ability of the instructor and the students to achieve successful outcomes. Amid all the high-minded talk of the purposes of liberal education, the overall goals of an academic program, and the specific objectives sought for the capstone course and its students, the issue of faculty-student ratio assumes substantial importance. As Smith succinctly observes, "Small class size enhances the collaborative nature of learning as well as the participants' satisfaction" (1993, p. 251). As we shall see, contemporary capstone studies routinely find that the size and nature of the institution and the corresponding size of the capstone course sections they can support remain important factors. Finally, Smith also raises a second fact that warrants further discussion: the page length of the major papers that are the most tangible identifiable product of most capstones. Smith notes that at Loras College, the standard page count at the time was fifteen to twenty pages, within the range we have found (Hauhart & Grahe, 2010, 2012) but at the lower end of the range within contemporary sociology and psychology programs.

Flint's (1993) comment directly challenges some of the earlier discussions. He does so through his willingness to acknowledge existing "deep contradictions in the discipline" (p. 254) of sociology that some of the prior authors, including Atchison, would not. Flint suggests that rather than gloss over these contradictions, the divergent positions held by different sociologists and schools of thought within sociology should themselves be made the fertile ground on which the senior capstone experience is built. Flint is direct in his criticism in this regard. Rather than wide consensus regarding the skills and knowledge sociology students should acquire through the capstone experience, Flint finds "broad disagreement" within the discipline (p. 254). With some latitude for extreme outliers on either side of the debate, Flint identified two antipodal positions within the discipline aligned with different capstone approaches: an ideology of professionalism versus an abiding concern with the "moral-political" paradigms of analysis that characterize modern social thought. The former, in Flint's view, lead to capstone designs that teach rational techniques of investigation through formal methodologies, an acceptance of late-twentieth-century capitalism, and the socialization of graduating seniors for entry into the occupational sphere within the existing economic, political, and state-controlled structures. Advocates for the latter position, as Flint sees it, develop senior capstone experiences that focus on raising social consciousness, encouraging students to envision and actively pursue the "good society," and teaching skills that enable students to accept and perform the role of active, concerned citizen within a democracy.

Flint (1993) is undeniably correct in concluding that neither sociology nor any other academic discipline can separate fact from values or science from politics and ideology. The implication for capstone design is that a significant part of the intentionality required for those responsible for the capstone experience must be directed at addressing the foundational divides that inevitably inhabit the pursuit of knowledge. Regardless of one's position on the scientific professionalism versus moral-political humanism continuum, one should be clear about one's views and conscious of their influence on the choices one makes for the graduating seniors' culminating experience.

Pulling It All Together in the Senior Capstone Experience

Finally, of particular interest for our purposes are the articles that identify important principles that support a typical one-semester capstone course. These articles explain and comment on the many pitfalls that even well-designed courses encounter. Moreover, many of the observations offered have now been confirmed by more contemporary studies across a wide range of academic disciplines.

Dickinson's (1993) report on the capstone at Rider College in the 1980s and 1990s offers a thumbnail sketch of such a capstone structure. As Dickinson relates, the capstone at Rider College was in place prior to the explosion of interest in senior capstones in the early 1990s. Moreover, the college's sociology capstone was embedded in a sociology curriculum that had been extensively restructured in the early 1980s that consisted of six required core courses. That core shared the twin goals of integrating the disciplinary study around theory and method and doing so through research and writing.

The Rider College senior seminar Dickinson described was limited to twelve students to permit an intensive research and writing experience, echoing the advantages Wattendorf (1993) and others describe arising from small class sizes for the capstone course. The primary goal was for each student to identify a topic of interest and a method for researching that topic, and then produce by the end of the one-semester term a report that summarized his or her capstone experience. The seminar meetings consisted of some shared readings used to form the background for student topic selections, drafting and presentation of two-page written topic proposals, individual meetings with the instructor to develop the research plan further, oral reports regarding the progress and findings by each student, and final submission of the completed research report. Each of these features of the capstone reflected essential core practices that our own research has subsequently identified as typical of contemporaneous capstone courses within sociology and psychology. Finally, Dickinson documents the most common limitations of this capstone model: under-prepared students, insufficiently motivated students, time limitations due to the one-semester iteration, faculty limits due to the intensive nature of the mentoring process, and resource limitations with the department.

In addition to the example offered by sociology of the way in which disciplines debate the range of goals that should properly imbue a capstone course, the 1993 *Teaching Sociology* articles also note the absence of answers to some of the critical questions that have been influential in inspiring us to write this book—for example:

> The desire to include a capstone course within a department's curriculum is one thing, but the reality of doing so is another. Incorporation of a capstone course requires departments to reexamine and restate their goals and philosophy. It also necessitates addressing some practical issues. How should the capstone course be structured? What materials are appropriate? What specific learning objectives will be achieved? How will we know if we achieved them? Do we have the resources to staff it? Who should teach the capstone course? (Tiemann, 1993, p. 258)

In short, although the articulation of goals for the capstone course is an essential initial step in building a culminating experience, expression of a series of course goals will not automatically provide answers to the many other important questions that must be addressed. Hartmann's (1993) brief comment is not the last word chronologically in the *Teaching Sociology* 1993 special number, but it deserves to be the last word because of the important summary statement it offers, then and now. Hartmann's piece, "A Next Step," makes the point that while well intentioned and informative, the articles under review "fall far short . . . of telling us what works and what doesn't" (p. 253). This remains the critical task today and one we take up in ensuing chapters.

Process and Result: Lessons Learned from Sociology's Self-Examination

Our review of the capstone adoption, creation, development, and redesign processes within late-twentieth-century sociology provides a case study of the manner in which a single academic discipline addressed the question of purpose and goals within the senior experience. There are five instructive points to remark on as we next take a broader look at capstone course goals across the liberal arts curriculum. Adoption of the senior capstone course as a focal experience within academic sociology involved (1) articulable dissatisfactions with current academic outcomes; (2) discipline-based and higher education policy initiatives that provided the framework for academic departments within institutions to develop capstone courses; (3) a departmental process leading to capstone course development that ranges from externally driven and expedient to internally conceived, deliberate, and consensus based; (4) instructor influence on final capstone design based on a matrix of disciplinary disputes, alternative learning theories, and substantive curricular considerations growing out of the nature of the field; and (5) a recognition by instructors, departments, and institutions that course designers must make value choices within resource limitations and existing institutional systems. There are good reasons to believe that factors and forces like these have been instrumental in driving the interest in capstone courses among many fields. We offer the following general observations.

First, the drive to develop senior culminating experiences within contemporary American higher education seems to have been propelled by dissatisfactions with graduation rates and other tangible outcomes and supported by discipline-wide or national education commissions. This is an understandable trajectory for social change. Typically social movements demanding social action arise in the United States only after a persuasive case is made that a substantial problem exists. When a possible solution is proffered and legitimized by blue-ribbon panels, the clarion call may be taken up more widely. This is what happened with widespread adoption of the capstone course. The fact is that undergraduate education as a whole during the late 1980s was considered to be underachieving by many observers using a number of measures. Many in academia believed that a malaise permeated higher education that required radical action. Committees, task forces, and commissions were convened to investigate the causes and consider the possible alternatives. This attitude demanding accountability from higher education has resurfaced and continues to drive issues relating to the senior capstone, particularly the trend toward reliance on the capstone for program assessment.

Second, the policy and value statements that disciplinary societies and higher education commissions generated in their reports established a foundation on which academic disciplines and individual departments typically built their own iteration of the senior capstone experience. This is a common basis for social action and should likely be anticipated as a precursor to curricular change. Generally, institutions are inherently conservative. Since change does not come easily, will likely disenfranchise some groups, and carries other risks, the legitimacy and imprimatur provided by policy and value statements emanating from professional bodies is often a prerequisite for change. Once the policy aims are formulated, typically those responsible for the operational arm of the institution are authorized to develop the change—in this case, creation and adoption of a senior culminating experience.

Third, the initial capstone design, or its redesign, may be more or less conscious and intentional with respect to both the goals sought and the means adopted. A rational model of organizational action and curricular restructuring might suggest that a careful and comprehensive assessment of university and department goals, weaknesses, staffing, resources, and competencies should drive the process. While this might be an ideal model, anyone familiar with higher education institutions will recognize that even under the best of circumstances, this idealized process is hard to achieve. The fact is that different actors wield different degrees of influence with respect to divisions and departments within universities and, in particular, with respect to curricular decisions. Moreover, as the case study of sociology indicates, while there were guides for restructuring in terms of broad goals (study in depth, synthesis of learning across the discipline), there was very little evidence-based research discussed in 1993.

Fourth, the goals one chooses to pursue within the senior capstone experience are likely a reflection of one's theory of knowledge, theory of society, and theory of education. While one cannot sever the connection between fact and values, science and morality, or professionalism and citizenship, one can be aware of the contradictions inherent in most disciplines with respect to one or more of these dimensions. There is, for example, the continuing debate about whether academic subjects should be taught primarily as theoretical or applied. Most students clearly will not pursue a life of detached knowledge for knowledge's sake. Should the sociology capstone be structured so that it prepares students to enter the real world of applied sociology as low-level social caregivers, minor bureaucrats, corrections guards, police officers, grassroots activists, and the like? Or should it be more theoretical? Or should it be some combination of both? Psychology and many other disciplines share their own version of this debate.

Finally, design of a capstone is an exercise of choice within the preestablished structure of American higher education that inevitably places limits on the approaches one can adopt, the details of what one can implement, the outcomes one can seek, and the successes one can achieve. In a perfect world, one would hope to have a free hand in curricular restructuring that would permit radical innovation and creative energy to unleash a substantial change driven by significant momentum. The truth, of course, is that there are certain bounded limits in place within the institutional environment that can be adjusted only modestly in one direction or another. In sum, all of these stages found in this case study are valuable lessons to keep in mind as we discuss designing or revising the senior capstone course.

Contemporary Capstone Goals Viewed across the Liberal Arts Curriculum

The modern series of comparative capstone studies across institutions in American higher education can probably be dated from a brief paper published by Cuseo in 1998. Relying on values expressed in program proceedings from four national conferences on the senior-year experience sponsored by the University of South Carolina's National Resource Center for the First-Year Experience and Students in Transition, Cuseo (1998) identified a set of themes that pervaded the individual presentations. Cuseo concluded that three major themes could be identified: (1) bring integration and closure to the undergraduate experience, (2) provide students with an opportunity to reflect on the meaning of the college experience, and (3) facilitate graduating students' transition to postcollege life.

Cuseo (1998) also understood that these broad goals embraced a series of more targeted initiatives. He identified ten relatively discrete goal objectives:

1. Promoting the coherence and relevance of general education
2. Promoting integration and connections between general education and the academic major
3. Promoting integration and synthesis within the academic major
4. Promoting meaningful connections between the academic major and work (career) experiences
5. Explicitly and intentionally developing important student skills, competencies, and perspectives that are tacitly or incidentally developed in the college curriculum (e.g.,

according to Cuseo, leadership skills and character and values development)

6. Enhancing awareness of and support for the key personal adjustments seniors encounter during their transition from college to postcollege life

7. Improving seniors' career preparation and preprofessional development, that is, facilitating their transition from the academic to the professional world

8. Enhancing seniors' preparation and prospects for postgraduate education

9. Promoting effective life planning and decision making with respect to practical issues likely to be encountered in adult life after college (e.g., according to Cuseo, financial planning, marriage, and family planning)

10. Encouraging a sense of unity and community among the senior class, which can serve as a foundation for later alumni networking and future alumni support of the college

While Cuseo believed that each of these ten goals should be a part of the "senior-year experience," he also understood that some of these goals were more suitable within the context of a capstone course than others. Although there is certainly room for debate regarding several of the goals, Cuseo identified the first four goals as particularly suited for inclusion within a senior capstone course.

Through his discussions with college faculty, Cuseo (1998) found that the major vehicle used to bring coherence and closure to the general education curriculum was the senior capstone course. Thus, institutions that were pursuing an interdisciplinary initiative to bind the elements of a general education program to a senior experience commonly chose to do so through the capstone. The anecdotal support Cuseo gathered for this conclusion has been supported by later studies. He also concluded that the goal of integrating students' general education with their major concentration was suitable for inclusion within a senior capstone course. This integration, he believed, provided a curricular anchor that boded well for seniors' transitional experience from an academic world to a occupational world. This objective too seems to be reflected in later studies suggesting that interdisciplinary senior capstone courses often pursue this goal.

Cuseo (1998) also found that synthesis of the academic major was an initiative suitable for the senior capstone course. This is the most common contemporary stated purpose of the senior capstone course. Cuseo knew, of course, that synthesis or disciplinary integration was identified as an important goal for the capstone course beginning a decade earlier with the national reports that inspired major curricular restructuring. Its persistence as a goal seems to mirror a reliance on the capstone to address some of the gaps that arise across the range of individual courses that constitute the curriculum.

Finally, Cuseo (1998) concluded that senior courses of one kind or another were also suitable vehicles for providing graduating students an opportunity to connect their study in their academic major to the world of work. Although he also recommended a number of supplementary initiatives that would augment this goal, courses tied to research or professional development that were linked with existing corporate or professional organizations were among his preferred formats for achieving this goal.

In the end, Cuseo (1998) believed that his ten goals for the senior experience would enable students to develop a series of interrelated benefits: (1) a more comprehensive understanding of the role of general education, (2) a desire to better grasp the connections between general education and course work in the academic majors, (3) a more comprehensive appreciation of course work in the major, and (4) an understanding of the connections between course work in one's academic major and the transition to a career. His examination of the predominance of these themes led him to focus attention on the fact that the senior year constitutes the final opportunity for higher education institutions to provide meaningful support to students and contribute to their emerging skill sets. Consequently, he believed that institutional-level programming during the senior year assumes an importance far beyond that of the students' simple completion of his or her major requirements.

Cuseo's work has been influential with respect to the identification of learning goals suitable for the senior capstone. Henscheid, Breitmeyer, and Mercer (2000) created a list of nine goals following those that Cuseo had identified for use in their national survey. Respondents who reported on a discipline- or department-based course stated that the most important goal by far was "fostering integration and synthesis within the academic major" (Henscheid et al., 2000, p. 54). Over half of the schools reported integrating learning within the academic discipline as a primary goal. A distant second goal was promoting integration and connections between the academic major and the work world. A mere 13 percent of institutions reported the connections between the academic discipline and the world of work as the primary goal. The remaining seven goals were identified as "most important" by fewer than 10 percent of the institutions responding. Although Henscheid et al. examined how these goals were rank-ordered differently according to institutional size, there were never statistically reliable differences in the primary goal in discipline-based capstone courses. Henscheid et al. did find that respondents who reported offering an interdisciplinary capstone course identified "promoting the coherence and relevance of general education" as the primary goal.

Our own research measured goals consistently across institutions within sociology and psychology programs and found the top two stated purposes for the capstone to be, "Review and integrate learned material" and "It helps students extend and apply learned material" (Hauhart & Grahe, 2010, 2012). Thus, our research supports the general pattern that has emerged. Researchers whose work is intended to simply document the characteristics of their discipline's or department's capstone experience report similar findings (Johnson & Halabi, 2011; Upson-Saia, 2013). Although there are minor distinctions in the terminology used in various studies, the goal of integration and synthesis of the substance of the major academic field remains relatively constant across most multi-institutional studies.

In 2011 Padgett and Kilgo (2012) revisited the senior capstone experience on behalf of the University of South Carolina's National Resource Center for the First-Year Experience and Students in Transition. This was the first major reconsideration and survey on this topic conducted by the National Resource Center since Henscheid et al.'s (2000) extensive survey. In the 1999 survey reported by Henscheid et al., the most common capstone was identified as a discipline- or department-based course in which the primary goal was "fostering integration and synthesis within the academic major" (Henscheid et al., 2000, p. 54). Padgett and Kilgo's (2012, p. 12) follow-up survey asked respondents to identify their "three most important capstone or course objectives."

It is somewhat unclear if this change in wording, from *goals* in the 1999 Henscheid survey to *capstone or course objectives* in the 2011 Padgett and Kilgo (2012) survey, was intended to introduce a meaningful distinction. Moreover, regardless of the researchers' intent, there is the question of whether and to what extent the respondents believed they were answering the same or a different question about their capstone course. Perhaps the remarkable consistency in the top goal identified by Henscheid et al. (2000) is the reason that the 2011 follow-up to the 1999 study relied on measured course objectives rather than learning goals or purposes.

Ultimately Padgett and Kilgo (2012) reported on nineteen common capstone objectives (eighteen plus "other"), including five "dominant" objectives: critical thinking, analytical, and or problem-solving skills; the ability to conduct scholarly research; career preparation; professional development; and proficiency in written communication. Though these were the top five, their popularity differed among institution types. Private schools were more likely to report research as an important objective (32.5 percent versus 19.4 percent) and public schools more likely reported professional development as the most common objective (33.7 percent versus 17.5 percent). Increased critical thinking, analytical, or problem-solving skills remained the dominant objective for both private and public institutions. All other differences were less than 10 percent, and the biased sample relied on suggests that priority should be given to overall rank ordering rather than categorical differences. Furthermore, relying purely on public and private distinctions ignores the existing confound between type of school and highest degree awarded.[1]

Schermer and Gray's (2012) review of the capstone experiences at four liberal arts colleges (Allegheny College, Augustana College, Washington College, and the College of Wooster) also reported a range of goals consistent with the prior studies. Allegheny College, for example, suggested its capstone sought to "put into practice the analytic, creative, and expressive habits cultivated in [their] major fields; integrate the discipline-specific knowledge with communication and research skills." Washington College noted as its capstone goal, "Integrate knowledge and skills to produce sense of mastery and intellectual accomplishment," and the College of Wooster also specified as a core goal "the culmination of a four-year academic journey . . . that brings cohesion to the curriculum" (Schermer & Gray, 2012, p. 27). Although all four colleges that constituted the subjects of this study required completion of a capstone experience from every graduating senior, their capstones are predominantly disciplinary-based senior capstone courses that share integration, synthesis, and cohesion within the academic major as primary goals.

Connecting Capstone Goals to the Rest of the Curriculum

Generally the goals sought for the senior culminating experience are highly dependent on and related to the type of capstone course supported by the institution. Since the most common capstone course is disciplinary based and tied to an academic major, most capstones emphasize learning within the content and substance of the major field. The question of whether this goal should predominate is an important philosophical issue, but the best evidence available suggests that most capstones, which are disciplinary based, adopt this goal as the principal desired capstone course outcome.

Although there are occasional efforts to tie the disciplinary capstone to other learning experiences outside the major, these are generally limited. Rather, it is in the interdisciplinary capstone experiences—whether those driven by an emphasis on general education or some combination of foci across two or more disciplines—that adopt capstone goals that emphasize a broad accumulation and synthesis of knowledge. As Henscheid et al. (2000) observed, it is generally only capstones of this nature that adopt a primary goal other than integration of learning within a discipline. Thus, the distinction between disciplinary-based capstones and interdisciplinary capstones remains a sharp demarcation typically reflected directly in the differing goals that the two major types of capstone experiences seek.

Connecting Capstone Goals to Life after Graduation

Few capstone courses appear to explicitly emphasize the connection between disciplinary knowledge or more broad-based learning across the curriculum to the students' postgraduation transition, whether to the world of work or extended postgraduate education. Although this finding is contrary to the early support for these approaches offered by Cuseo (1998), Henscheid et al.'s (2000) finding that fewer than 10 percent of capstones report this emphasis as a primary goal appears reliable. While the senior capstone course would appear to be suitable for pursuing these purposes, only a few institutions appear to have developed these initiatives. This is a significant research finding that warrants further investigation and consideration. It may suggest that given the limitations inherent in a one-semester or even one-year senior experience faculty members have chosen to restrict the number of goals identified for their capstones. Faculty who are designing or redesigning their senior-year experience may wish to specifically discuss whether the transition from college to life after graduation should be part of the course their program wishes to deliver.

Conclusion

Our examination of the role of the capstone course has led us on a brief historical odyssey to locate the educational goals that have been identified and proposed for the senior experience. We used two approaches to guide us in this inquiry. First, we provided a capsule summary of the process pursued within academic sociology in the early 1990s that led to the widespread adoption of capstones within that discipline. Second, we examined recent studies of the senior experience movement in American higher education that seek to identify across the spectrum of disciplines the most common goals and structures developed for senior courses. Taken together, these approaches have offered a number of important insights regarding the manner in which senior capstone courses are conceptualized and developed.

The first impetus we identified from the movement to incorporate capstone course into the modern university curriculum was the need to develop courses that address dissatisfactions with current academic outcomes. This observation recognizes that the growth of inclusion of the capstone course into the curriculum was a response to other changes in higher education. As capstones in their modern form have been common for only a short period, the emphasis on outcome-based assessment of performance has occurred even more recently. As disciplines and accrediting agencies cycle through assessment, invariably changes in policy will follow regarding identifiable weaknesses in curricular programs. For instance, the American Psychological Association (2013) is considering a new framework for learning goals and outcomes for the undergraduate major. Any changes will likely have an impact on the development of new courses and other curricular changes in psychology departments that use these learning goals to guide their future plans. The association is not unique in reviewing its learning goals, and other examples likely exist, or soon will, where disciplines change their guidance for majors due to recent emphases on assessment.

As one of the premiere influences on administrators and program developers, we anticipate that the recent Liberal Education and America's Promise (LEAP) initiatives regarding the need for transformational education experiences will trickle down through individual institutions, and eventually, departments.[2] If so, it will be another example of discipline-based and national association policy goals continuing to provide the philosophical foundation for departments and institutions to develop capstone courses as one curricular alternative to perceived problems within their education programs. Naturally within a given institution, changes in cultural climate or administrative oversight can alter not only the expectations but also the resource allocation for support of curricular changes such as the adoption of capstone courses. This too should be expected based on our illustration of the curricular change process within academic sociology.

The third observation arising from our review of sociology's restructuring process in the 1990s was that curricular development does not always approximate the rational, ideal process envisioned. Although influenced by departmental, institutional, or association-level resource allocation, the change process can be co-opted by other agendas or disrupted by unexpected forces, and ultimately implementation rests on faculty instructors. While a given course could be developed by a department or follow an institutional model, the course instructors are the sole interaction point for the students as they engage the course. Although there are predominant trends that we discuss in the following chapter, there exists variability in both capstone implementation and common formats that are reflected in both institutional studies (Henscheid et al., 2000; Padgett & Kilgo, 2012) and discipline-related findings (Hauhart & Grahe, 2010, 2012; Schermer & Gray, 2012). Hence, regardless of the specific direction that future curricular changes take, the tension between articulating goals and implementing those goals effectively will not abate.

There are many ways that the fourth impact we identified in our sociology case study can change the contours of a deliberately designed senior capstone course. As instructors wade through their own conflicts among personal, departmental, disciplinary, and institutional expectations, they impose additional expectations through delivery of the course itself. This can reflect variability within a department as different instructors weigh the value of emphasis between, for example, student initiative versus content mastery or skill development. Different instructors may even urge the creation of distinct capstone types depending on the department's conception of its mission, thereby imperiling goals such as disciplinary integration. Finally, there may well be tension between academic and interdisciplinary capstones at the same institution.

The final impact on capstone course values that we observed is that instructors, departments, and institutions make value choices within resource limitations and institutional systems. This is a critical consideration when integrating any new curricular initiative. At Monmouth College in Illinois, all students take an interdisciplinary capstone course, and they are expected, if not required, to take the course from an instructor in a different department from their own declared major. In addition, students complete a discipline-level capstone course where they focus on a research project directly related to their major. These dual capstones can exist only because the faculty and administration concluded that this type of program was worth the extra costs associated with staffing twice as many courses. Other institutions have made other value choices. Such choices at each institutional level are inevitable, and any change process must anticipate that they will have an impact on implementation even after disciplinary, institutional, and departmental goals have been announced.

While these findings are relatively well established, they do not provide an answer to the question of which goals should be sought for a particular department or school's senior capstone experience. The selection of goals for a capstone experience is intimately connected with the nature of the underlying curriculum and the tangible work students will engage in within the course. There is no simple formula for composing a three-pronged strategy that will unite curriculum, capstone goals, and capstone substance for every academic discipline, general education program, and project that supports a capstone experience. Moreover, uncritical adoption of the goal of integration of learning across the discipline does not offer a panacea for every disciplinary-based capstone course delivered.

The fact is that the use, or reuse, of borrowed or shop-worn goals like "integration" can produce an experience that is less than ideal simply due to the uninspired, limited aim that can come to inhabit such trite and facile statements of purpose. It is true that the goal of integration of learning across the discipline will confer a sanctified legitimacy supported by the weight of the research evidence, but unless such a goal is invested with theoretical sophistication, creative energy, and intellectual curiosity, the product may take the form of a moldy rehash rather than a bold, innovative intellectual tour de force. Therefore, one challenge of creative capstone design is to articulate a goal worth pursuing that can be reasonably sought and achieved through identifiable objectives tied to specific assignments.

CHAPTER THREE

CHARACTERISTICS OF THE CAPSTONE COURSE

This chapter focuses on the capstone model that a majority of American higher education institutions have adopted and represents the typical format represented in the sciences, social sciences, and humanities, This format, which we have characterized based on our research as the "typical capstone course," requires a major project or paper associated with substantive course content that is integrative of the major, requires a minimum page length, relies on peer-reviewed sources, and is submitted in an approved format and style.

Nevertheless, to a certain extent it is a misnomer to suggest that there is a truly typical capstone course. Although we focus on the discipline-specific, project-based course shared by a majority of institutions, other contemporary approaches exist and deserve our attention as well. For instance, a consistent, although lesser, number of institutions maintain an interdisciplinary course approach to the capstone. These courses can provide exemplary learning opportunities, but they also include unique resource and management costs that make them prohibitive for widespread adoption by some schools. Other consistent but less frequent capstone course types include using professional experiences such as an external internship or the presentation or display of artwork or musical skills. Since a significant number of students engage in these alternative capstone course options as well, this chapter will comment on the characteristics of each model.

As we have noted, we began our research into capstone pedagogy focused on sociology and psychology capstones (Hauhart & Grahe, 2010, 2012). We consistently presented our work without distinguishing the two disciplinary approaches because we found very few discipline-specific structural differences. For instance, although psychology capstones were slightly more likely to collect data and sociology capstone courses were slightly more likely to require extended papers, the differences were otherwise minimal. Thus, there were rarely differences in the size, dominant features, or administrative structures of the course. There were no differences in the likelihood that a class lecture was guided by students, as opposed to faculty, or that student papers were not required to conform to a particular citation and writing style. A major project was required by both psychology and sociology, and in both disciplines, evaluation and grading were typically the sole province of an individual instructor.

As we approached the capstone course from a larger institutional lens, we searched for studies that considered more than one discipline while describing the capstone course. We found three studies that approached the question from a broad multidisciplinary and multi-institutional scope (Henscheid, Breitmeyer, & Mercer, 2000; Padgett & Kilgo, 2012; Schermer & Gray, 2013). When we examined these reports, we found that their results confirmed many of our own findings across other social science, natural science, and humanities disciplines. Furthermore, at the institutions where we have taught and in a number of institutions that have been studied, the capstone can be part of the general education program. Although disciplines control their course administration, a general education capstone course follows norms guided by the university rather than the division or department since the course is asked to conform to a general education protocol. Still, across many institutions and all of the more traditional liberal arts disciplines, a majority of capstone courses have shown a remarkable core consistency. This is what we will refer to as the typical capstone course that constitutes the subject of this chapter.

Although our review of the literature suggests a typical capstone format across many disciplines, the fact that we will be summarizing what is commonly found in contemporary capstone courses does not suggest the model presented here is ideal in every instance. Rather, we believe there is substantial benefit in knowing how other educators have conceived of the capstone course and are teaching it in their respective disciplines. Current practices constitute a benchmark even if it is in some instances a negative one. In the following discussion, we focus on the similarities between institutions and disciplines first and then briefly consider the differences that exist between capstones in some disciplines.[1] In later chapters, we focus on the capstone course characteristics that constitute best practices in design and teaching the course. If your interest as a reader is in primarily identifying practical tips for designing and teaching the best possible capstone course, you may wish to look ahead to those chapters.

Multidisciplinary, Multi-Institutional Studies

Henscheid et al. (2000) presented the first modern empirical evaluation of capstone courses based on a national sample. Although they report on three earlier studies, those comprehensive investigations found only 3 percent of American higher education institutions in the 1970s offered capstone courses (Levine and Carnegie Council on Policy Studies in Higher Education, 1978). Consequently, the lack of data about the composition of those early contemporary capstones made comparisons to modern course formats untenable. The only other prior capstone investigations were qualitative, often anecdotal. Although these studies provided the intellectual framework for the commonly accepted notion of capstone courses as important integrative experiences for students, they did little to create a baseline set of capstone data that would help us assess the range of standard practices prior to Henscheid's work (Cuseo, 1998). Study protocols that examine multiple disciplines across multiple institutions produce results that can more reliably be generalized to capstone courses nationally as compared to single-department reports regarding a capstone course at a single institution. This is why we rely primarily on multi-institutional, multidisciplinary studies in this chapter.

Henscheid et al. (2000) measured capstone experiences at 707 institutions nationwide, with an impressive 42 percent response rate. Their study measured both institutional demographics and course structures. Their approach represents, in our view, a reliable empirical measure of capstone courses nationally. Hence, we consider their study as representing the baseline data of capstone course characteristics at the dawn of this century. More recently, Padgett and Kilgo (2012) completed a follow-up study, contacting the academic officers at the same institutions that participated in the Henscheid study. Their sample was not an independent one and was smaller overall, with only 276 institutions, with a low 8 percent response rate. Still, their report provides a useful multi-institution comparison of capstone courses given the relative paucity of such studies. Although they did not measure all the same variables, they did identify and confirm many basic structural components of the majority of capstone courses.

The only other in-depth study of capstone courses with an institutional scope is one of four liberal arts institutions (Schermer & Gray, 2012). The primary purpose of this study was to examine the impact of capstone courses on student learning at these four institutions. Schermer and Gray (2012) measured all majors at each of the four schools since every student at these colleges was required to complete a capstone course. Their report provides a generalizable estimate of the characteristics of capstone courses even though they examined only four institutions because they reviewed a substantial number of different capstone courses at the four schools.[2]

There are, to our knowledge, no other large-scale studies of capstone courses using an institutional unit of analysis that also included surveys of multiple academic disciplines. We therefore rely primarily on these few studies as we investigate the question of what constitutes the contemporary capstone across institutions and disciplines. Since these studies found that the typical outcomes from the course commonly included a major project with an associated major paper, their findings bear directly on one of the core features we independently identified as typical of contemporary capstone courses (Hauhart & Grahe, 2010, 2012).

Defining the Typical Contemporary Capstone Course

The typical capstone course is identified along a series of characteristic elements that reappear across capstone courses in many disciplines.

Percentage of Institutions Offering Capstone Experiences

If we consider the weighted average of the four samples measuring more than one discipline (Hauhart & Grahe, 2010, 2012; Henscheid et al., 2000; Padgett & Kilgo, 2012), we would estimate that 81.1 percent of all American higher education institutions offer capstones (see table 3.1). When considering that the Padgett and Kilgo study was not an independent sample, we might be more comfortable with an estimate excluding their data, suggesting that 76.7 percent of all institutions offer a capstone course. This is slightly higher than the 70.25 percent estimate we found when examining the websites of a national stratified random sample of psychology department websites (Grahe & Hauhart, 2013). If we take the unweighted average of the estimates that we found (whether from a

TABLE 3.1. PRESENCE OF CAPSTONE AND INSTITUTIONAL DIFFERENCES

	N_{Disc}	N_{Inst}	%capstone	%private	Size Effect
Hauhart & Grahe (2010)	Two	95	61.00%		
Hauhart & Grahe (2012)	Two	187	80.70%	+22%	Curvilinear
Henscheid et al. (2000)	Institution	707	77.60%		Curvilinear
Padgett & Kilgo (2012)	Institution	276	97.10%	+3%	Curvilinear
Brown, Pegg, & Shively (2006)	International study	140	72.10%	+5%	
Jones, Barrow, Stephens, & O'Hara (2012)	History	30	96.00%	−3%	
McGoldrick (2008)	Economics	254	60.00%		
Perlman & McCann (1999b)	Psychology	400	63.00%		
Stoloff et al. (2010)	Psychology	374	40.00%		

single discipline or across multiple disciplines), we could conclude that almost three-quarters (74 percent) of institutions offer some form of capstone. In sum, we conclude that the vast majority of contemporary baccalaureate-granting institutions require undergraduate students to complete some form of a capstone course.

Other factors can influence the likelihood that a particular institution will require completion of a capstone course. For instance, we found in our national survey sample that private colleges are 22 percent more likely than public institutions to report having a capstone (Hauhart & Grahe, 2012). Henscheid et al. (2000) do not provide data that allow us to make this comparison, but Padgett and Kilgo (2012) report a slight bias (3 percent) in this direction as well. Although these findings are preliminary because they need further replication, the likely explanation for this difference arises from the different resource allocations available to these two types of institutions. Thus, private colleges and universities tend to have smaller student populations, better faculty-student ratios, and higher tuition. Each of these factors contributes to a better educational climate and setting for support of a senior capstone experience.

In our national survey sample, we also found that the type of degree offered influenced whether a capstone was part of the curriculum (Hauhart & Grahe, 2012). We found that universities offering doctoral programs were less likely to offer these courses (70.4 percent) than master's (89.6 percent) or baccalaureate (86.2 percent) institutions. This finding too could benefit from further study since detailed data regarding similar comparisons are not available. Generally we can speculate reasonably that resource allocations at the different types of institutions are influential in creating this difference. Thus, doctoral institutions tend to be larger in many instances, with correspondingly higher faculty-student ratios. Moreover, faculty at doctoral institutions tend to be more strongly invested in graduate education than undergraduate education, thereby reducing the faculty available for guiding undergraduate capstone courses. The reverse is true for baccalaureate institutions, where faculty have no pull from graduate duties and can therefore dedicate their efforts exclusively to the undergraduate program, including the senior capstone experience.

Finally, research suggests the size of the institution alone bears on the likelihood of a capstone course being offered. Both Henscheid et al. (2000) and Padgett and Kilgo (2012) reported a curvilinear relationship with institution size. They found small schools between one thousand and five thousand full-time-equivalent (FTE) students were most likely to offer the course, with a diminished likelihood as the size of the school increased. Although we did not test this relationship in our original report of our national survey sample (Hauhart & Grahe, 2012), a reanalysis of the data demonstrated a correlation, $r(185) = .17, p = .02$, between the likelihood of offering a course and the size variable squared (Grahe & Hauhart, 2013). Thus, our data replicate this curvilinear relationship with respect to institution size and support the inferences we made.

Types of Capstone Experiences

We found small changes in the array of course structures that are identified as a capstone course since the Henscheid et al. (2000) study. Henscheid reported that most of the courses (70.3 percent) are discipline specific.[3] Padgett and Kilgo (2012) reported similarly that the discipline-based course was most prominent (84.7 percent), with interdisciplinary courses (12.9 percent) and senior theses or undergraduate research papers also present at this distant second level (12.9 percent).[4] However, both studies found a number of other alternative format capstone courses offered, although with only modest frequency.

Although we found traditional discipline-based classroom courses most common, we found both internship experiences and comprehensive exams were listed as capstone experiences by a minority of respondents in our studies of sociology and psychology departments (Hauhart & Grahe, 2010, 2012). Online capstone courses remain relatively rare, however, although reports regarding online senior experiences may be found in the literature. Healey (2014), for example, describes a distance education capstone course offered by a community engagement and governance program where students are enrolled from across England and Wales. Also, Tappert and Stix (2010) describe the transition of their capstone course at Pace University from a traditional classroom-based course to an online course to reach more students. Many recent single-discipline papers remark on internship or comprehensive exams as options for capstone experiences, however. A quick review includes the following: accounting (Johnson & Halabi, 2011), economics (McGoldrick, 2008), psychology (Stoloff et al., 2010), public administration (Reid & Miller, 1997), and religious studies (Upson-Saia, 2013). This may suggest an increased trend of using internships or senior comprehensive exams as a capstone experience and warrants further examination. Another option not specifically examined in the Henscheid et al. (2000) and Padgett and Kilgo (2012) studies was identified in a survey of international studies capstones where study abroad can constitute the capstone experience (Brown et al., 2006). While infrequently reported, study abroad may fall within the capstone course option for other majors as well (Sill, Harward, & Cooper, 2009).

Discipline-specific courses sometimes include an alternative option of a lecture-based, integrative course. In psychology, a sizable minority of programs (up to 20 percent: Grahe & Hauhart, 2013, Stoloff et al., 2010) use a History and Systems of Psychology course as the only capstone course or one alternative from a list of options. In this course, students are exposed to the primary and basic historical figures and theories that shaped the field into its current form. In psychology as well as other fields, this lecture-based, integrative alternative also manifests in slight variation as a senior seminar course (Berkson & Harrison, 2001; Brown et al., 2006; Obringer & Kent, 1998; Upson-Saia, 2013), where students investigate recent papers or cases around a topic. For instance, Berkson and Harrison (2001) report on a capstone course designed for conservation biology majors at Virginia Polytechnic Institute that is designed to expose students to "issues not discussed within the traditional conservation biology or natural sciences' curriculum" (p. 1461). Students address one of a series of basic questions and integrate the material through daily readings and classroom discussions. Brown et al. (2006) report that 41.6 percent of the courses in their study of international studies programs included a seminar approach which is similar (45.8 percent) to what Ishiyama and Breuning (2004) found in their examination of international studies programs in the Midwest. These courses follow the same goal of helping students integrate and apply material to better prepare students for their transition to a professional setting. Another modest variation within this approach more explicitly focuses on providing a career-oriented course (Hartmann, 1993) or courses more generally oriented to preparation for "life after college" (Hathaway & Atkinson, 2001).

Finally, the capstone experiences also emerge from arts programs such as theater, fine arts, and music. These senior experiences tend to be radically different in both substance and process from those we will be discussing as the typical capstone course. For these, the experience often includes demonstrations or displays of skills in the form of a recital, performance, exhibition, or play (Roens & Young, 2014; Posnick, 2014). Compared to other disciplines, there are comparatively few empirical studies focused on capstone courses in the arts. For that matter, there are few published papers that even address capstone courses within artistic academic programs. Consequently, there does not appear to be as strong a model or expectation for undergraduate research in arts (or some humanities programs) as in the sciences and social sciences (Corely, 2013).

Two books published by the Council on Undergraduate Research (Crawford, Orel, & Shanahan, 2014; Klos, Shanahan, & Young, 2011) provide some examples of work in these disciplines. Given the lack of widely available published discussion of capstone courses in the arts, in 2014 we interviewed Jeff Bell-Hanson, orchestra director and primary capstone instructor in the Pacific Lutheran University (PLU) music program. PLU offers four undergraduate concentrations in music (bachelor of music in performance, bachelor of musical arts, bachelor of music education, and bachelor of arts). The four majors reflect the breadth of potential intersections with music.

Two PLU programs (bachelor of musical arts and bachelor of arts) have project-based capstone courses typical of other academic disciplines. The music education students' capstone experience is tied to their student teaching and does not involve research but rather focuses on teaching practice. Students completing a performance major also do not engage in research project. Instead, their performances at multiple recitals serve as their capstone experience.

Bell-Hanson noted that the department only recently eliminated the research component from the performance capstone because faculty felt it did not match the other goals of that concentration. He observed that this a complex issue that reflects challenges in "trying to integrate music performance into the mainstream of American university life." Generally, Bell-Hanson noted, it is difficult to find a balance between the requirements of rigorous music training and the liberal arts curriculum, which encourages broad exposure to many topics. As Bell-Hanson stated, "The most fundamental characteristic of a musical scholar is to be a capable musician. We further agree, I think, that musicians first need to learn to think musically."

This disciplinary debate is beyond the scope of this book, although it does explain why there are fewer performance-based arts capstones organized along the lines of the more typical thesis or research capstone. To address this dearth, Crawfod, Orel, and Shanahan (2014) prepared an edited volume on initiating and sustaining research and creative inquiry in undergraduate education. A chapter in that book by Steven Roens and Gregory Young discusses examples of research capstones for music majors.

Though the form of the major project is less data collection and review of primary resources than display of artistic expression, the major project in performance-based disciplines aims, implicitly if not explicitly, to connect the students' learning to real-world application. As Christ, Malinauskas, and Hunt (1994) explain, "As a culminating experience, the production of a play prompts the individual to bring together all of the course-specific experiences learned in the areas of the liberal arts theatre experience: dramatic theory/criticism, performance, design/technical theatre, and administration" (p. 325).

Kindelan (2010) similarly describes a student's "thesis on dramaturgy and *The Laramie Project* (a play by Moisés Kaufman and the Tectonic Theatre Company)" as promoting "intentional learning through emphasizing critical thinking and analytical skills as well as developing leadership and citizenship skills" (p. 35). The purpose of such a project, says Kindelan, is similar to other capstone research goals: "She moved beyond the hypothetical research experiences found in a curricular script analysis course and faced the authentic problems of a dramaturgy working with an artistic team on an actual production of *The Laramie Project*" (p. 35).

Sill, Harward, and Cooper (2009) suggest that this active interaction with art is preferable to merely generating a portfolio of previous work. Though such an exhibition portfolio provides some evidence of student learning, Sill et al. (2009) argue that without a reflection on previous learning, students fail to achieve one of the primary capstone goals. Instead, Sill et al. report that the senior exhibition became transformative when the portfolio was integrated into a broader capstone course based around a shared classroom experience. This intentionality and corresponding importance helped students understand the course's "crucial place in the art program, putting the experience into a larger context, and making integration, breadth, application, and transition the intention" (p. 52).

The Prominence of the Major Project Capstone

Although this modest possible trend regarding the proliferation of other forms of senior experiences is intriguing, we found that the vast majority of the published papers across all disciplines describe capstone courses that are discipline specific and formed around a major project, commonly involve a literature review, often include research or data collection, and result in a substantial paper that is subjected to peer review and one or more oral presentations. Though the project may take other forms, this major project capstone course format still predominates. Moreover, though there are substantially fewer interdisciplinary capstones reported, these still overwhelmingly rely on major projects as the primary outcome.

Administering the Capstone Course

With many capstone course types to choose from, it is not surprising that the approach to administration of those courses is similarly varied and highly dependent on the type chosen. As we have discussed, capstone experiences range from independent study projects and senior theses to lecture and discussion-based classes with dozens of students in the classroom.

Course Credit

In Henscheid et al. (2000), the range of credits included one- and two-hour weekly courses (quarters/semesters) receiving from one to four credits or units. We similarly found that capstone experiences ranged from one- to three-hour weekly courses, with students receiving from one to nine credits or units (Hauhart & Grahe, 2010, 2012). Some of this variation in academic credit (three versus four hours) depends on the normal credit structure of the institution (semester or quarter system). The most extreme variation might be institutions such as Colorado College, where students take one course at a time intensively for one month, or eight times per academic year. Colorado College offers a one-month capstone course, and it counts as one unit just like all their other courses. Some of this variation in credit assignment is also due to whether the capstone course is structured as a single semester-long course (three or four credits), two single-semester courses (six to eight credits), or even three (nine to twelve credits).

In rare instances, this variation also reflects that some institutions provide little or no credit for course completion. At PLU, the faculty voted, and the administration adopted, a motion in 2006 that the capstone course must be considered part of the instructor's teaching load and that students must receive course credit for completion. Thus, only after thirteen years as part of the general education program requirements was the course administered with minimal credit available campuswide. Prior to that time, both students and faculty were completing the course as a required overload.

If the capstone course is the apex of the student's major experience, it deserves to be recognized with appropriate academic credit. It is inconsistent to suggest to both faculty members and students that the capstone course is the "culminating course" of the undergraduate experience and then not award suitable compensation and credit. However, where the course becomes part of a series of courses (Theory I, Theory II, Methods and Presentation, Capstone Course) it becomes less of a capstone experience than one part of an integrated core sequence. Multiple schools that Schermer and Gray (2012) reviewed reported that the capstone experience was part of a two- or three-semester sequence (as an independent research project at the College of Wooster and as a set of courses called Senior Inquiry at Augustana College). Though we focus our discussion primarily on the single-course capstone because it represents the majority of courses, we acknowledge the importance of sequencing. Generally we favor supporting the capstone course with a sequence of courses but suggest that further research is necessary to compare the learning benefits attributable to a traditional academic major versus one that has an integrated course sequence leading to the capstone course.

Class Size

The issue of course size has been investigated across institutional types. Henscheid et al. (2000), for example, reported on relative enrollment within capstone courses. Their reported categories ranged from low (up to nine students) to high (more than one hundred). The category with the greatest frequency was twenty to twenty-nine students in 33.2 percent of courses within their sample. However, a sizable number of respondents reported smaller class sizes (ten to nineteen, 27.4 percent; up to nine students, 20.6 percent), with very few schools offering larger sections (forty to seventy-five, 6.4 percent; seventy-six or more, less than 1 percent). This range and distribution were consistent with our own findings (Hauhart & Grahe, 2010, 2012). Though Henscheid et al. (2000) disaggregated the findings between public and private institutions there were no significant differences of note. In contrast, they did find the unsurprising result that larger institutions generally enrolled more students per class. However, even the biggest institutions were most likely to offer capstone courses with thirty or fewer students per section. This is a pedagogical and resource administrative decision that has wide-ranging impacts. If the number of students declaring a given major increases, the enrollment limits begin to have an impact on staffing decisions and, arguably, the quality of the capstone experience.

Beyond the relatively simple equation,

$$N_{\text{seniors in major}} / N_{\text{enrollment limit}} = N_{\text{capstone sections}}$$

that determines how many instructors are needed to staff the course, departments need to find faculty who will elicit high academic performances from students and thereby maintain academic standards in the course. Henscheid et al. (2000) addressed this concern by asking questions regarding the type of instructional staff assigned to capstone courses and found the vast majority were FTE faculty (85 percent). The other options included "career professionals, community leaders, other student affairs professionals, and graduate students," with career professionals and community leaders being the most common of these additional types (p. 15). Henscheid et al. (2000) also reported that responsibility for the capstone course was more likely to be the exclusive responsibility of one instructor (67 percent) rather than shared as part of a team. These findings were consistent across the disaggregated categories such as public or private and between institutions of various sizes. These findings are consistent with our own studies. We also found that the vast majority of capstone classes were taught by one person rather than shared as team or by the whole department (Hauhart & Grahe, 2010, 2012). The single model of a FTE faculty member as instructor is also consistent across the single-discipline papers. The question of whether a single-instructor model is best depends on a number of factors and cannot be easily answered. Certainly one issue is class size, as we have already suggested. A second issue is the degree to which a department is concerned about course consistency across a number of sections within a given academic year. Finally, there is the question of whether it is optimal to place the important responsibility of managing a department's capstone course within the hands of a single faculty member when the department's productivity and reputation are collective concerns.

In chapter 2, we observed that an important design implication was that all decisions regarding capstone course implementation occurred within the framework of institutional resources and cultural expectations. Depending on the course goals and expected outcomes, institutions need to provide support for the capstone course from the limited resources available to support all courses. The number of students registering for a capstone course is affected by a number of factors, including the academic major's popularity. For example, at an institution where all majors require a capstone, students taking a course in a major with fewer students (such as philosophy) might complete the course with only a few classmates, whereas students with popular majors (such as biology and psychology) enroll in classes at or exceeding the maximum enrollment cap of twenty students. The willingness to offer a course with only one or a few students enrolled places high educational value on the capstone experience; the other extreme of high enrollment reflects the low, or lesser, value of the course to the institution generally, and the department specifically.

Location and Method of Delivery

A notable change in research questions regarding capstone administration is the location of the course offering. Although distance learning has been part of the higher education landscape for two decades, only recently have online courses been feasible to the point of displacing traditional brick-and-mortar course offerings. Henscheid et al. (2000) did not even address the question of whether the capstone course was offered as an online option in their 1999 survey. More recent investigations were more concerned with the frequency with which these two primary options are now offered. Padgett and Kilgo (2012) found substantially more online course activity than we did in our national survey of sociology and psychology departments (Hauhart & Grahe, 2012). They also found that almost 40 percent of their respondents reported some form of online activity within capstone courses. Colleges and universities with large senior classes were more likely to employ significant numbers of online courses. About 25 percent of public higher education institutions offered online-only capstone options versus 10 percent of private schools. In contrast, we found only 5 percent of institutions offered capstone courses as an online option in our national random survey of sociology and psychology departments (Hauhart & Grahe, 2012). Our survey sample likely underrepresented for-profit and online-only institutions, which may account for the discrepancy in our findings. This is an administrative issue that deserves further study.

Classroom Activities

When considering what happens within the classroom, Henscheid et al. (2000) again provide the critical baseline for comparison. In their survey, they ask respondents to "check all that apply" to a list of potential classroom activities. In table 3.2, we see their responses as well as the figures from comparative studies conducted by Hauhart and Grahe (2010, 2012), Padgett and Kilgo (2011), and Schermer and Gray (2012) that measured classroom activities similarly. The general conclusion from their findings

TABLE 3.2. PERCENTAGE REPORTING THE PRESENCE OF COMMON ACTIVITIES AND OUTCOMES OF CAPSTONE COURSES ACROSS STUDIES

Instructional Components	Henscheid et al. (2000)	Hauhart & Grahe (2010)	Hauhart & Grahe (2012)	Padgett & Kilgo (2012)	Schermer & Gray (2013)
N_{sample}	864	58	151	276	105[d]
Major project[a]	71.9	76	64.6	64.6	86.6
Oral presentation	75.1	69	69.2	[c]	64.4
Internship	15.2	19	19.9	46.6	8.0
Exhibition of arts				58.2	32.6
Final exam	39.7	[b]	[b]	20.1	19.4

[a] This category was measured as "extended paper" by Hauhart and Grahe (2010, 2012), "senior thesis/research paper" by Padgett and Kilgo, and "written thesis or substantial paper" by Schermer and Gray.

[b] Hauhart and Grahe did not include this as a primary option, but numerous open-ended responses included a comprehensive or final exam as a capstone activity.

[c] Unlike other studies, this was measured as "choose the most important" rather than "check all that apply," so comparisons cannot be made.

[d] The number represents the various departments that completed a survey across four campuses rather than the four institutions.

is that capstone students should expect to complete a major project or extended paper and will likely present those results in some form of oral presentation. However, the range of actual classroom activities pursued within capstone courses is otherwise very broad.

Beyond the common goal of producing a major project and presenting it orally, there is relatively wide variability in what a student might expect to do in a capstone course. Henscheid et al.'s (2000) "check all that apply" option makes it impossible to examine whether certain course elements are more or less likely to co-occur. These authors note that many students will complete one or more of several complementary tasks: portfolio development (37 percent), visiting the career center (16.6 percent), explicitly considering graduate school (13.9 percent), leadership training (11.6 percent), or service-learning (10.8 percent). All of these course activities are reported as occurring in at least 10 percent of capstone courses.

In our own regional and national surveys of capstone course activities in psychology and sociology departments (Hauhart & Grahe, 2010, 2012), we confirmed Henscheid et al.'s basic findings. Although our respondents reported somewhat less likelihood of having a major project, this result was probably due to definitional or terminological confusion. Psychology and sociology majors are likely to engage in a research project, but the phrase "major project" may not have translated to respondents as incorporating the standard senior research experience in those disciplines. However, all multi-institutional or multidisciplinary studies suggest that over 70 percent of students complete an extended paper as part of the capstone course.

We asked about pedagogical activities and found that although instructor lecturing occurred in about half the cases (Hauhart & Grahe, 2010, 2012: respectively, 53 percent, 52 percent) classroom discussions were more common. Our respondents reported that these were led by either the instructor (84 percent, 80 percent) or the students (67 percent, 63 percent). These ratios did not differ between the two disciplines, but lectures were less common at four-year institutions compared to PhD-granting institutions and more common at private than public institutions. Also our findings suggest that students were likely to have common reading lists (55 percent, 47 percent). To a lesser extent, students also experience peer review of final papers (26 percent, 18 percent) or, more often, oral presentations (48 percent, 39 percent). These were unaffected by type of institution or department.

Padgett and Kilgo (2012) measured many of these variables in their 2011 follow-up survey to the Henscheid et al. (2000) multi-institutional study. Although their research produced a low response rate, their results show a strong consistency in reporting on a range of common classroom activities. One area where they noted a substantial difference was between institutions where the senior capstone course was the most heavily enrolled (primary) experience as compared to simply one of several options students could choose among to fulfill their senior obligation. For instance, although 64.6 percent of the institutions offered a senior thesis or research paper experience, only 12.9 percent had it as the primary experience. This pattern was similarly pronounced with internships (46.6 percent offered, 3.9 percent primary), comprehensive exams (20.1 percent offered, 2.4 percent primary), and exhibition of performing arts (58.2 percent offered, 1.2 percent primary).[5] This pattern partially reflects differences between numbers of students enrolled in majors where these outcomes are critical. Not all science majors are planning a postgraduate career in research or other professional career where completing a research paper or internship is necessarily the primary display of disciplinary skills and knowledge. The same is true for exhibition and the arts: the proportion of students who will be professional fine arts performers is small relative to the institution size and even within the major itself. For instance, music education majors' capstones might be more likely related to teaching materials preparation as compared to public performance demonstrating musical mastery. Consequently, many senior courses may incorporate such activities as part of a larger capstone experience or as an option for interested students rather than rely on it as the primary capstone within the department.

Schermer and Gray (2013) present findings consistent with the other studies we have reviewed.[6] Their findings are somewhat constrained by the fact that departments ($N = 100$) are nested within only a limited number of institutions ($N = 4$). As we discussed earlier, institutional culture guides capstone development and thus has an effect, although an indeterminable one based on the present data, in how the capstone is conceived and implemented. Even though three of the four institutions state they have little or no oversight over departmental capstone choices, there is likely to be some interdependence between respondents not reflected in other multi-institutional studies.

Completing the Major Paper

While there is a need for additional multidiscipline, multi-institution studies to more fully explore the variation of capstones between types of schools as affected by source of funding, degree offered, institutional size, or institution selectivity, existing studies present a consistent image of the typical capstone. The most consistently reported component within the major project capstone course is the production of a major paper or senior thesis. In this section, we consider other common elements of the typical capstone experience: factors that determine how the project topic or issue gets selected, how (or if) a mentor is assigned, and how that project is shared with others either in or beyond the classroom.

A common question asked by faculty is, "Which comes first: the topic for the major project or the mentor to guide it?" Results suggest that the answer to this question is determined by whether there is any contact between the student and faculty beyond the primary capstone instructor. Since survey results consistently report that most capstones are taught by a single instructor, guidance from another faculty member is not a primary goal, or a guaranteed option, for most students within capstone courses. We did ask this question in our national survey of sociology and psychology departments and found that most respondents reported "no meetings" with faculty (66 percent) other than the course instructor (Hauhart & Grahe, 2012). However, the rest of the respondents reported a range (from one to fifteen) of frequencies. The most common response from our respondents was one meeting (16 percent).[7] Unfortunately, neither Henscheid et al. (2000) nor Padgett and Kilgo (2012) investigated this question in their surveys.

Alternatively, Schermer and Gray (2012) report explicitly on this format. In all four of their participating institutions, some, if not all, students work with both the instructor of record and a faculty mentor to complete their capstone project. They detail slight differences in how the mentor is assigned and the expectations of the mentor, but they are consistent in reporting the need and value of a mentor in the capstone experience.[8] The Schermer and Gray (2012) report is also helpful in documenting variation in standard expectations for the mentor-student relationship. Three institutions have no formal statement of the role that mentors should fulfill, but the College of Wooster identifies explicit expectations with substantial detail, including expectations that the mentor will help identify the topic; meet regularly with the student, often weekly; assist with thesis editing; and provide a written evaluation of the work.

Of perhaps greater value for institutions considering their own capstone-related workload issues, each of these four schools also has a system to count faculty mentorship as part of the standard faculty teaching load. For instance, at the College of Wooster, faculty members received one course release for advising five students within the capstone experience. At Washington College, faculty members received one course release for every twelve capstones supervised. At Allegheny College, the administration assigns differential points for the project director (3 points) and the second reader (1 point) for each student. Forty-four points are equivalent to a course release. Only at Augustana College among the four colleges studied is the capstone workload not predetermined as part of the standard teaching load.

The mentor assignments have some impact on the major project selection, but results suggest that topic selection still varies greatly along a continuum. In our own surveys of sociology and psychology departments, we found that the student is the primary source of the capstone project topic in most instances. In our regional survey (Hauhart & Grahe, 2010), student selection (40 percent) was reported slightly more frequently than selection as an extension of the faculty member's research area (34 percent). In our national survey (Hauhart & Grahe, 2012), respondents rated students as solely responsible for selecting the topic ($M = 2.71$, $SD = 1.13$), higher than any other option. Student decisions among small student groups ($M = 1.56$, $SD = 0.82$), student research within a faculty research project ($M = 1.77$, $SD = 0.79$), and instructor decisions ($M = 1.72$, $SD = 0.92$) all produced lower response rates. Schermer and Gray (2013) confirm the predominance of students as the most common source of ideas for the project topic.

Characteristics of the Major Paper

Although many studies document the major or extended paper's centrality to the typical capstone course, we found few studies other than our own that investigate the characteristics of the major paper. Although our studies focus only on psychology and sociology departments, single-discipline capstone papers suggest that the patterns are likely consistent across other disciplines given the consistency of other capstone-related characteristics. With respect to sociology and psychology capstones, we found that where a major paper was required, over 50 percent of respondents said students were often also expected to meet minimum production standards (Hauhart & Grahe, 2010, 2012). While the range was sometimes great, the averages provide an indication of the typical capstone project in these disciplines. There was generally a minimum page requirement ($M = 18.46$, $SD = 10.91$) and often a minimum number of references ($M = 12.10$, $SD = 6.63$).[9] Students were commonly expected to work on the project for a considerable amount of time ($M = 78.80$, $SD = 63.48$). Even more consistent was that students were expected to follow some discipline-guided writing style such as American Psychological Association (APA), American Sociological Association (ASA), Modern Language Association, or *Chicago Manual of Style* guidelines. Type of citation and reference style were normally determined by major: psychology, for example, followed APA style, sociology chose ASA style, and combined departments reported a range or mix of choices. There was great consistency between our regional and national surveys regarding these findings. We estimate with some certainty that over half of the capstone courses in these disciplines provide some guidance regarding minimum writing standards to their students. Although the format, length, number of citations, and writing style will be variable across all disciplines, there is likely a shared set of minimum standards within each discipline on each of these four components.

Grading

The completed project is most often evaluated by the instructor of record, but often the instructor receives feedback about the student's performance from a second reader. Alternatively, some departments grade the capstone using a committee or even members of the entire department (Hauhart & Grahe, 2010, 2012; Henscheid et al., 2000; Schermer & Gray, 2013). While grading can occur through classroom presentations and the final paper, a popular destination for capstone projects is an on-campus conference where students either orally present their findings or (primarily in the sciences) share a poster of the findings.

These public presentations provide members of the department faculty, other students, and potentially the entire academic and local community to share in the senior culminating experience. Both of our institutions engage in some form of capstone conference. At Saint Martin's University, students may apply or be nominated for selection as participants at a university-wide Scholar's Day where they present their research. Classes are cancelled, an academic awards ceremony is held on the same day, and students selected to make presentations (and their guests) are invited to a faculty-sponsored luncheon. At PLU, all capstone projects include a public presentation component but they are not necessarily open to the entire university community. Departments typically plan their own sessions. These range from in-class presentations where others are invited to attend to conference-style activities with talks or posters in multiple sessions accompanied by awards ceremonies and refreshments. Where the outcomes are performance rather than research based, the capstones are presented as recitals, art shows, or theater performances.

Although not always used for grading purposes, public presentations of senior work are common. Schermer and Gray (2012) include descriptions of each mode of "celebrations/recognitions of completed projects" at the four liberal arts schools they investigated. Two of these institutions hold campuswide events. Augustana College holds "Scholars' Day," and the College of Wooster cancels class for that day in a massive celebration that includes a "parade of seniors who have submitted their projects . . . [where] 'I did it' buttons are worn" (p. 31). Allegheny College and Washington College do not have campuswide celebrations, but they do electronically archive all capstone projects as a means of honoring completion of the projects.

Conclusion

In this chapter we began by reviewing studies that examined capstone courses from a multidisciplinary, multi-institutional perspective in order to describe capstone course characteristics broadly at a general level of abstraction. Although only a handful of studies meet these criteria, these studies are largely consistent with each other in suggesting the features of a typical capstone course common to many programs. Furthermore, when we compared these studies to other single-discipline, multi-institutional studies or even single-discipline, single-institution studies, we found little divergence in capstone descriptions across institutions or disciplines. Thus, we feel confident that the typical contemporary capstone experience generally includes the core characteristics we have discussed. It is important to state that we are not proposing that what the great majority of higher education institutions do currently is necessarily, in every instance, the best practice from a pedagogical point of view. However, we do believe that knowing what other educators, departments, and institutions are doing is a valuable point of departure.

Based on our review of the literature, the typical capstone experience is one in which students complete a major research project that most likely produces an extended paper with some minimal length and research criteria. The experience will generally count as a single full-semester course, though it might be extended through course sequencing. The primary goal of the course is to integrate and apply material from the discipline, but there are consistent secondary goals that include improved oral and written communication and research skills. Most often the student will work alone in the context of a small class or seminar, and there is commonly a single course instructor or faculty mentor. The project topic is most often generated by the student, but the topic selection might follow a topic identified by the instructor or mentor. The major project will be conceived within the content of the student's major discipline, conform to its writing and citation styles, and could include portfolios of professional work or presentations of creative expression in fine arts disciplines. On completion, the student likely presents the completed work to classmates or the university community.

CHAPTER FOUR

THE ROLE AND DESIGN OF RESEARCH PROJECTS LEADING TO THE CAPSTONE EXPERIENCE

The reason that approximately three-quarters of all capstone courses include a major research project is threefold. First, professional academic work everywhere includes a research component, and in many instances research is hailed as the sine qua non of work within a discipline. Second, the research project is an important learning tool. Third, the majority of discipline-specific capstone courses in existence already incorporate research as an essential component of the course.

This chapter's review of the literature regarding the ways undergraduate research courses can be developed within the curriculum is intended to advance the use of research experiences in anticipation of, in conjunction with, and during capstone courses. Research capstone course outcomes will be measurably improved by early and frequent student exposure to research opportunities. Capstone courses can offer a single-semester research experience or can serve as the final phase of participation in a major research project that extends over one or more prior semesters. Moreover, success within core research courses is highly predictive of learning outcomes and long-term performance generally.

Capstone Experiences and Undergraduate Research Opportunities

To understand the distinction (or lack of distinction) between capstone experiences and undergraduate research generally, it is important to review the status of research opportunities in the academic environment. In many traditional academic majors, learning to conduct research is part of the core curriculum. Although scientists have always needed to learn about their discipline-specific methodology, this impetus for students to engage in hands-on undergraduate research is relatively recent. Many writers suggest that the drive to incorporate research opportunities for undergraduates rose to its recent fervor beginning in the 1990s after release of the Boyer Report (Brownell & Swaner, 2010; Merkel, 2003; Rowland, Lawrie, Behrendorff, & Gillam, 2012; Webber-Bauer & Bennett, 2003). Merkel (2003) suggests that the contemporary emphasis on undergraduate research began even earlier, "in 1969 when MIT established the country's first campus wide program" (p. 1). Merkel documents important moments in the history of this movement, including the emergence in the 1980s of such key programs as the National Science Foundation Research Experiences for Undergraduates (REU) and organizations such as the Council on Undergraduate Research (CUR), the National Council on Undergraduate Research, and Project Kaleidoscope. His history recap ends with a description of the Boyer Commission of the Carnegie Commission on Higher Education report (Kenny, Boyer Commission, & Carnegie Foundation, 1998), which encouraged institutions to increase their research opportunities for undergraduates. In short, this undergraduate research history time line mirrors the capstone course history we presented earlier. Thus, some of the same outside forces encouraged both to become more common in the 1980s and 1990s. Capstone courses were often viewed as one way to increase opportunities for students' undergraduate research experience.

The Range of Undergraduate Research Opportunities in the Curriculum

A look at several disciplines reveals a pattern that many research-based areas of study have followed with respect to undergraduate research. Research courses are already part of many traditional academic disciplines. Often, however, the study of research methods is camouflaged by their submersion in substantive courses as well. In studies of the psychology curriculum, an introductory research course was present in over 90 percent of the institutions measured (Perlman & McCann, 2005; Stoloff et al., 2010). Curricular studies have also shown that students were likely to experience multiple opportunities to learn about empirical research as part of the major. In chemistry, the American Chemical Society (2008) recommends that students complete multiple laboratory courses where they practice completing research activities. Though biology does not appear to have a standard set of learning guidelines as psychology and chemistry do (Rowland et al., 2012), a report by the National Research Council (2003), *Bio 2010: Transforming Undergraduate Education for Future Research Biologists,* suggested changes to improve future biology education, including changing laboratory experiences to be more interdisciplinary and more integrative.[1] It does not require elaborate citation to reliably assert that sociology and many humanities disciplines, like history and English, also include research courses or research components within their major offerings.

Extending Undergraduate Research across Disciplines

This expectation for undergraduates to engage in research opportunities beyond sciences that historically embraced undergraduate research opportunities (UROs) has found much support. CUR supports undergraduate research across many academic disciplines.[2] As documented on the CUR website, it was organized in 1978. CUR defines undergraduate research as "an inquiry or investigation conducted by an undergraduate student that makes an original intellectual or creative contribution to the discipline" (CUR, 2013). This broad definition for research enables the organization to work in arts and humanities disciplines that historically define research distinctly from the sciences (Crawford & Shanahan, 2014).

CUR supports undergraduate research by providing small grants and travel awards, workshops and conferences focused on advancing methodological and pedagogical techniques, and publications and publication opportunities for faculty and student researchers. The organization also advances undergraduate research opportunities through advocacy with the federal government. In sum, it provides a source of support for individuals at institutions without strong research programs or individuals in disciplines who are historically less likely to embrace UROs. CUR is organized across all disciplines in the sciences, social sciences, and humanities.

This brief description of CUR highlights the prevalence and increasing prominence of undergraduate research across the contemporary curriculum. Given the predominance of research-based capstone courses in most disciplines, the prevalence of undergraduate research opportunities in core courses will enhance the ability of students to complete high-quality scholarly research in capstone courses. This will be especially true if the research opportunities are maximized by the institution and department by sequential alignment with the capstone experience. The potential for establishing strong UROs across disciplines is a common theme among academic writers. Brownell and Swaner (2010) state, "Although undergraduate research had its inception in the sciences, such opportunities now frequently extend to the arts, humanities, and social sciences" (p. 31). Although these experiences exist beyond the sciences, they seem to be less frequently offered in some other disciplines (Corley, 2013; Davis & Sandifer-Stech, 2006; Langford, 2014; Rodrick & Dickmeyer, 2002; Seymour, Hunter, Laursen, & DeAntoni, 2004). For individuals in these disciplines, a recent book edited by Ian Crawford, Sara Orel, and Jenny Shanahan (2014) addresses this gap by focusing ten chapters on methods for including URO experiences across arts and humanities disciplines. Generally UROs that are developed in support of the research expected within the senior capstone experience will contribute to preparing students for a more successful project.

Rodrick and Dickmeyer (2002) note a drive to incorporate UROs in fields beyond the natural sciences but point out many potential barriers. For instance, they note nonscience students' fear of statistics and students' difficulty seeing the relevance of research as two intertwined, major issues to address. We expect this observation is applicable to many fields. Rodrick and Dickmeyer (2002) point to their own effort to enhance UROs for students in the communications major who, they observed, often encounter research methods as an elective rather than as a required course. They present their scaffolded, sequential research curriculum as one that can better support a capstone course because it increases students' experience with research methodology through two required courses in the core program. It is also notable that they found that increased research methods in the curriculum improved both the quality of the capstone research projects and department morale. They noted an increase in "the [positive] energy the faculty feels when student projects are proposed" and commented that "more research collaboration has occurred among faculty members than ever before" (Rodrick & Dickmeyer, 2002, p. 48). Similar approaches with accompanying success are reported in descriptions of how history (Scott & Orel, 2014), art (Lightfoot, Sand, & Wilbur, 2014), and communication (Hay, Snowball, Varallo, Hilton-Morrow,

& Klein, 2014) departments can successfully scaffold research across their curriculum. Further examples from Chamely-Wilk et al. (2014) discuss scaffolding across multiple departments—accounting, biology, and political science—at Florida Atlantic University.

These examples provide guides for those interested in addressing the disparity in research opportunities among disciplines acknowledged by academicians writing within a number of fields. Corley (2013), for example, also suggests that UROs should occur more routinely in history departments and argues that history departments can and should create similar types of UROs as those that exist in the sciences. In history, he writes, a major impediment is the idea that "historical research is inherently non-collaborative . . . thus deemed as something done alone; the monastic scholar sits in archives and various studies while developing the illuminated manuscript that promises to shed new light on the sacred past" (p. 401). Corley perceives his colleagues in the humanities as less likely to believe undergraduate students can develop sufficient skills to complete such a project. Finally, he suggests that faculty do not receive sufficient incentives to work with students. Scholarly collaborations require time that must be subtracted from other activities that are central to the faculty review and promotion process. For there to be faculty support for undergraduate research, there must be corresponding support for faculty to undertake the task. This is a recurring theme in descriptions of how to build strong research programs across disciplines (Karukstis & Hensel, 2010; Taraban & Blanton, 2008).

There are barriers that limit the exposure of more students to UROs in practical fields such as family studies (Davis & Sandifer-Stech, 2006) and nursing (Hagen, Awosoga, Kellett, & Dei, 2013). Davis and Sandifer-Stech state, "This persistent problem lies in the inadequate quantitative research curricula of many family studies programs" (p. 57). As a result of limited course options (specifically the lack of advanced methods courses), this dilemma yields two types of students who turn into two types of professionals: swimmers or sinkers. As the terms imply, *sinkers* are those who complete required quantitative training but never internalize the material, avoid conducting any future research, and often do not attend graduate school. In contrast, *swimmers* succeed at quantitative methods, but they often attend applied, non-research-based graduate programs. Davis and Sandifer-Stech indicate that even these students are unlikely to use research in their careers.

To address this problem in their field, Davis and Sandifer-Stech (2006) describe a research training curriculum that includes basic statistics as a required course early in the major, followed by two research courses in the spring of the junior year. This sequence is intended to prepare students for their capstone course in the senior year. The result is that by the time students begin their senior capstone course, they are neither anxious nor unprepared to complete a major project. They generally found that students' confidence with using research methods increased as they progressed through the research course sequence.[3]

Across disciplines, whether they are natural or social sciences or arts and humanities, departments face challenges in administering undergraduate research. In Crawford et al. (2014), these themes are considered in many arts and humanities disciplines: classics (Langford, 2014), English (Swift, 2014), history (Scott & Orel, 2014), religion (McNary-Zak & Peters, 2014), visual arts (Lightfoot et al., 2014), music (Roens & Young, 2014), and theater (Cavanagh, Quarmby, & Unwin, 2014). Although each discipline responds uniquely to the question of how to incorporate UROs, the book collectively can be used to help aspiring or established programs evaluate how best to integrate and administer UROs in their curriculum.

The Rationale for Undergraduate Research: A High-Impact Practice

The Association of American Colleges and Universities identifies both undergraduate research experiences and capstone courses or experiences as high-impact practices that should be encouraged in all liberal arts programs (Brownell & Swaner, 2010). The literature suggests that such practices greatly improve students' attainment of institutional learning goals through deeper learning and immersion in their discipline. Brownell and Swaner also suggest that outcome gains related to personal development from these high-impact practices are consistent, "regardless of the students' major, whether in the sciences, social sciences, arts, or humanities" (p. 34). Taraban and Logue (2012) recently noted the importance that agencies such as the National Science Foundation and the National Research Council place on having all students participate in these experiences because all students are expected to benefit. They call this expectation that any student benefits from high impact practices the "unconstrained model." In their own constrained model some students benefit more than others. The constrained model, if accurate, suggests that faculty may need to offer assistance to underprepared students who might not otherwise benefit as substantially. In either model, however, it is clear that research projects benefit students, although perhaps some more than others.

Healey and Jenkins (2009) suggest that UROs can range on two important dimensions: the degree to which the students are participants, as opposed to merely an audience to the research, and the degree to which the emphasis is on research content, as compared to understanding common processes and problems. Their model can be illustrated as the intersection of two axes that yield four quadrants representing distinct types of student experiences. Characterizing research experiences in this manner focuses attention on the benefits that students acquire from the experience rather than the academic discipline that supports the research itself. These research experiences can occur inside an established classroom or in a laboratory course, but they may also occur through an independent study project, capstone course, or as a paid or unpaid research assistant without credit (see figure 4.1).

There appears to be general agreement that in an ideal curriculum, undergraduate research experiences should occur across the college career, although in practice, not all students are introduced to these experiences (Brownell & Swaner 2010; Davis & Sandifer-Stech, 2006; Elrod, Husic, & Kinsey, 2010; Russell, Hancock, & McCullough, 2007). A significant consequence of the disparity in research opportunities is that not all students experience the same learning benefits (Hartmann,

FIGURE 4.1. THE NATURE OF UNDERGRADUATE RESEARCH AND INQUIRY

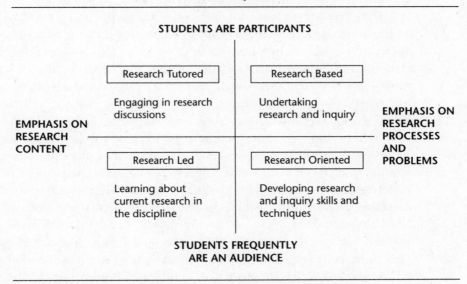

Source: Reprinted with permission from Healey and Jenkins (2009, p. 7).

Widner, & Carrick, 2013; Taraban & Logue, 2012). The upshot for most commentators is that students across disciplines are encouraged to complete research both within the existing curriculum and as additional opportunities outside the structure of the major. Regardless of how undergraduate students are involved in research, the essential point is that the greater the number of research experiences a student has, the greater learning benefits he or she attains, and the better prepared he or she is for a capstone research project.

Many studies have documented the benefits that students attain from research. In a comparison of the impact of various types of undergraduate research, Russell (2008; see also Russell et al., 2007) reported on a series of surveys completed by undergraduate, graduate, and faculty participants in National Science Foundation (NSF) undergraduate programs. The authors distinguished between research projects by discipline: STEM (science, technology, engineering, and math) and SBES (social, behavioral, or economic science). The researchers compared the responses of STEM ($N = 3,400$) and SBES ($N = 3,200$) graduates in the United States. They identified three groups: students who participated in sponsored (i.e., funded) research (approximately 6 percent), those who participated in nonsponsored research (approximately 46.5 percent), and those who did not participate in research (approximately 47.5 percent). Research activities included summer research, hands-on in-class-based research, internships with hands-on research, and a junior or senior thesis.

These results suggest little difference in the percentage of STEM and SBES students participating in internships and thesis projects. NSF and sponsored-research students did complete more hands-on in-class projects than nonfunded research students did (Russell, 2008). Notable differences emerged when they compared types of activities the student researchers completed (see the table on p. 67 in Russell, 2008). Although the majority in all groups reported collecting and analyzing data, SBES-sponsored researchers reported doing so the least. NSF researchers were the most likely (and nonsponsored research the least likely) to prepare a final report or a poster or to deliver oral presentations. There were no clear differences between STEM and SBES researchers in participation in these activities. STEM- and SBES-sponsored researchers were more likely to have a choice of project and to have input or make decisions about the project. They were also more likely to write a proposal about the project and have primary responsibility for its completion. When comparing STEM and SBES directly, more SBES students reported gains in "increased understanding about," "increased confidence in," and "increased awareness of" their discipline (Russell, 2008, p. 68). This is an interesting finding because it suggests that while STEM students might have more undergraduate research opportunities, SBES students might experience greater benefits. STEM and SBES students both reported benefits, the precise outcome that UROs are intended to deliver.

Webber-Bauer and Bennett (2008; see also Bauer & Bennett, 2003) examined undergraduate research from the University of Delaware. Their study examined student evaluations, faculty and alumni accounts, and a longitudinal study of research experiences in science and engineering departments. The survey results echoed other conclusions, with large percentages of faculty suggesting that UROs led to "cognitive and affective development including intellectual curiosity, understanding scientific findings, thinking logically about complex material, and synthesizing information from diverse sources" (p. 92). They also reported that faculty observed that the "cost in terms of time" and "financial cost" were substantial. Alumni reported that more research was associated with greater academic gains as well. These benefits appeared greater for those who experienced formal programs or completed a senior thesis compared to "self-reported" research participation (those who were not listed in the University of Delaware Research Program Database).[4]

Seymour et al. (2003) used interviews to examine benefits to students who participated in summer UROs. They categorized gains from students' reports as personal/professional, thinking/working like a scientist, skills, career path clarification, career/graduate school preparation, and changes in attitudes toward learning/working as a researcher. Their findings confirm many previously established benefits of undergraduate research, but their subjects did not consistently identify others. They found little evidence of publications (whether as conference presentations or authored papers) and little evidence that UROs helped students choose a career. But they conclude that students describe UROs as having a "profound significance for their emergent adult identity and sense of direction" (p. 531). The students told the researchers that their research experiences helped increase their independence. Arguably, experiences that improve maturity and autonomy better prepare students for their success in a senior capstone experience.

In a single-institution study, Taraban and Logue (2012) identified factors that augment the research experience for biology and psychology students. Students with more research experiences, those with better relationships with their mentors, those with higher grade point averages, and those who were intrinsically motivated reported increased benefits from UROs. Like Webber-Bauer and Bennett (2008), this report documents that more research involvement begets greater learning benefits. Furthermore, better students benefit more from research experiences than poorer students do. This suggests that as students enter the senior capstone, they come with a range of performance and motivational differences that will likely influence the benefits they receive from any capstone-based research experience.

In sum, these studies provide strong evidence of the varied benefits of undergraduate research and suggest that the associated costs are worth the effort.

Types of Research Experiences and Differential Outcomes

In chapter 3, we noted that capstone project topics could be determined by either the student or the faculty or some hybrid of the two. Healey and Jenkins (2010) also incorporate a student- or faculty-led research dimension in their conceptual framework for inquiry-based learning, a term that reflects UROs as well as other active learning procedures (figure 4.2). They suggest a second dimension also has an impact on the nature and type of project pursued. Thus, students may participate through research directed at either "building of knowledge" or "exploring or acquiring existing knowledge" (p. 26).

This model, like their model regarding type of experiences, yields four quadrants: pursuing, identifying, authoring, and producing. The framework deftly represents the possible roles that students will pursue in activities that form the capstone courses. *Authoring projects* are those in which the student is attempting to contribute a novel piece of knowledge to academic discourse. The quality of the question and the student's resources have a clear impact on the value of those contributions. *Producing projects* represents research where the faculty mentor is making a novel contribution to public discourse and the student is completing a project in support of the faculty-driven question. We will focus on these quadrants because they offer students the most benefit and the scientific method anticipates creating shared knowledge.

The distinction between authoring and producing projects is the degree to which the student assumes a responsibility as the primary investigator on a particular project. A few of the Healey and Jenkins (2009) case studies provide examples of projects that participate in building

FIGURE 4.2. INQUIRY-BASED LEARNING: A CONCEPTUAL FRAMEWORK

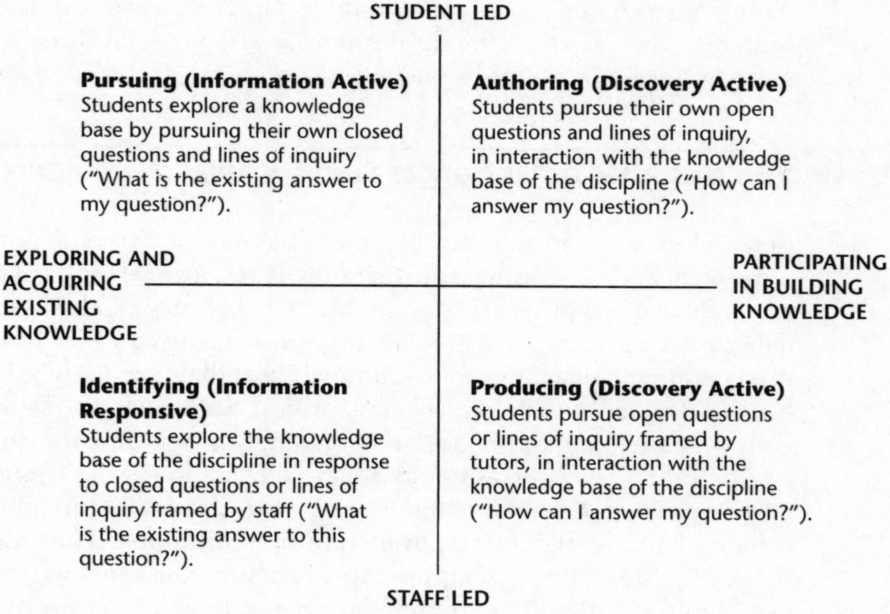

STUDENT LED

Pursuing (Information Active)
Students explore a knowledge
base by pursuing their own closed
questions and lines of inquiry
("What is the existing answer to
my question?").

Authoring (Discovery Active)
Students pursue their own open
questions and lines of inquiry,
in interaction with the knowledge
base of the discipline ("How can I
answer my question?").

EXPLORING AND ACQUIRING EXISTING KNOWLEDGE ——————————— **PARTICIPATING IN BUILDING KNOWLEDGE**

Identifying (Information Responsive)
Students explore the knowledge
base of the discipline in response
to closed questions or lines of
inquiry framed by staff ("What
is the existing answer to this
question?").

Producing (Discovery Active)
Students pursue open questions
or lines of inquiry framed by
tutors, in interaction with the
knowledge base of the discipline
("How can I answer my question?").

STAFF LED

Source: Based on Levy (2009) printed in Healey and Jenkins (2009). Reprinted with permission.

knowledge, but hover on the line of authoring and producing. One example is a series of team-based problem-based projects employed at the University of Queensland as part of the capstone course. Here students work in small groups as consultants on projects that originate through faculty effort. Projects are formed as "staff solicit suitable 'problems' and clients among their contacts, for instance from government agencies, non-government organizations, land care groups or the private sector" (p. 32). Student groups meet for a year with their "clients," often off campus, and ultimately share with them their final reports. Another example is an alternative final-year project at Durham University in the United Kingdom developed by Stefan Przyborski for students not interested in the "traditional laboratory-based project" (p. 42). "Students use their knowledge and understanding of science to develop and research their idea into a technology that can be readily commercialized, e.g., a diabetes breath test, a biodegradable chewing gum" (Healey & Jenkins,

2009, p. 42). If students are the primary originators, this is authoring, whereas if faculty members generate the research hypothesis, students assist in producing.[5] In either instance, high student investment and direct engagement in research produce substantial learning benefit for students. This factor distinguishes the projects between those requiring more or less intensive involvement in research.

Costs and Benefits of Undergraduate Research Projects

Research projects in the social, behavioral, and natural sciences include some or all of the following types of inquiry: literature review, meta-analysis, research or grant proposal, case studies or program evaluation, empirical data-gathering theoretical project, or performance-artistic projects. These projects might fall in any of the four quadrants that Levy (2009) discussed, but the ideal senior capstone research project would be high on the "participating in building knowledge" continuum. Research in core curriculum research methods courses would more likely fall in the "pursuing knowledge" quadrant. Each mode differs in the amount and nature of required resources for the student, faculty mentor, and institution. The various configurations also differ in their potential benefit to the student, faculty, and institution. Whether these traditional types of research activity directed at building knowledge are incorporated in a capstone course or not, either authoring or producing offers challenges that have been previously identified as high-impact learning experiences. Knowing the resource and design limitations of the various forms of research activity is a distinct advantage in selecting research experiences for inclusion in the core curriculum, electives, or the capstone experience.

We briefly consider each common phase of most research projects with respect to the associated costs and potential outcome.

The Literature Review as Independent Project

Thomas and Hodges (2010) remind us that a literature review may take either of two forms: a general conceptual review that serves as background for an empirical project or a systematic review that "aims to provide a synthesis of the main trends or findings in a carefully selected groups of studies on a topic, using procedures intended to limit bias and random error" (p. 107). Thomas and Hodges offer students a guide to conducting a literature review. Their summary begins with the early processes of refining the topic and conducting a search for appropriate articles and continues through evaluation of relevant studies leading to a final written review. Other potential resources for supplementary textbooks guiding literature reviews as the major project are also available (e.g., Galvan, 2004; Landrum, 2012). Jones, Barrow, Stephens, and O'Hara (2012) suggest that history majors use "research-and-writing advice manuals offered by textbook publishers" generally (p. 1103).

A literature review that is the sole basis for a secondary research paper does not include any independent empirical data collection. Consequently, the only tangible resources necessary are research time and library access to primary materials. While it is true that access to these articles can take days or weeks depending on the speed of the interlibrary loan requests, information-sharing systems have improved markedly. Thus, in a standard fifteen-week semester, this should not present students with an insurmountable problem. Although a project of this nature is not as academically challenging as pursuit of an experimental design, it does offer academic benefits that may be more suitable for some students and may be an acceptable scholarly exercise for undergraduates within some disciplines. Generally any research activity that challenges students to work beyond the academic level they have already attained will produce benefit. Literature reviews have potential high value for student learning and varying demand on faculty time, but they add little value to the institution or faculty research productivity.

When students complete literature reviews for class projects, they are not likely to be published or contribute to the academic discourse. Thus, a literature review that constitutes the final product for a capstone course must be carefully distinguished from the literature review that is incorporated as a step in a larger process. Stephens, Jones, and Barrow (2011) increase the experience of authentic research and student motivation as well by including research papers incorporating disciplinary literature but arguing a thesis in a "book project." Here, the literature reviewed must examine and either support or contradict the thesis pursued. The students experience the process of preparing a professional essay intended for publication (the work is self-published by Virginia Tech) but not the rigors of external, professional peer review. Though we have found no research documenting the proportion of capstone projects that are eventually published in professional journals, undergraduate student-faculty collaborations can occasionally yield such an outcome. (For an example of student work that produced a novel and interesting thesis that achieved eventual professional publication, see Hauhart & Choi, 2012.)

The Meta-Analysis

A meta-analysis is a type of literature review using published results as data for an original analysis (Thomas & Hodges, 2010). The findings from multiple published studies are tested comparatively to explore the reliability and generalizability of propositions beyond the conclusions of each individual study. The procedure has been developed considerably since early demonstrations of the potential benefits to be derived from drawing conclusions based on systematic examination of previous work (O'Rourke, 2007). More recently, access to software that can conduct statistical analyses has led to increased prominence of this approach in many disciplines (Cooper, 2010). Although a meta-analysis employs quantitative procedures, there is no original empirical data collection. This means that meta-analysis has the same basic resource requirements as the literature review, although it requires a substantially more sophisticated understanding of statistics and methodological complexities.

Since meta-analytic procedures are more complex and challenging, they require increased faculty training and resources for students to complete a project along these lines successfully. To address this, faculty will likely employ supplementary support texts such as Harris Cooper's *Research Synthesis and Meta-Analysis* (2010). This book is directed at researchers who want to conduct literature reviews or meta-analyses and guides students through the process of finding adequate literature and basic meta-analysis statistics. While student-level meta-analyses are infrequent, they have the potential to contribute to the academic discourse, a positive outcome for the student, the faculty member, and the institution. However, the increased faculty time necessary to train students to complete meta-analyses might not make the potential gain worth the increased resource cost. Successful implementation of this type of research might require reduced research course enrollments or teaching loads.

The Research or Grant Proposal as a Major Project

Research proposals can also be treated as artificial, independent research exercises. They can vary from simple proposals that include a literature review and planned methodology to complex assessments offering a fully developed plan for data analysis, expected results, contribution to the discipline, and anticipated difficulties. Although we are primarily focused on capstone projects and the sequence of research courses leading up to the capstone, it is worth noting that Peterson, Anderson, and Mitchtom (1996) found that using research proposals for introductory earth science courses was beneficial to student learning. Pergram (2006) also extols the benefits that can accrue from requiring research proposals to help students learn basic research. He states, "Not only does it give students proper context for their research but it also helps them develop valuable creative-thinking skills" (p. 18). Pergram describes projects that could be used for high school through the senior year of college.

The intended audience for the proposal can range from fellow students and the course instructor to businesses and agencies beyond the institution. The proposal could also be structured as a grant proposal and include associated components such as a budget. Oh, Kim, Garcia, and Krilowicz (2005) provide detailed direction about the process of writing a National Institutes of Health– or NSF-style grant including weekly benchmarks for progress, which could be used as a learning model for student proposals. Finally, students could engage in peer review and panel judging of research proposals to extend the level of professional experience gained (Oh et al., 2005; Pergram, 2006; Peterson et al., 1996).

Using the research proposal as a project in its own right does not include implementation of the project; thus, there is no data collection. Under these artificial project proposal conditions, the resource costs are similar to those in a literature review or meta-analysis. Students simply need to devote time to library or elementary research, analysis, and writing. The demand on faculty time and resources can be modest, particularly if outside volunteers can be enlisted to mentor students through an internship or practicum-type course. These projects do contain the potential for a partnership arrangement with an organization. A number of courses in business and engineering enlist the cooperation of alumni or other volunteer professionals to provide a real-world setting or problem that is the basis for the research proposal. If a student is sharing a proposal with a nonprofit organization or a company, a successful proposal might eventually generate interest within the organization and gain support for implementation. If the project is a grant proposal, it is even possible that a motivated student could submit the proposal for potential funding. Consequently, these projects have the potential to make eventual contributions to academic discourse by leading to future empirical projects. The connection to alumni or other community volunteers provides a special benefit to the institution.

Case Studies and Program Evaluations

Case studies and program evaluations are substantially similar types of inquiry projects. Each focuses on background literature and theory to address a research question through a methodology that examines in depth a single entity or subject. In business courses, case studies often examine a single organization that faces a critical problem (Lee, 2012); in behavioral sciences, the focus often is on a single individual or client. Program evaluation, present in both business and the behavioral sciences, examines whether a system or organization is functioning according to its mandate. These projects can take the form of either a literature review, if the project is conceived of as limited exclusively to library sources, or include an empirical study if there is an agency or institution that is willing to be the subject of organizational analysis by student researchers (Campbell & Tantro, 1998). The costs and benefits of either of these approaches vary depending on the nature of the project and the nature of any data shared by an agency for a program evaluation.

One issue that can arise regards the standards that should be used to evaluate student research projects that do not constitute fully developed and implemented research studies. Multiple Pacific Lutheran University psychology department meetings have been devoted to discussing the challenge of applying the department's grading rubric to literature reviews, research proposals, and program evaluations. After multiple iterations, the rubric allows for a reasonable comparable evaluation of these projects with empirical projects.

Empirical Data-Gathering Theoretical Projects

The project that provides the greatest potential benefit to the student, faculty mentor, academic discourse, and institution is the development of a research plan and its full implementation. In our national survey of psychology and sociology capstones (Hauhart & Grahe, 2012), we found that about half of the capstone major projects in those disciplines included some form of data collection. Perlman and McCann (2005) estimated that over 90 percent of students engage in some form of data collection activities when completing a psychology major. Other reports of students collecting data as part of their capstone project may be found in other disciplines (Burnette & Wessler, 2013; Barry, Drnevich, Irfanoglu, & Bullock, 2012; Schroeder, et al., 2009), though we discussed earlier that the frequency with which full research projects are required for undergraduates varies across disciplines.

Empirical projects take longer to complete, sometimes require additional approvals (e.g., institutional review board approval for human or animal participants), and can include materials and laboratory costs. In some cases, these costs can be considerable. Particle accelerators and electron microscopes are expensive and not likely to be used widely by students. Even students conducting inexpensive studies could have copying costs for research materials.

Across multiple disciplines, costs are among the issues that must be addressed in building undergraduate research programs (Hunter, Laursen, & Seymour, 2008; Karukstis & Hensel, 2010; Locks & Gregerman, 2008). Even with these additional costs, institutions are clamoring to offer undergraduate research experiences because of the associated student learning and student satisfaction benefits. Perhaps the most common, although not fully quantifiable, additional cost for supporting quality empirical research is the additional faculty time and expertise required. The demand for faculty involvement can be high, thereby limiting enrollment to a manageable student-faculty ratio and increasing costs to the department and the institution.

The Performance-Artistic Project as a Research Experience

In chapter 3, we described a range of capstone experiences that included creative performances and reflection papers associated with internship experiences. Kindelan (2010) reminds us that performing arts majors engage in research projects as well: "The curricula of many performing arts programs support interdisciplinary and independent research projects, encourage reflective pedagogies of civic engagement, include service learning activities and study abroad programs, and offer distinctive experiential ways of learning" (p. 31). Plays and films can require students to gather, analyze, and synthesize knowledge as in many other disciplines. Works of art are often social commentaries that encourage students to think about the world and conduct analysis. Kindelan offers other examples that encompass dance, theater, art, and music projects that establish observable benefits for critical thinking, communication and literacy, and values development. While less common, capstone courses can be fashioned for art and music curricula. Lightfoot et al. (2014) regard this experience as critical to visual arts students' development as professionals and suggest that "the development of a final body of work, whether for a gallery show or for a first professional portfolio, constitutes the final stage in the scaffolding" (p. 65). This sentiment is echoed by Roens and Young (2014) when they discuss research in music performance programs.

Incorporating Undergraduate Research in the Curriculum

Research projects should not—and really cannot—be limited to the senior capstone experience if that experience is going to be successful, even transformative. Rather, the senior capstone course must be the pinnacle of a sequential process of research experiences that create the foundation for the final capping research experience. The questions become: How many undergraduate research experiences can be supported? Where, and in what order, should these research courses appear in the core curriculum to best prepare students for their capstone course?

Departmental Considerations

The decision that a department makes regarding the major project in the capstone course is typically in response to asking, "What projects best match the department goals for graduating seniors within the available resources?" The question of achieving departmental learning goals requires a decision regarding whether majors are expected to conduct data collection (and analysis) or whether it is sufficient to complete a paper based on secondary sources.

Many departments have addressed this question. For chemistry and other physical science majors at York College, the critical component has been defined as consumption, interpretation, and communication of published work (Harrison, 1994). As such, the major project requires students to investigate a current topic through the lens of published studies and then to present that material to peers in an oral presentation with an accompanying paper that the instructor reviews. For biomedical science majors at California State University-Los Angeles, students complete a research grant proposal in groups determined by the instructors (Oh et al., 2005). The goal is to create an authentic professional experience, but one that is couched within the available resources and student limitations.

Each of these approaches reflects settings in which department choices guided by a realistic appraisal of available resources ultimately govern what is important for students to complete within the senior capstone experience. To our knowledge, there is no current research comparing the success of achieving capstone learning outcomes depending on whether data collection was required as compared to senior thesis–style capstone courses based on secondary sources. Yet if a department intends to offer or require a research capstone course, then supporting other courses that involve undergraduate research is critical.

To foster research, it is valuable to focus resources where they will potentially produce the most beneficial effect. Mancha and Yoder (2014) interviewed and then surveyed faculty and student researchers in order to identify critical factors for successful undergraduate research programs. They categorized the factors according to whether faculty, students, or both identified the factor as critical to a successful project. Consequently, departments may consider mechanisms in the curriculum that encourage those factors that are controllable. Though many of the student factors were not under a department's control (such as motivation and enthusiasm) student factors did include availability of resources and institutional support. The most critical faculty list also included availability of resources, as well as better student-faculty relationships and reduced faculty workload.

Faculty Instructor or Mentor Resource Allocation

What we have said so far regarding undergraduate research suggests that it is resource limitations, not lack of benefit from a potential learning experience, that dictates many of the decisions regarding the nature and number of UROs that an institution or department can support. This is certainly true from the faculty's point of view. Faculty members typically are expected to engage in teaching, research, and university and community service. There are discernible limits to what a faculty member can be expected to achieve within each of these areas. Their decisions will therefore often be governed by resource husbandry. Since the primary resource they possess is their own time, faculty will want to expend their capital wisely in influencing the selection and nature of undergraduate student research within the curriculum.[6]

An example of the manner in which a department can manage its research workload is through collegial support among faculty. Rodrick and Dickmeyer (2002) describe a collegial effort within their communications department. First, there was an effort to match expertise so that the student could receive better feedback. Second, by having many faculty members provide feedback, the workload on the instructor was made more manageable. Assigned mentors met regularly with their student charges throughout the semester. By sharing mentorship responsibility, each faculty member was responsible for only a small allocation of his or her time resources.

Faculty members can also be encouraged to support research capstones through the creation of incentive and support systems that reward them for generously investing time in undergraduate research. Ramirez and Dickson (2010) suggest the following are critical considerations for assessing and providing the resources needed for faculty support: teacher responsibilities that allow ongoing research, support of a full-year paid sabbatical, well-funded professional development resources, a strong grants and development office and infrastructure, and a tenure reward system that recognizes meritorious research contributions.

Faculty instructors have some control over the course experience after a research-oriented course is codified by the department. This limited control may allow the instructor to determine the structure of the research project. If possible, an instructor may choose to encourage or require students to engage in research projects that are beneficial to both the student and the instructor in two ways. First, instructors could encourage topics that are within the expertise of the faculty member. Second, they could encourage students to complete research that is directly within the instructor's own research agenda. Burnette and Wessler (2013) describe such a course where introductory biology students are exposed to research procedures associated with active research at the institution. In this manner, both faculty and students can benefit from the research.

Student Controlling Factors

Capstone research can become transformative for the student and possess the potential for producing an influential impact on the future of the sciences or humanities (Karukstis & Hensel, 2010). The capstone course can do so, however, only when student limitations are taken into account. Successful projects can be defined by students along a continuum from earning a passing grade to being published. However, a truly transformative research experience can be achieved only when student factors with the greatest impact on academic success are addressed. Research suggests that the most important factors are student long-term goals, prior academic performance, and motivation or interest in the topic. Although interest in the topic might appear to be the most critical determinant, it is constricted by the other two factors.

The decision of whether to engage in a research course and the definition of future goals occur within a rather narrow time span for students. Though some students are sure of their graduate school or career aspirations early in their college experience, the spring and summer before the senior year are typically when many students make longer-term plans. Graduate school admissions deadlines are often in late fall or winter. Given the arduous task of identifying a school with the best fit, students must start investigating options if their aspirations include graduate education. If students have no graduate school plans, investigations into first job or career opportunities also begin at this time. Simultaneously, students should be making decisions about how a capstone project might be useful in presenting their case for either a graduate application or a future job application. A capstone project demonstrating important laboratory skills or deep integration of theory might impress a graduate school committee.

Students should be guided to select research projects that are within their performance parameters. This means that capstone course instructors and mentors must actively advise students regarding their choice of research questions and the scope of their projects. Since it is increasingly common for a number of academic disciplines to have a sequence of research-based courses (Stoloff et al., 2010; Rowland et al., 2011), students should first be advised to adhere to the sequence in order to prepare properly for the pinnacle of their undergraduate work, the senior capstone course. This is especially true where the capstone course is elective or multiple options for completing the course exist. Thus, students in the research capstone course should be those who have pursued the research sequence available to them and whom the department has deemed to have the basic skills necessary to complete the major project. Students who complete a thoughtfully developed research course sequence will be capable of completing the major project in the capstone course. However, there can be wide variation in student ability even among those with the same grades. This suggests that some students will benefit from a tightly structured framework to support their capstone efforts. However, if students are unwilling to face their own skills limits, the department or the instructor should be honest in communicating to students their academic limits and how those may influence a suitable research project choice.[7]

Thus, students of modest academic ability should choose projects or participate in an instructor's projects that allow them to demonstrate and improve their skills rather than engage in projects that may end up exposing their academic limitations. In psychology, that might mean choosing an empirical project with a simple design or working in a research assistant capacity on a faculty member's research. High-performing students should be encouraged to choose a project that is sufficiently challenging that they can showcase their abilities rather than choose a project that is simply easy for them to complete. Students who are graduate school bound should choose a research question that the instructor considers potentially publishable, whether in a student or a professional journal. In many disciplines, this will mean an empirical research study. Advanced students who seek admission to highly rated graduate schools in a discipline will benefit significantly from having completed quality undergraduate research that has led to a paper that is either accepted for publication or under review by a journal by the time graduate applications are due.

Students should address, whenever possible, questions that they are passionate about answering. Even if a student is able to complete a research project that has the potential for contributing to the advancement of disciplinary knowledge, if the experience is not meaningfully related to the student's learning goals, this work may discourage further interest in research rather than encourage it. When studying student outcomes from UROs, there are persistent reports of students who find the experience lacking. Russell (2008) reported that 6 to 13 percent of students in large samples reported that they "did little or nothing that seemed to me to be real research" (p. 67). Another 7 percent "reported a decreased interest in a STEM career" and "17 percent of follow-up survey respondents "reported that . . . 'research is not for me'" (p. 71). Webber-Bauer and Bennett (2008) report that only 62 percent of respondents felt that UROs were more beneficial than standard science courses. The other 38 percent left unimpressed. Lopatto (2008) also found that a small minority (4.7 percent) found that the research experience guided them away from science. When comparing these groups, Lopatto found that students who "changed for" versus those who "changed against" were more prepared, worked more independently, and had higher self-confidence. This is perhaps the strongest argument in support of offering alternative capstone experiences, including internships and practicums.[8]

Internal motivation to complete a task produces a feeling of self-efficacy. Moreover, persistence on tasks increases both task performance and satisfaction. These outcomes are well documented by experimental psychologists (Freedman & Phillips, 1985; Parker, Jimmieson, & Amiot, 2013; Puca & Schmalt, 1999). Parker et al. (2013) provide a very recent demonstration using a within-subject design with a job simulation where participants responded to e-mails as though they were a human resources manager. The results showed that intrinsic motivation, task performance, and satisfaction are highly correlated and complexly intertwined. The authors concluded that self-determined students can better handle workload dynamics and maintain their intrinsic motivation with less anxiety, but those who are not self-determined function better with more constraints, including higher extrinsic motivation. Because major research projects typically require extended study in depth, researching a personally meaningful question greatly increases a student's willingness to stay focused on completing the research. Since completing a major writing project will be required within the research capstone course, every research course should be designed to inspire student interest rather than exhaust it.

Mapping Student Journeys onto the Generic Undergraduate Research Project

Students, however academically skilled, have seldom been asked—or asked themselves—to develop and carry out significant research within a field prior to the start of their undergraduate research experience. Thus, it is the faculty's responsibility to create frameworks within which student research work can be accomplished. For a generic research project, this would typically include work that would complete the following stages: identifying a research question, gathering appropriate background support and information, designing the research method or protocol, conducting the study, analyzing results, interpreting the findings, integrating the material with the broader literature, and creating a finished report of the entire project. While this elementary scientific model is well known, students need guidance and guideposts for successful implementation.

A visual representation of the model is one method to convey the simple reality of the project as process for novice researchers. In figure 4.3, lines represent the potential focus for students as they work on these projects. Though these do not suggest the only areas of the research process completed by the student when working on a project, they do suggest the likely strengths of a student project that employs each project type. For instance, a literature review provides opportunity to explore the literature and suggest possible empirical studies that are needed, but they are not well suited to draw inferential conclusions. In contrast, a refined empirical study is not likely to be devised and executed in a typical academic course time frame. Therefore, students are likely going to start with a topic already identified, and the bulk of the learning will occur as part of the design, collection, and analysis stages. Depending on the student, instructors, or departmental resources or goals, these

FIGURE 4.3. MAPPING PROJECT TYPES TO THE PATH TO COMPLETING RESEARCH

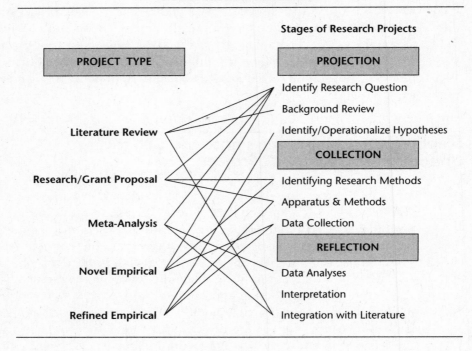

primary foci could be radically different, but this figure highlights that each project need not excel at every stage of the research process.

The visual representation of the research process can also act as a reminder that less ambitious, partial research projects can be carved out of the full research arc. For instance, in the Pacific Lutheran University psychology program, students can complete projects ranging from literature reviews to grant proposals to empirical projects. The empirical projects can range from being wholly student developed to replications as part of an established faculty member's research. Projects never intended for submission into public scientific discourse may involve more creative methods or pose more difficult questions. For such projects, students will be focused on the projection phase more. Where projects are intended for publication, students are likely already addressing a refined question, and their work may already involve collection or even reflection.

Undergraduate Research as Preparation for the Capstone Course

In our view, capstone courses should require completion of some prerequisite courses. Although students may struggle connecting their learning across multiple classes, research courses found in the core curriculum are designed to help prepare students for their coming capstone experience. The actual practice of course sequencing is one of the more important preparatory steps for conducting a successful undergraduate research program. A brief survey of the literature offers several examples of how students may be assisted in overcoming a weak course sequence preparation. These discipline-specific approaches cannot be analogized directly to every field. They can, however, suggest variations that might be successfully adapted.

Jones et al. (2012) help students work on their research project in history by measuring students' present knowledge by having them complete a "'research résumé' during the first week of class" (p. 1107). There, students address a series of quantitative and qualitative questions about their prior research experience and familiarity with research tools, sources, and databases. This is intended to provide students with an easily accessible assessment of their strengths and weaknesses so that they can better seek help through the semester. When compared to their posttest of the same material, Jones et al. report that students often overestimate their initial skills.

Woodard (2011) describes an approach for guiding successful theology capstone projects. The basic premise is to set attainable learning goals and use specific tasks to address targeted skills. Woodard states, "Regardless of the learning objectives, this framework can be used to assist faculty in creating meaningful goals, designing tasks that are directly linked to the learning objectives, and providing effective feedback mechanisms to evaluate the incremental progress involved in the attainment of those goals" (p. 382). He provides an example of seeking out quality sources by introducing basic search guidelines and then having the class go to the library together. The students share their sources and receive immediate feedback regarding the quality of the sources, as well as their summary of them. Another example is teaching students how to write an introduction. Students receive instructions from lecture, review examples in published literature, and then practice by outlining and writing their own introduction. Students then engage in peer evaluation in small groups, thereby providing immediate feedback with less workload for the instructor, while simultaneously providing students with the benefits of giving and receiving peer review. Woodard reports using the peer review process for the final report, with students paired together for the semester and required to use the instructor's rubric to provide each other feedback.

Communication about the Capstone Experience to Students

There are multiple ways, both formal and informal, for students learn about their major's required courses and associated expectations. It is noteworthy that students feel this is a critical component in their preparation for successful research (Mancha & Yoder, 2014). They can view the description in the institution's course catalogue, talk to their academic advisors, consult with instructors for the current term, and talk to each other about what classes they are taking and should take. For capstone courses, unlike many other courses, they might be able to learn about the research project assignment from an academic conference or public presentation of the current senior projects.[9] All of these sources can collectively establish a research culture within the discipline and the university. These sources include those that are intentional and official (such as the course description or advisor meetings), as well as those that are peripheral and informal (such as peer-to-peer discussions). In either case, lower-division students can acquire knowledge about the department's research sequence leading to the senior capstone experience and begin to acquire the attitudes necessary to support an undergraduate research culture at the institution.

In short, students do not enter a course without some prior knowledge and expectations. When those expectations are better informed, the students will experience a more productive and less anxiety-ridden capstone experience. Thus, faculty should take every opportunity to communicate the nature of the capstone experience to their majors.

Guiding the Research Course Project and Sequence

Once students begin the research course, at whatever stage of project planning, they have a limited period in which to complete it. They will be learning not only about discipline-related content and skills but also project management. While many class projects have deadlines and consequences for failure, there are few that occur so close to graduation.

Beyond these structural components, which students can ignore at their own peril, the instructor is responsible for providing guidance for the student to complete the major project. While the capstone instructor may have help from a faculty mentor or through coteaching, often one instructor will guide many projects (Padgett & Kilgo, 2012; Schermer & Gray, 2012).

Although the research course instructor is well practiced at conducting research, teaching others about managing a research project is a different process. In the Pacific Lutheran University psychology capstone course, students are assigned to read a research or writing guide in addition to the sources gathered for their major project. In recent years, students read *Designing and Managing Your Research Project* (2010) by David Thomas and Ian Hodges, an excellent monograph that explains many of the pitfalls of poorly conducted research. Their book provides distinct examples and practice activities. Guidance from this book can help students independently frame their own projects and complement the instructor's advice.[10]

Conclusion

There is a shared history between the emergence of support for UROs and capstone courses. Moreover, there is a convergence between the major research project inherent in most capstone courses and the call for students to complete more research. Research capstones are favored for many reasons, but the most important one is that a research experience provides a high-impact learning situation that produces the most cognitive development. Unfortunately, there is a disparity in research experiences and expectations across disciplines: some students may engage in several UROs before the capstone, while the capstone project may represent the only hands-on experience some students have. Our review of the literature suggests that more undergraduate research experiences lead to better capstone experiences. Multiple research opportunities better prepare students for graduate school and better transfer valuable job skills. Thus, better-integrated research programs increase benefits for students, faculty, and the institution.

CHAPTER FIVE

RESEARCH PROJECT IMPEDIMENTS AND POSSIBILITIES

This chapter considers the potential outcomes from research projects and ideal outcomes for student learning and professional advancement for both students and faculty. We briefly review factors that interfere with successful completion of undergraduate research projects and consider how recent innovations in collaborative science might ameliorate some of these impediments. To the degree that the ultimate goal of successful empirical research is a contribution to public knowledge, a possible approach to capstone research is to coordinate student questions so that data can contribute to the discipline generally. We focus a second chapter on undergraduate research because of the important benefits it offers to both students and faculty and the opportunity it provides to demonstrate competence and excellence within a highly respected, shared academic enterprise. Readers who are more interested in our nuts-and-bolts dissection of the contemporary capstone and our research-based recommendations for constructing the best capstone experience may wish to focus their attention on those chapters.

As we have discussed, the undergraduate research sequences leading to integrative capstone projects have become an increasingly common model for the capstone experience, almost regardless of discipline. Since the research capstone has become the typical capstone, issues that pervade contemporary research more generally relate to students' pursuing research or relying on the research produced in their field. Professionals grapple with these issues as they conduct their own research. However, PhD academicians have the advantage of advanced training, extended experience, and professional colleagues to guide them. Students are new to the research process, lack research experience, and are dependent on their capstone instructor or mentors. This chapter summarizes a number of the issues, pitfalls, and prospects that capstone students face and capstone instructors should anticipate addressing in the undergraduate research sequence or capstone course.

Reduced to a crisp phrase, the goal of the capstone course is often said to be a transformative learning experience in one way another. By this, educators mean that the experience will be life changing to a degree; the learning experience will make a "high impact" on the learner (Kuh et al., 2005; Kuh, 2008). In recent years, the word *transformative* has also been adopted to describe certain types of scientific research. The National Science Board offered the following definition of *transformative research* in a 2007 report:

> Transformative research is defined as research driven by ideas that have the potential to radically change our understanding of an important existing scientific or engineering concept or leading to the creation of a new paradigm or field of science or engineering. Such research also is characterized by its challenge to current understanding or its pathway to new frontiers. (p. v)

The two uses of the word *transformative* share a sense of positive and important change in learning or research.

The typical capstone course can contribute to transformative research and create a transformative learning experience only when students experience a collaborative, ethically based, professional research capstone. We focus attention on the ethical foundation of good research because integrity of method is inextricable from the scientific or professional model. Good results can arise only from good procedures.

A Crisis of Confidence in Empirical Research

Students of the scientific method learn that the ultimate test of a concept's contribution to the field is whether a research finding is replicable. The search for the ability to convert lead into gold defined the field of alchemy.

Yet in the hundreds of years that alchemists used their knowledge as a source of fiscal and social power, none learned how to make the conversion from tantalizing to demonstrable. Alchemy's influence waned, and its failure led to the establishment of the field of chemistry. The reason is simple: when a person achieves outstanding results in a study, those outcomes should be capable of replication. Research submitted for peer review has thus become the test for disciplinary recognition. Furthermore, measures of academic performance, and therefore career advancement, are often associated with the frequency and importance of peer-reviewed research publications. At their best, these motivational factors lead to high productivity and high-quality work; at their worst, they can lead to bad professional practices, including the worst academic sin of all: falsifying data.

In psychology, discussion of the crisis and its possible solutions has become a recurring theme. The Association for Psychological Sciences broached its concern regarding the shortage of replication studies in a special issue of its lead commentary journal, *Perspectives on Psychological Science*, and selected the topic as a theme at its twenty-fifth annual conference. Pashler and Wagenmakers (2012) highlighted a number of recent events that corresponded to the emergence of a scientific crisis in psychology. Recent disciplinary debates regarding the inability to replicate certain effects led the way:

> The Diederick Stapel fraud case . . . the publication . . . of an article purporting to show evidence of extrasensory perception . . . , reports . . . that psychologists are often unwilling or unable to share their published data for reanalysis . . . and the publication . . . [shows] how easily research can . . . obtain statistically significant differences through [adoption of] various questionable research practices. (p. 528)

While announcing the crisis, Pashler and Wagenmakers (2012) try to bring a modicum of comfort to the psychology audience by pointing out that "over the same period, similar concerns have been arising across the scientific landscape" (p. 528). Concerns regarding publication bias and poor scientific practices led John Ioannidis (2005) to survey the problem across all sciences and conclude, "It can be proven that most claimed research findings are false" (p. 696). Although Ioannidis undoubtedly overstates his conclusion, further evidence of the widespread nature of these concerns abounds. Fanelli (2010), for example, examined statistical reporting practices across thousands of articles randomly selected from all scientific disciplines and found that with increasing subjectivity in the framing of the research question, papers were more likely to report positive results. Practices such as these jeopardize the viability of the scientific enterprise across the curriculum. Subsequent studies have concluded that most retractions of scientific journal articles are not due to honest errors but rather research fraud (Saey, 2012).[1] Students, who are new to the research experience, will need guidance to navigate the research literature responsibly.

Impediments to Successful Project Completion

Though it is beyond the scope of this book to fully explore impediments to good science and good research in all disciplines, this crisis has led to some exciting new opportunities. And though all academic research is ultimately conducted by trained professionals, it is possible for students to participate in good science or professional research as they complete their undergraduate training. There are, however, some impediments that students face routinely in completing research projects. In our national survey of sociology and psychology capstone courses, we asked respondents to rate the degree to which each item from a brief list "interfered with completing the capstone project" (Hauhart & Grahe, 2012, p. 230). Our list included (1) students being unprepared academically, (2) difficulty synthesizing a coherent paper, (3) difficulty getting institutional review board approval, (4) obtaining sufficient literature review in available time, (5) students not being motivated, (6) coming up with the research idea, (7) lack of time to collect data, (8) lack of time to analyze data, (9) finding appropriate methodology and/or study materials, (10) student's maturity or emotional level, (11) faculty background being limited relative to student interests, and (12) not enough time for faculty supervision. We reported our findings from a principal components analysis that yielded four factors (items loading on each factor in parentheses): student motivation and preparedness limitations (1, 2, 5, 10), student time limitations (3, 7, 8), research methods limitations (4, 6, 9, 11), and faculty limitations (11, 12).

Experienced capstone instructors, regardless of discipline, can likely call forth memories of specific events and students where each of these four factors was manifested. In a conference talk for the Geological Society of America, Jones and Haywick (2010) discussed impediments for guiding undergraduate research and identified similar issues. They remarked on difficulties in research arising from designing studies specifically for students, students choosing a topic without enough experience in the discipline, time constraints with other course requirements, and resource limitations if funding is not available. Bos and Schneider (2009) identified a similar range of limitations in their interviews of faculty who were guiding research projects in political science. Eliminating barriers to student participation in research is therefore crucial for good research and for good student learning experiences.

Although it is critical to address problems with student motivation and preparedness, faculty limitations also present difficult problems impeding student engagement in research. Most faculty limitations arise from conflicts that revolve around time constraints. Thus, a mismatch between student project topic and faculty expertise constrains time because the faculty member must learn a new area with enough sophistication to address methodological and theoretical questions about the project. Faculty time is further limited by how much intellectual energy a mentor can devote to a student project given other responsibilities. The fact that a student project may or may not be valuable enough to present at a conference or publish in a paper may also bear, consciously or unconsciously, on a faculty member's willingness to invest time in that project when other pedagogical and research activities demand time as well. Schermer and Gray (2010) identified similar costs associated with capstone course research projects. Specifically, they noted that 31 percent of faculty mentors reported negative experiences as capstone mentors arising from factors like these.

Sharobeam and Howard (2002) discuss these faculty limitations as part of the "eternal dilemma" (p. 436) between research and teaching. They note that toward the end of the twentieth century, additional scrutiny regarding faculty time emerged from many state governments. Legislative committees were formed to investigate faculty time, and legislation dictating how faculty can use their time was offered in a number of states. Measures of teaching and community service are now "influenced by external factors such as cost, public pressure, state policies, institutional reputation, and academic ranking" (p. 437). Research productivity, often measured as number of publications or amount of grant money received, becomes pitted against teaching and service in the competition for faculty time.[2] Karukstis (2004) similarly reported that the preponderance of responses to a survey about major barriers to faculty research productivity identified time limitations associated with conflicting professional roles as primary. The Council on Undergraduate Research devoted a special issue of the *CUR Quarterly* (June 2004) to this concern.

One possible solution to this dilemma is to integrate research and teaching time. This method is more applicable to the question of teaching capstone courses than simply undergraduate research courses because of the increased sophistication of the student researchers by the time they are seniors. When students and faculty are jointly engaged in completing projects of high quality that may ultimately deserve publication, faculty are more productive, students are more engaged, and their learning is enhanced. Everyone benefits, especially students, who receive a more intensive, high-impact senior experience.

Responding to Research Impediments

Research impediments such as identifying a good topic, obtaining appropriate resources, time constraints, and institutional review board hurdles are orthogonal to the problems of integrity that challenge professional and scientific work. While the publish-or-perish culture and the allure of flashy novel research over experimental and research replications contribute to the general malaise, these do not routinely affect students directly. The sequence of undergraduate research opportunities leading to senior capstone projects, however, offers an ideal process to train students to consider and respond to what will become professional challenges for them. Efforts from faculty researchers directed at eliminating these impediments can create learning models for capstone students. Of special interest are efforts to increase collegiality through shared data and shared results where students can learn the ethically based collective nature of the research enterprise.

In a *Perspectives on Psychological Science* special issue in November 2012, a number of commentators urged revision of the publication process. Brian Nosek and his colleagues (Nosek & Bar-Anan, 2012; Nosek, Spies, & Motyl, 2012) also have argued that the existing incentive and communication structures are impediments to open scientific practices and deter the search for knowledge.[3] The desire to improve the publication and review process is a problem not only for psychology. Rather, the emergence of open source journals is one response to the problems inherent in status quo academic publishing. Stakeholders interested in changing the publication process include not only researchers and publishers but also funders. Both the National Science Foundation (NSF) and the National Institute of Mental Health adopted procedures within the past decade to require that any research funded by their agencies is made publicly available. The National Institutes of Health policy issued in October 2003 requires all funding requests over $500,000 to include a data-sharing management plan (http://grants.nih.gov/grants /policy/data_sharing/data_sharing_guidance.htm#goals). NSF, in a May 2010 press release (http://www.nsf.gov/news/news_summ.jsp?cntn_id= 116928), announced that all research proposals needed to include a plan to increase access to publicly funded data. In 2011, a task force for the National Science Board explained in detail procedures for implementing this paradigm shift in its report, "Digital Resource Data Sharing and Management." The report calls for the dedication of more resources to expand support for digital data sharing and management. The open science and open source movements have bearing on the participation of undergraduates in research experiences. The relaxation of historically artificial barriers to disseminating research data and analyses creates opportunities for novice researchers to participate meaningfully in confirming, creating, and disseminating quality research.

Michael Nielson in his recent book, *Reinventing Discovery: The New Era of Networked Science* (2012), argues that shared science "increase[s] our collective intelligence" (p. 20). There is no principled reason that undergraduate students cannot contribute to answering important research questions. Nielson introduces examples of successful collective research such as the Polymath Project. There, a blogger posted unsolved math problems and invited readers of the blog collectively to attempt to answer them. Nielson reports that in a little over a month, "27 people wrote 800 mathematical comments, containing more than 170,000 words" (p. 2). By so doing, they collectively and cooperatively had solved the problems. Nielson reports that the project continues: "Nearly a dozen [other] . . . Polymath-like projects have been launched." Nielson also offers as an example projects where organizations offer small rewards to amateurs to address computer science and engineering problems. One program, InnoCentive, inspired over 160,000 people from 175 countries to sign up when prizes for more than 200 challenges were awarded. These and other examples of crowd-sourcing science where colleagues or amateur scientists help answer questions that are difficult to address by a single researcher are becoming commonplace. While many do not accept student contributions, there are many instances where these projects are being developed for student participation.

Capstone Projects and Their Potential Contributions to Professional Research

The Center for Open Science emerged from psychology, but the founders are interested in activating changes across all scientific disciplines. Similar open science initiatives are emerging in other disciplines, and capstone research projects can benefit from these changes. When thoughtfully designed, capstone projects arising from a sustained undergraduate research program are conducted within established professional protocols. Success depends, however, on the introduction of authentic research experiences in core courses and capstone projects generally. The nexus between the emerging drive to share more data publicly and encouraging undergraduate research is a fragile one that has not been completely worked out. Yet advances in research must be shared to enrich any discipline and students must be introduced to the importance of sharing their research. The capstone course is clearly one place to do this.

Introducing students to content that could make a contribution to their field has potential benefits for the students, faculty, institution, and discipline. From the student perspective, completing a research project with even the potential for publication provides a competitive advantage in gaining admission to graduate school or demonstrating discipline-related skills for the job market. In addition, projects that are real to students help address the major student impediment we have noted: motivation. This is one of the premises of problem-based learning and internships and practicums as well. When students believe in the importance and legitimacy of the task, their psychic investment is higher and their motivation improves. If faculty members can benefit because their hard work in guiding research projects is documented for promotion and tenure applications and institutions can benefit from research published by their affiliated faculty and students, undergraduate research can prove its worth to all concerned. Finally, a discipline can benefit by accumulating greater knowledge through student participation. Auchincloss et al. (2014) described these offerings as course-based undergraduate research experiences and identified five dimensions that distinguish them from typical classes or more independent forms such as summer programs or independent studies: use of scientific practices, discovery, broadly relevant or important work, collaboration, and iteration. We focus here on examples of these types of courses and associated projects so that others may adopt or modify them.

Research support for collaborative student engagement in professional-quality work abounds. Trosset, Lopatto, and Elgin (2008) discussed the value of classroom-embedded research experiences in the core curriculum. They found that integrating meaningful science activities into advanced laboratory courses led to similar benefits as summer research experiences. They presented possible research-related undergraduate activities across a spectrum, ranging from "learning about research" to "doing research" (p. 35). Activities focused on "learning about research" included a lecture course, directed lab, and a literature and seminar course, whereas collaborative research courses and individual research were termed "doing research." They described activities in three advanced laboratory courses (two biology courses and a chemistry course) that were employed not only for learning but also to develop the potential for publishable findings. They found that "items on which these courses received a higher mean than summer research included understanding how knowledge is constructed, the ability to analyze data, understanding that assertions require supporting evidence, and skill in scientific writing" (p. 41). They suggest that gains in scientific understanding and research skills could be made through student reports and faculty assessment of performance.

In another natural science class, Rowland, Lawrie, Behrendorff, and Gillam (2012) similarly discussed a system that bridged the typical independent URO and canned classroom lab demonstrations. They offered students a choice to learn about science through either more canned activities or engaging in a URO-type laboratory activity where the findings contributed to scientific knowledge. This approach was specifically developed to bring more authentic research to students at a large institution where hundreds of students pass through the basic research courses. Though only a percentage of students experienced the URO, one benefit provided by the experience was that highly motivated students could get research experience as they progressed through the major where this had not otherwise been available.

Authentic research activities are not limited to natural sciences. Corley (2013) describes three models for getting history students involved in archival work: faculty-driven partnership, faculty collaboration, and student-driven collaboration. These range in the degree to which the faculty or students identify the question and guide the direction of the project. For these undergraduate research efforts to be successful, he suggests learning to create opportunities based on four principal propositions: (1) design studies with undergraduates in mind, (2) find motivated students by matching interests during other courses, (3) reevaluate projects to determine how they might be segmented, and (4) look for collaborations that are likely to occur beyond a one-semester course. He compares these lab-oriented undergraduate research opportunities in the core curriculum to capstone courses and suggests that they should be coordinated to work in harmony. Corely acknowledges that good faculty-student collaboration can happen in the capstone course, but suggests that undergraduate research should be recognized as more than a simple prelude to the capstone experience. Undergraduate research, in his view, should be conceived more broadly.

Collaborative Undergraduate Research across Multiple Institutions

In a similar approach melding student learning with doing science, Alan Reifman coordinated psychology research methods instructors across multiple institutions to enlist students as researchers to measure school spirit indexes. The activity was geared to teach students about psychological methods while also generating publishable findings (School Spirit Study Group, 2004). Recently Grahe et al. (2012) suggested that students regularly participate in science by combining data samples from projects students conduct for course credit across multiple institutions.

Following this call, Grahe, Guillaume, and Rudmann (2014) describe a partnership between Psi Chi, the international honors society in psychology, and Psi Beta, the national community college honors society in psychology, where the two groups collaborated on their National Research Project replicating the International Situations Project (Guillaume & Funder, 2012). In that study, students from ten institutions collected data using a shared protocol to examine potential cultural differences within the United States. The purpose of this replication project was to give undergraduates an opportunity to learn research methods while at the same time engaging in meaningful science. In the spring 2014 semester, two students who collected data as part of the project (one from Pacific Lutheran University and one from Hunter College) collaborated on a paper reporting findings from this project for their respective capstone courses with the intention of submitting the paper for publication. Another recent initiative developed specifically to allow both introductory methods and capstone students to share in research is the Collaborative Replications and Education Project (CREP; Grahe, Guillaume, &

Rudmann, 2014). Here, students are invited to dedicate their course research projects to science by directly replicating one of eight recently published studies.[4]

These collaborative projects transition well into other fields where data from multiple sites are valued and can occur as partnerships with the community as well as other institutions. Cutucache et al. (2014) describe such a project at the University of Nebraska studying water pollution in a local watershed. In this crowd-sourcing science project, they used three groups of student researchers: high school students, students intending to replicate the study in Peru, and students in a microbiology class. The groups worked with the water samples at distinct levels of difficulty where the high school students primarily collected samples and the other two groups cultured and made preliminary analyses of them. Six coauthors on the publication were students. This type of project can provide capstone research experiences for students who work at different levels of assurance and competence: some students can limit their contribution to simple data gathering, while others can conduct the synthesis and analysis of the collected data, address larger questions, and correspondingly receive recognition as contributing coauthors.

These distinct levels of student involvement are also demonstrated in a large-scale coordination project providing undergraduates authentic research experiences in the field of genomics. Christopher Shaffer and fifty-two coauthors (2010) described the Genomics Education Partnership as offering opportunities for undergraduates to make novel contributions to science while providing scaffolding support for faculty wishing to offer these experiences. They describe the scientific details as well as the manner in which results are collected, the technical and instructor support needed, and the procedures employed for disseminating the results. This project is designed to allow students to work on projects as either guided laboratory activities (genomic annotation projects focusing on identifying biological information about specific areas of the genes) or independent study projects (genomic finishing projects that combine various areas to describe a complete gene sequence).

Shaffer et al. (2010) also assessed the quality of the student research and the student benefits arising from participating in the project. They reported that across the two project types, genomic finishing and genomic annotation, approximately 75 percent of the student projects were scientifically valid. This outcome highlights both the value of student research and the need to maintain quality control. In a comparison of learning outcomes, students in the more independent project type (genomic finishing) improved in both learning outcome measures (finishing and annotation skills), whereas the genomic annotation students improved only on the annotation skills measure. Shaffer et al. (2010) also documented that students benefited from this research consistent with other studies: students experienced greater identification as scientists, acquired better research skills, and demonstrated increased independence. Faculty members generally responded favorably regarding the quality of support received, the increased access to novel technology, the benefits to their home institution in genomics research capacity, and their own improved reputation in their department. This highlights the potential advantages of collaborative projects over single campus projects: the multi-institutional networking exposes contributors to other resources not available when working solely within the home institution.

In their summary of lessons learned from implementing their program, Shaffer et al. (2010) note three primary factors that help sustain the program. First, they reported needing "centralized technical support" (p. 66) to deliver and receive research materials. Second, they noted the need for courses to include enough time to allow students to complete the steep learning curve necessary to complete the research tasks and skills. Finally, the unique contribution of this multi-institutional approach "is the idea of 'common tools, different problems'" (p. 66). "Common tools" represents how the system allows instructors to employ the same research techniques across the various institutions and class types. "Different problems" refers to the fact that students can answer distinct questions as well as learn from the inevitable glitches that arise in conducting research. Challenges to implementation included student resistance to participating in a novel learning style by completing authentic research and that "some faculty and students do not consider computer-based analyses as 'real research'" (Schaffer et al., 2010, p. 67). Other challenges included problems of technology and the "unpredictable nature of experimental work" (Schaffer et al., 2010, p. 67).

Transformative Student Experiences from Authentic Research

The concept of engaging students in authentic research experiences is clearly evident in multiple disciplines and there are multiple levels within which this can occur. Even small contributions that are published in undergraduate journals or shared at professional conferences provide students with an opportunity to see the connection between their personal inquiry and the profession generally. Thus, projects that do not truly meet contemporary standards for professional work can contribute to students' acquisition of a professional identity and support their transition beyond the undergraduate curriculum.

The most impressive participation in building knowledge occurs with transformative research, but student learning is not limited solely to projects that generate publishable findings. In *Transformative Research at Predominately Undergraduate Institutions* (2010), editors Kerry Karukstis and Nancy Hensel urge that projects that enlist students to participate in research projects that are conceived as capable of contributing to the development of new knowledge are not wholly defined by the scientific success actually achieved. They provide examples of manageable yet scientifically sound projects and explain how and why undergraduates should participate in what has been characterized as transformative research.[5]

As we argued at the start of this chapter, transformative research projects and transformative learning experiences are mutually reinforcing initiatives. Authentic, professional-quality research integrated within a capstone course can diminish the negative impact of some student limitations. First, when faculty provide base questions that are scientifically interesting to students, students do not struggle as much with finding appropriate methodology. Furthermore, if the materials are publicly available, faculty mismatch is minimized by employing materials from coordinated studies (e.g., the CREP or Genomics Project) or by employing projects where the faculty already have a strong background. Although authentic projects can reduce many barriers, they will not address poor motivation or disinterest in every instance. Nonresearch-based capstones still have their place in certain programs and institutions for this reason. As we have previously urged, while the research capstone and major paper have become the typical capstone experience, faculty members should design their senior capstone experience with the particulars of their own department, institution, and field clearly in mind.

Conclusion

In this chapter, we noted some concerns but also potential opportunities in the way we conduct research. We also identified impediments that interfere with the completion of any project, including undergraduates' capstone projects. Changes to how we conduct science and other professional work are already coming because of the adoption of digital sharing technology, the way funding agencies award grants, changes in how publishers and editors evaluate research papers, and the manner in which institutions and faculty value interconnected scientific relationships. As those changes come, undergraduates can benefit from participation in research projects that are intensive, collaborative, and broadly contributory in nature.

The examples provided here were often drawn from the second author's field of psychology, but the potential contributions in other fields are no less dramatic. Nielson's (2011) examples included mathematics, engineering, and computer science. The Genomics Project and other examples of biology or chemistry authentic research provide clear examples of potential applications for many fields. Corley's (2013) suggestions were drawn from history. We concur with Frank and Saxe (2012) that undergraduate students can contribute to their professional field by focusing research projects toward potentially transformative questions (Grahe et al., 2012).

CHAPTER SIX

DESIGNING THE CAPSTONE COURSE

We know from previous research that institutional size and major department have an impact on whether and how the capstone course is offered. Other factors include whether one faculty member, several, or all members of the department teach the course. In contrast to other courses (with the exception of introductory courses), the capstone course is shared in a certain sense, even when it is taught exclusively by a single faculty member. How do factors like these affect the structure or administration of the course? How should a course be designed to create consistency of learning outcomes while minimizing restrictions on autonomy for instructors? Where and how should the capstone course design process start? In this chapter, we examine the factors to address in the process of designing a capstone course, with special emphasis on factors that research suggests are crucial for effective organization, including those that bear directly on student success.

Interest in designing a capstone course generally arises under one of two circumstances. In the first instance, an academic department, division, or institution without an existing capstone begins to explore the process of developing one. In the past, this decision has been driven by national trends in curriculum revision or program evaluation and assessment. Alternatively, it can be driven by a department, division, or institution with an existing capstone that is revisiting or replacing the current capstone with a new course. In both cases, there are common considerations that will warrant review if the capstone course is to mesh well with the existing curricula and achieve its goals. In our view, the place to start is with an acknowledgment that any capstone course must fit with the existing curriculum, department and institutional mission, and professional culture.

Four Foundational Components of Capstone Course Design

Intentionality

Capstone courses do not arise in a vacuum, or magically appear in a department or program. At the same time, too many capstone courses are a sort of a half-gesture, a not fully articulated after-thought. There can be a tendency to adopt or initiate action to revise a capstone course simply because it has become a standard of the discipline or because institutional pressures for assessment have come to bear. Research has suggested, for example, that course design has often been less than intentional and that issues related to student learning have been pushed aside, often by outdated adherence to untested faculty beliefs and assumptions (Stark, Lowther, Ryan, & Genthon, 1988). This is, to a degree, quite understandable, if regrettable. In our rational, postmodern age, we are dismissive of the unconscious forces at work and sometimes rather blithely unaware that our rational self-image is not fully in accord with the plans we are so busily developing. We should, however, resist these forces driving us to be less than fully intentional with respect to creation, or re-creation, of a senior capstone experience. This, then, is the first rule of capstone course design: be intentional (McNair & Albertine, 2012).

Curricular redesign, including the introduction of a senior experience into an existing curriculum, should not be lightly pursued. Rather, the decision to incorporate a capstone course or revise an existing one should proceed only after a comprehensive examination of the reasons that exist for doing so and an equally thorough review of the current curricular offerings. Generally this process will return us to the questions raised earlier: What are the goals and objectives sought by adopting (or revising) the capstone course? Does the interest in a capstone course arise primarily within an academic department or more generally within the university or a division of it? In other words, is a discipline-specific capstone under consideration or an interdisciplinary, perhaps general education–based, capstone? What structural framework for the course will successfully conform to the existing curriculum? Should adjustments be made to the existing curriculum in order to support the planned capstone experience? These questions and many others need to be raised, openly considered, and then intentionally resolved before moving on to address the details of a proposed new course or revision. Ultimately, developing a purposeful basis for the innovation and an intentional implementation plan is one key to the successful launch and sustainable pursuit of a capstone course (McNair & Albertine, 2012).

Collaboration

The second guiding principle of capstone course design or redesign is collaboration among the principals who are stakeholders in the outcome. Thus, a deliberative process must be conducted by the principals within a department, a division, or the university depending on the origin and impetus for addressing the senior culminating experience. Moreover, while practical considerations will eventually be brought to bear on the decision, the collaborative discussions at the beginning of the process should be restricted to issues of educational purpose, scholarly objectives, pedagogical impact, and academic rigor. In short, the collaboration that matters at the early stage must consist of a searching inquiry that addresses substantive questions central to the educational enterprise: Why are we here? What are we doing? What is it we wish to achieve? Contrary to what some might see as an unnecessary expenditure of limited time and resources on broad curricular questions that should have already been resolved and the answers in place, the initiation of a senior culminating experience in the form of a capstone course requires reconsideration of many fundamental academic issues. These issues cannot be dismissed or only summarily addressed if the resulting senior course is going to be successful.

Moreover, some capstone proposals require university stakeholders to go further to develop collaborative relationships with external stakeholders. The most obvious circumstance in which this occurs is when the senior culminating experience under consideration is in the form of an internship, a field practicum, or a sponsored project. Every educator who has experience with external collaborators and the capstone experience has commented on the importance of evaluating the course from their point of view and accommodating their interests within the course design (Allard & Straussman, 2003; Campbell & Lambright, 2011; Gorman, 2010; Schachter & Schwartz, 2009). Todd and Magleby (2005) describe their process for incorporating externally sponsored projects in an engineering capstone at Brigham Young University. Their experience, while not directly applicable to other capstone models, illustrates well the idea that every capstone model must effectively incorporate the interests of vested stakeholders.

Brigham Young University has required a two-semester senior design capstone in engineering since 1990. One purpose of an engineering capstone is to prepare graduates for engineering work in industry. A fundamental principle of engineering design for a new product is to engage in preliminary work to identify the product's stakeholders. A new product's group of stakeholders obviously includes consumers but also the suppliers, manufacturers, distributors, other users, and, ultimately, anyone else who may be affected by the product since there may be environmental or safety issues that extend beyond those who are expected to be the final end users for the product (Todd & Magleby, 2005). Thus, an essential phase of product design engineering is to identify the needs, wants, desires, and values of the various stakeholders. The core principles of product design suggest that engineering resources should not be devoted to producing something no one needs in a form that no one wants. Todd and Magleby suggest that these sound principles for new product design constitute sound principles for capstone course design as well.

These considerations lead Todd and Magleby (2005) to analyze the needs and desires of the various stakeholders, especially including industry representatives who can sponsor the projects. Briefly, they identify three primary industry interests: (1) access to a pool of good graduates among whom the industry representatives may find new employees; (2) affiliation with an engineering school and its faculty, including the engineering and research laboratory facilities, which may offer future help with industry's products and processes; and (3) supporting academic programs when that support coincides with perceived company needs. Ultimately Todd and Magleby argue that a successful internship, practicum, or project capstone that relies on external collaborators will need to create a capstone course that satisfies some or all of these stakeholders' interests.[1]

Curricular Fit

The introduction or revision of a capstone course raises the issue of curricular fit between the capstone and the curriculum as a whole. We have made the point that a course can cap a curricular experience meaningfully only to the extent that there is a coherent core academic experience to top off. Although full curricular redesign is perhaps not intended, and in some instances more or less consciously avoided by the principals early on, introduction or revision of a capstone course in the context of an existing curriculum is not a process that mimics a clean surgical implant. Rather, one of the foremost elements of a successful capstone course introduction to a curriculum is the coordination and complementarity between the courses leading up to the senior capstone course and the course itself. For example, Upson-Saia (2013) concludes, based on her study of religious studies capstone courses, that alignment with the existing curriculum, along with coordination with the university and department mission statements and feasibility in terms of available resources, is among the most critical underlying factors in supporting, or disempowering, a capstone experience. Issues of sequencing and redundancy, for example, clearly must be articulated and addressed. Departments or universities that overlook or ignore the importance of this phase of capstone course development and design take the risk of grafting on a senior capstone course that is at odds with, rather than an enhancement of, the existing direction of the curriculum. As Jones, Barrow, Stephens, and O'Hara (2012) note, "A gratifying outcome for students and teachers cannot be achieved if the capstone course is merely plunked atop an otherwise unchanged content-laden curriculum" (p. 1110). While it is tempting to short-circuit this phase of the capstone course design process, it is rarely a good idea. Only to the extent that there is a working merger between existing courses and sequences and the new or revised capstone course will the senior culminating experience likely produce the outcome sought.

Professional Standards

Many academic disciplines that lead to professional practice now include ethical norms or other guidelines as part of their curriculum. Engineering programs, for example, must assure the Accreditation Board for Engineering and Technology (ABET) that their graduates have an understanding of professional and ethical responsibility (Catalano, 2004). Similarly, accounting and business capstones frequently have professional orientation foci that address ethical issues within professional practice (Johnson & Halabi, 2011). Just as curricular fit constitutes a reasonable criterion and goal for the development of a new capstone course, many disciplines will need to consider whether a new or revised senior culminating experience should include design elements that teach, and meet, professional standards for practice, including ethical standards. While it is possible to meet external accrediting standards by establishing ethics and professionalism components within other courses (Catalano, 2004), the integrative nature of a senior capstone augurs in favor of introducing these issues there.

Structural Characteristics

Only after the preceding four elements of capstone course design or redesign have been incorporated and pursued will questions of external and internal course design present themselves in a context where those issues can be successfully addressed. Here too it is tempting to rush ahead and begin to consider the detailed features that the new or revised capstone course should offer students, but there are clear reasons not to do so without thoughtful deliberation regarding the overall framework.

The structural framework and mechanics of a course exist to serve the learning objectives of the senior culminating experience. Until the purpose and specific objectives sought have been articulated through an intentional, collaborative examination of the existing or newly reorganized curriculum the capstone course is intended to serve, the appropriate, or best, structure for the course cannot be determined. Since the learning objectives ultimately will need to be pursued by students, an analysis of student interests and goals should be a part of the preplanning phase of design. Todd and Magleby (2005) describe their own student interest analysis while constructing their capstone course in engineering design.

The capstone course that Todd and Magleby (2005) created at BYU relies on industry sponsorship that supports a design-and-build project. In considering creation of their externally sponsored capstone, they identified five stakeholders: students, faculty, industry, academic administrators, and others.[2] Engineering students, Todd and Magleby point out, are engaged in a rigorous curriculum that places heavy demands on their time. Consequently, one thing students want is relevant courses that contribute to their goal of a meaningful engineering education. Thus, the capstone course in senior design should be one that prepares students for transition to a role as a successful engineer ready for practice. Correspondingly, students are interested in developing skills that will appeal to prospective employers when these are recorded on their professional résumés. Design engineering students also want experience in fabricating actual prototypes to test their ideas. However, since students have limited resources, engineering students value opportunities to use someone else's equipment to create mock-ups and test them. Since fabrication is a missing feature of many theoretical courses in engineering curricula, students will want to gain opportunities to design and construct prototypes to build some confidence in their ability to do so. Finally, Todd and Magleby (2005) note that most design engineering is done in the context of teams, so students want experience working with a team in a real-world design situation. Students have experience in the artificial teams that are used in some engineering classes, and they know that not every student makes an investment in teams when there is no stake in the outcome. Therefore, students want to work on a team where the product outcome matters and every team member will be forced to work effectively and cooperatively.

Van Acker and Bailey (2011) found that eleven different instructors had disparate and sometimes conflicting approaches to effectively communicating the work-related skills in the capstone course. This is an example where planning and communication could vastly improve the delivery and experience of capstone experiences. By analyzing the academic and professionals goals of students prior to the actual design phase of the capstone course instructors will increase the likelihood that the goals for the course will incorporate and reflect student goals. This is an important element of a successful capstone course.

Practical considerations cannot obtrude into the process too early. The most important structural characteristics of the course must address student learning and the student experience. The issues relating to faculty staffing for the course then can be evaluated along the lines of the potential impact that different staffing equations will have on the senior culminating experience for students. Ultimately there will be an accommodation or compromise between what has been emerging as the ideal capstone course design for a particular curriculum. However, by emphasizing students' interests first, the strengths and weaknesses of the various staffing alternatives can be more easily envisioned, compared and contrasted, and finally evaluated.

Recent research suggests that curricular innovation is limited by the realities and constraints of the particular educational environment in which change is sought (Hora & Ferrare, 2013). It is apparent, for example, that the basic organizational and institutional facts of American higher education delimit the broad nature of any curricular changes that can be conceived, let alone implemented. Hora and Ferrare (2013, p. 214) emphasize that "faculty do not operate in isolation but instead function within distinct cultural and organizational contexts at the institutional, departmental, and classroom levels." The fact that the range of course design choices along some dimensions is limited does not mean those choices are unimportant. Rather, it means the exact opposite: while the range for certain choices is very constrained, the narrow range suggests that the impact of any choice will be relatively great. This means that a poor choice will have a decidedly substantial impact in one direction, just as a good choice will have a significant influence on outcomes in the opposite direction.

Upson-Saia (2013) found that religious studies capstones that ignored solving fundamental questions regarding foundational structural characteristics like curricular fit, mission alignment, and resource availability foundered rather than prospered. The result was that faculty members were unhappy with their own capstone courses, a rather clear indication of poor planning. One key, therefore, is to choose course design elements that evidence has shown produce good outcomes within institutional structures (Brownell & Swaner, 2010). "Getting it right" at the design stage may be more important than the instructional phase, although many believe the opposite.

Building the Internal Structure of a Senior Capstone Course

Many readers may consider creating the internal framework of the course the actual design work. Yet we believe the previous steps are critical. We have cautioned against minimizing the importance of the early steps we have set out or disregarding the sequence we have recommended. We also believe that establishing a sound internal framework for delivery of the senior culminating experience is a crucial step in achieving successful outcomes for students.

The early design process steps are necessary for various constituencies, and some stakeholders will benefit more than others. The most important beneficiaries of the early steps are clearly the faculty who will ultimately be responsible for delivering the course. Thus, in cooperative deliberation, the relevant faculty must have clearly articulated their goals for the senior capstone course, determined that the course will fit with and enhance the existing curriculum, and will meet the requirements of any external accrediting bodies, professional associations, or other stakeholders. For this reason, it is the faculty that will take most interest in the early design stages and influence those phases of the design process the most.

The equation is slightly different for the internal structural characteristics of the course. Faculty members will still inordinately influence the design choices; however, it is the student audience that will be the direct recipients and primary beneficiaries. This means that each of the internal features of the course should be chosen based on the impact it will have on the students who will experience it. Relevant research suggests that a highly structured capstone course is supportive of student success and that students recognize this positive effect on their learning (McKinney & Day, 2012). Here, then, the focus is on selecting policies and practices that will support student learning within a course framework that can best deliver student success. This is the stage where the cumulative weight of the best practices found in the literature with respect to student learning must be applied. Having studied the relevant literature, we recommend the following with respect to internal structural elements of a capstone course.

Restricted or Select Admission

An early but often neglected consideration is whether a policy to restrict admission to the senior culminating experience beyond the requirement of senior status should be adopted. This is one of many considerations where the philosophy behind the senior experience will guide the course designers to select the right choice for their program.

The question of restricted or select admission is most likely to occur within the context of a disciplinary capstone course rather than an interdisciplinary or general education–based course. Generally, institutions that have chosen to support interdisciplinary or general education–based senior capstone experiences seek to encourage universal participation. Portland State University, for example, requires each of its three thousand graduating seniors to complete one of approximately 230 capstones offered annually (Kerrigan & Jhaj, 2007). Having established its primary goal as requiring every graduate to complete a capstone, Portland State has no institutional interest in narrowing accessibility to these courses. Institutions are less likely to consider approaches that limit admission when their goal is to broaden and support engagement and participation in the senior experience.

Academic departments may share these broad participation goals as well. Some departments envision one of the essential goals of the senior culminating course as offering a unifying learning experience that every graduate within a discipline shares. Carlson, Cohn, and Ramsey (2002) argue that the economics capstone should be required for every major. These departments too will be disinclined to restrict admission because it would be counter to a primary objective (McGaw & Wechsler, 1999). At one and the same time, departments may act to regulate admission to the senior capstone course by establishing a sequential core of prerequisites required for enrollment in addition to senior status.

Some academic departments, however, may choose to place specific entry requirements on admission to the senior seminar rather than emphasize the universal requirement that all majors must complete senior seminar. Siegfried (2001) writes about an economics honors capstone that is conceived as not for every student (see also Siegfried et al., 1991; Siegfried, 1991; Siegfried & Wilkinson, 1982). Departments and units that wish to serve multiple goals and a variety of student interests with a senior culminating experience may elect to develop alternative senior capstone experiences while sharing the requirement that all seniors must complete one of several senior courses offered. Thus, a department might offer an internship or practicum senior course, a career transition model senior course, and a more typical research- or thesis-style senior capstone course and permit graduating seniors to choose among them. A variation within this approach may involve creation of an honors seminar that is limited to students who have demonstrated through their academic work an exceptional ability and motivation to perform at the highest academic level (McGoldrick, 2008).

Capstone Course Prerequisites and Core Course Sequences

A second, sometimes related, consideration is whether there should be an introductory sequence of prerequisites that must be completed before admission to the senior capstone is permitted. The theory behind such a sequence is that students will have acquired, through the prerequisite courses, a solid preparation in the skills necessary to complete the senior capstone course successfully. Typically the prerequisites involve technical skills, such as statistics or research methods or advanced writing courses, or all three. At this point, questions regarding the content of the existing curriculum, faculty load, and best practice intersect.

Most self-studies of departmental capstone courses, regardless of discipline, suggest that the best practice is to support a senior cap-stone course with one or more prerequisites. Jones et al. (2012), for example, discuss four sequential history capstone courses in their survey of thirty departments. In each of the four departments (University of Missouri-Kansas City, Carleton College, Yale University, and Virginia Tech) one or more prerequisites to the capstone course exists. The Histori-ography and Method course is a preparatory requirement at University of Missouri-Kansas City. Carleton students are ushered through a tight sequence of prerequisites beginning with a six-hour colloquium during their junior year, a three-credit-hour senior research proposal in the first semester of their senior year, and a six-credit Advanced History Writing course as well as the Integrative Exercise course (the title given to the capstone where senior papers are actually written) in the final semester. At Yale, the senior culminating experience, called the Senior Essay, is a full academic year rather than a single semester. The fall term is devoted to developing a proposal, learning the historiography that will enable the student to complete the proposal, and completing a series of sequential assignments that support successful completion of the essay project in the second semester. At Virginia Tech, the completion of a senior paper that will become a chapter in the department's book project is preceded by a course in historical methods as a preparatory prerequisite (Jones et al., 2012). The Virginia Tech history department book project was created to provide an opportunity and incentive for highly motivated students to develop a high-quality senior project. The authors conclude that preparatory courses that are sequenced with the capstone course at their pinnacle constitute a practice that produces successful student outcomes.

Schermer and Gray (2012) tell much the same story in their comprehensive study of four liberal arts institutions: Augustana College, Allegheny College, Washington College, and College of Wooster. At Allegheny College, they report that "many departments construct their curriculum in part to prepare their majors for the senior project"(p. 7). They note, for example, that "every major but one" at Allegheny required a junior seminar in anticipation of the capstone project. These junior seminars typically enabled students to begin the early stages of their work on the senior project (Schermer & Gray, 2012). At the College of Wooster, the senior project formally extends over an entire academic year. Schermer and Gray (2012) report that most departments at the College of Wooster still require majors to take a research methods course prior to the formal commencement of the senior year project. In their summary statement regarding the four schools, Schermer and Gray (2012) note that most departments in the four schools have one or more courses explicitly designed as preparatory courses for the senior-year project. They characterize this approach as "extensive [student] preparation" through prerequisite courses before undertaking the senior experience.

Bos and Schneider (2009) analyzed student and faculty surveys regarding knowledge and preparation for application of research methods skills in political science. Faculty members characterized students as poorly prepared for advanced, self-directed research. While there were areas of more or less competence identified, the results suggested that stating a good research question, conducting a suitable literature review, assessing the quality of existing research, proper sampling methods, difficulty in establishing acceptable norms for measurements and use of statistics, and difficulties in presenting research findings all constituted to one degree or another significant barriers to research for undergraduates. Students generally agreed with the faculty assessment. Results like these strongly suggest that a series of sequenced prerequisites in research methods (and statistics for some disciplines) would be advisable for a research capstone experience. Without belaboring the point, our reading of the relevant literature on capstones from across the university curriculum supports the proposition that preparatory prerequisites support the study in depth that senior capstone courses are expected to provide.

Capstone Course Length

A related issue to the question of preparatory prerequisites is the length of the senior capstone course. To a certain degree, the issue is a red herring. Yale University's history capstone extended over a full academic year. Yet the first semester of the course was not unlike many preparatory prerequisites at other schools: an opportunity to choose a topic for the senior project, conduct initial research, formulate the research question, develop a working set of references, create a proposed methodology, and draft early sections of the proposed senior paper (Jones et al., 2012). Is Yale's history capstone a full year long—or is it a single semester supported by a one-semester preparatory course? The answer does not really matter.

Surveys across institutions and departments generally show that capstone courses are most often described as one semester (or one quarter) long. Henscheid, Breitmeyer, and Mercer (2000) state that 86 percent of their respondents reported capstone courses that were one semester in length. The dozens of individual capstone course case studies summarized in our online appendix lead to the same conclusion. To the extent there are preparatory prerequisites specifically designed and intimately connected to the senior capstone course, it matters little whether these are incorporated directly into the capstone, as in Yale's history capstone (Jones et al., 2012), or treated as entirely separate courses. Many disciplines offer a research course or advanced research course as the immediate precursor to the capstone course where initial work on the capstone project begins. Carleton College's history sequence is one example (Jones et al., 2012). This, in effect, makes a one-semester capstone a year-long experience as well.

Enrollment Size

Deciding on an appropriate size for student enrollment in a senior capstone course is an exercise in balancing limited faculty resources against the creation of an optimal learning environment. Prior to this juncture, we have emphasized that design decisions should be driven solely by criteria that define an optimal learning experience. The reality of higher education today now intrudes. Although there is no one-size-fits-all solution, several considerations will guide the decision process: the number of graduating seniors annually, on average, who are required to complete the senior capstone course; the number of faculty available to teach the capstone course; whether the senior capstone will be team-taught or taught by a single instructor; whether adjunct faculty will teach the senior capstone course as well as tenure-track faculty; and whether practices like team grading are supported even when the course is led by a single instructor.

The baseline starting point for deciding the issue of section size within the senior capstone experience is the number of graduating seniors expected annually who are required to take the course. For example Jones et al. (2012) report that approximately 150 history majors graduate each year from Virginia Tech. Based on this figure and taking the size of the faculty and other factors into account, the Virginia Tech history department chose to offer the senior capstone course in both fall and spring semesters and cap sections at twenty students (Jones et al., 2012). These same authors report that the University of Missouri-Kansas City, a public institution with thirteen thousand students, and Carleton College, a private liberal arts institution with fewer than two thousand students, both cap their senior capstone course sections at fifteen students. While these schools required all seniors in history departments to complete the capstone course, one national study has produced results that show about 70 percent of respondents reported their capstone courses were required (Henscheid et al., 2000).

National figures are available from several studies regarding capstone course section size. Henscheid et al. (2000) report the following results for 864 respondents across all types and sizes of institutions they surveyed in 1999:

0 to 9 students	20.6 percent of respondents reporting
10 to 19 students	27.4 percent of respondents
20 to 29 students	33.2 percent of respondents
30 to 39 students	11.6 percent of respondents
Other	7.3 percent of respondents

Thus, 80 percent of capstone course sections nationally have fewer than thirty students. Section sizes at public institutions are larger than those at private institutions (Henscheid et al., 2000). However, since sections tend to be larger at institutions greater than average size also, the controlling factor may well be institutional size rather than the public-private distinction. This conclusion is buttressed by the fact that the selectivity of the institution does not seem to appreciably influence capstone course section size (Henscheid et al., 2000).

National studies also have reported on the instructional format for senior capstone courses. Multiple studies suggest that capstone courses are led by single instructors in the great majority of cases. Padgett and Kilgo (2011) report that nearly half of the institutions (43.7 percent) reported that less than 10 percent of their capstone courses were team-taught, and no discernible differences were identified across all institutions when institutional size and type were considered. Overall, around 18 percent of institutions reported that their capstone courses were never team-taught, whereas only 5.8 percent of institutions reported they were always team-taught (Padgett & Kilgo, 2012). Henscheid et al. (2000) report, using a different method, that 72 percent of 864 respondents described their senior capstone course as taught by a single instructor; 28 percent of respondents indicated the course was team-taught. Our own data from a regional study of sociology and psychology departments suggest that about 10 percent of senior capstones in those disciplines are team-taught (Hauhart & Grahe, 2010).

There is no simple calculus we can provide to determine the optimal section size for the capstone course. Virtually all studies of pedagogical best practices suggest, however, that a critical factor in producing better student outcomes is high interaction between student and instructor regarding substantive academic matters. Clearly, large section enrollments are not conducive to high levels of one-on-one student-faculty interaction on substantive intellectual issues. Since we do not know the trade-offs that professors and various departments or institutions are willing to make or the resources available to invest in the capstone course, we simply recommend choosing the smallest section size the professor believes department and university resources can support.

Course Description

An important feature of the capstone course that is routinely treated as a relatively unimportant detail is the formal course description. The official description should constitute the connecting link between the university and department's goals for the course and the experience that students are intended to discover. It should not be confused with the name or title given to the course since, as we have seen, the labels range from "senior inquiry" to "senior comprehensive course" to "senior project" and beyond. Rather, the capstone course description should convey a succinct statement of the learning experience the student should envision, along with a capsule statement of the tangible outcome the student will be expected to produce.

The public statement of the formal course description appears in the university catalogue. A second important version can be delivered in materials directed at students who will experience the course. These statements can appear on a course website, in the course syllabus, in explanatory materials such as brochures prepared for potential majors, and so forth. It is not important if there are multiple versions of the course description (and it may even be quite helpful) so long as the various versions are mutually reinforcing.

At Saint Martin's University, the catalogue description of the Criminal Justice Senior Seminar reads in part, "Major research paper on approved topic under direction of department chair." Another version of the course description that appears as the very first lines of the course syllabus reads: "The Senior Seminar consists of research and writing on *a significant question of scholarly merit* in criminal justice or legal studies. You will select a research question; develop a methodology for addressing the question; research the literature; conduct your own research; summarize the results; work collaboratively with the Seminar advisor; and complete an approved thesis in the format required by the Department of Criminal Justice" (emphasis in original). This version of the course description, which is the one students will encounter on the first day of the course, identifies critical components of the learning experience that will constitute the capstone to their major curricula, including the core activity ("research and writing on a significant question of scholarly merit in criminal justice or legal studies"), a sequence of ordered tasks ("select a question; develop a methodology"), the expected nature and quality of the learning experience ("work collaboratively"), and the expected final outcome ("complete an approved thesis in the format required by the Department of Criminal Justice").

One may object that drafting a course description for the senior capstone at this juncture is a matter of minor detail that does not establish an important parameter for the structure of the course. To the contrary, a pithy description of the distinctive mission of the course with special reference to what students are actually expected to do is a critical structural component that establishes a solid foundation for the experience that will follow. Only when the course description establishes the broad outlines of the experience can subsequent defining statements demarcate the boundaries for the balance of the course framework.

A breadth of approaches to drafting the capstone course description can be located across institutions and departments. Washington College, for example, states in its catalogue that the Senior Capstone Experience (SCE) "requires students to demonstrate the ability to think critically and to engage in a project of active learning in their major field of studies. In the SCE, required of all graduating seniors, students integrate acquired knowledge and skills, in a senior project demonstrating mastery of a body of knowledge and intellectual accomplishment that goes significantly beyond classroom learning" (Schermer & Gray, 2012, p. 15).

The catalogue elaborates by adding that while formats or approaches may vary, all capstone courses at the school "will be informed by the following expectations":

- Demonstrated student initiative
- Significant preparatory work
- Active inquiry
- Integration of acquired knowledge and skills
- Culmination of previous academic work. (Schermer & Gray, 2012, pp. 15–16)

This statement focuses on the idealized learning experience at some length but offers little with respect to the more tangible outcome that is expected. Presumably such details are left to the individual major field of study that delivers the course. The contrast between the catalogue course description at Saint Martin's University (one succinct phrase focused on the task and product) and Washington College (an elaborate vision expounding the nature of the learning process) offers perhaps either extreme for framing the essence of the course. They share, however, an acknowledgment that the course description is an important structural component. A thoughtful statement that establishes realistic expectations regarding the experience is one element in fostering a suitably receptive set of student attitudes among incoming seniors.

Building a Framework of Sound Expectations

The balance of designing the capstone course consists of the construction of increasingly specific guidelines intended to shape the senior experience and create a dynamic learning environment of high academic expectations. The following elements contribute to the goal of achieving successful student learning outcomes.

Define the Major Project or Paper

Research has consistently found that the senior capstone course is predominantly centered on completion of a major project or major paper (Hauhart & Grahe, 2010, 2012; Henscheid et al., 2000; Jones et al., 2012; McKinney & Busher, 2011). The task for the course designer is to define the specific process and outcome expected. Is original research within a discipline required? May the "major paper" simply consist of an extended term paper in the form of a literature review? Can the final product of the project be delivered in some form other than a paper—perhaps as a performance or oral presentation?

There is not a definitive answer to the form that the major project or major paper should assume. McGoldrick (2008) reported that 70 percent of economics departments had a writing requirement and that the capstone course was frequently used to fulfill that requirement. In sociology and psychology, our regional study suggests the capstone course is even more frequently the site of a writing or major research paper requirement—as high as 95 percent (Hauhart & Grahe, 2010). The course design committee or course designer therefore needs to consider once again the goals that have inspired the move toward developing the capstone course. To the extent the course is a typical discipline-based course, the project chosen may well be defined as completion of a major paper in the format commonly followed within the discipline (Hauhart & Grahe, 2010, 2012). The remaining features to be decided will then reduce to whether original research is required, whether a real-world project is the centerpiece of the capstone course, whether more than one type of capstone (original research, library research or literature review only, a portfolio of papers) is acceptable, who will select the topic or question for research, and the specifics of form and format required for reporting the research.

The four choices most commonly adopted for defining the senior capstone project are a senior thesis, a research project, a portfolio (whether of illustrations, drawings, or papers), or some form of real-world problem-based learning. The senior thesis addresses an important question within the context of a discipline and marshals evidence to support the thesis statement. Typically in the thesis option, the evidence relied on does not need to be the result of original research on the part of the student, although some undergraduate theses are designed to accommodate original research as well as more limited thesis formats (Reynolds, Smith, Moskovitz, & Sayle, 2009). In the more common approach, the student writing a senior thesis may rely on secondary evidence collected and analyzed by other researchers. Generally there may be a preference for (or even limitation to) peer-reviewed sources for the evidence relied on, but this criterion is dependent on the discipline and within the province of the instructor to decide. Here, the primary focus is on the analysis (or reanalysis) of existing information or data plus demonstration of basic information literacy and writing skills. There are practical guides available for students and faculty members that offer tips on how to write a senior thesis (Lipson, 2005; Masiello & Skipper, 2013).

The research project capstone requires original research conducted by the student, as we discussed in prior chapters (Sullivan & Thomas, 2007). The primary distinction between the research project and the senior thesis is active engagement in conducting research that leads to original data generation plus the analysis of those data to answer a significant question within the discipline. Sullivan and Thomas (2007) describe a research-intensive capstone course of this type in psychology that requires students to design their own empirical research study, complete it, and report it publicly with a poster session or oral presentation. Other features of this capstone design remain the same as for the thesis option.

The portfolio option requires students to compile a representative collection of their work. The portfolio may consist of previously submitted course assignments or newly prepared work. Resner (2011) describes a capstone based on a portfolio of three papers, each about ten pages in length, addressing signal areas of competence in theology that forms the culminating experience for MDiv students at Hood Theological Seminary. The Grand Valley University School of Social Work requires completion of a senior capstone course that involves preparation of an e-portfolio, which requires the gathering and uploading of papers from each social work course, thereby demonstrating fulfillment of the competencies associated with that course (Schuurman, Berlin, Langlois, & Guevara, 2012).[3] A web-based portfolio has also been used as a capstone experience for preservice teachers (Herner-Patnode & Lee, 2009), and the portfolio development process has been discussed with respect to the history major as well (Carlson & Youngblut, 1998). Although the portfolio-based capstone course does not appear to have become as popular as the other three options, it offers a credible alternative for the capstone experience. It is more often used in fine arts, music, or performance courses.

Finally, a senior capstone course can consist of posing a real-world question and answering it or engaging in an exercise of problem-based learning that requires the student to tackle analytical problems in the process of creating a solution to a specified problem. This format is commonly found in internship or practicum-based senior capstone courses (see, e.g., Goldstein & Fernald 2009; Weis, 2004), fieldwork disciplines such as geography (Levia & Quiring, 2008; Hefferan, Heywood, & Ritter, 2002) or conservation biology (Berkson & Harrison, 2001), or fields that engage volunteer mentors or outside clients who consult with and monitor the capstone students' projects, such as business and engineering (Barry, Drnevich, Irfanoglu, & Bullock, 2012).

As with some other issues, it is not necessary to pose the four options as polarities that preclude a senior capstone course with more than one acceptable format. As Reynolds, Smith, Moskovitz, and Sayle (2009) point out, a capstone framework can support more than one option if the course is intentionally designed. Carlson, Cohn, and Ramsey (2002) agree and specifically laud the flexibility of their capstone model to accommodate multiple approaches within an overall framework. While a narrowly defined single-option senior capstone course may be preferable for those institutions or disciplines with large enrollments offering only larger sections, a multiple-option senior seminar can work at smaller institutions or in capped sections. The senior thesis projects of the four Saint Martin's University students mentioned in our Acknowledgments were quite different from each other, yet each was completed in a multiple-option senior seminar composed of both criminal justice and legal studies students.[4]

The key to supporting projects that embrace different methods, ask different questions, and produce different outcomes in a single section is a firm structural framework. Four senior projects from the Criminal Justice/Legal Studies Senior Seminar at Saint Martin's University illustrate the point. Stacia Wasmundt (BA, 2009), with her academic advisor's assistance, obtained an internship at Superior Court's Juvenile Probation Office in Thurston County, Washington. There, under the direction of the juvenile probation office supervisor, she created a method for reviewing hundreds of clients' cases with respect to the success achieved through four treatment modalities. The question of whether the various modalities worked or did not work was a real-world problem for the office. The internship lasted nearly a year. Senior seminar at Saint Martin's is a one-semester course.

Courtney Choi (BA, 2011) developed an interest in Fourth Amendment law. Specifically, she wanted to know how the federal courts applied the Supreme Court's good faith exception to the exclusionary rule developed in *United States* v. *Leon* (468 U.S. 897, 1984). Briefly, under *Leon,* violations of a criminal suspect's Fourth Amendment rights may be overlooked by a court if the police officer acted in "good-faith" reliance that he or she was acting properly and lawfully. Consequently, Courtney designed a method for selecting cases; read a representative sample of 175 US Circuit Court of Appeals decisions (of 698 such decisions from 1984 to 2010) reviewing the *Leon* good-faith question; and recorded how each court handled the *Leon* exception. This senior thesis was purely library research, case analysis, and data interpretation.[5]

Kim Menius (BA, 2012) and Jessica Flores (BA, 2012) also crafted distinctive senior projects within the senior seminar framework. Kim obtained an internship with a midsized local police department, and with the assistance of her academic advisor and the support of the police commander, she studied the department's evidence procedures, including DNA evidence handling. Kim designed and administered two surveys for officers (one a self-report survey, the second an objective ten-question test on DNA handling). She also developed a third survey for laboratory managers at the five full-service Washington state crime labs.[6] She found generally that local police officers had only modest knowledge of DNA-handling procedures.

Jessica Flores developed an interest in youth "hanging out" on the streets of Washington's capital, nearby Olympia. She developed a research proposal based on participant observation: she would hang out with the street youth and find out whether their involvement in street culture led them to have more engagement and more negative contact, including arrests, with Olympia's police. Thus, Jessica, a middle-class college student, donned suitable attire (flannel shirt, torn jeans, inexpensive shoes), mussed her hair, wore no makeup, and undertook traditional participant observation. The result was a sixty-page senior thesis that quoted from her conversations with Olympia youth, extensively supported with careful references to the many published studies of street youth, delinquency, and the police.

Cumulatively these four exemplary undergraduate research projects demonstrate that with a proper framework and admittedly the benefit of a modest enrollment, it is possible to have students work successfully with more than a single model in a single section of a capstone course. The key is a course structure that entails firm task completion guidance with an open approach to the questions asked, and methods pursued, to creating sound empirical work.

Some other national findings of interest apply here. In our research regarding sociology and psychology capstone courses, for example, we found that psychology departments reported requiring their students to do more data collection and data analysis than sociology departments (Hauhart & Grahe, 2012). If one were engaged in designing a new psychology capstone, one might wish to build in requirements for data collection and data analysis to conform to common practices in the field. One might do so by requiring senior capstone students to complete their senior work through participation as a research assistant on faculty research projects (Starke, 1985). This would achieve the goal of creating a capstone experience consistent with the practices of many other psychology departments while relieving students of the burden of topic selection or completion of individual "original" research.

While our findings (Hauhart & Grahe, 2012) are limited to these two fields, they suggest that academicians in other fields may wish to examine the practices of other professionals within their discipline to ascertain the general run, or specific approach, to defining the core activities normally included in the capstone. Participation in a profession by definition means an adoption of certain professional standards. Incorporating core professional practices and standards in the senior capstone is one obvious way to socialize graduating seniors into the profession. We have attempted to support that inquiry across the curriculum by providing summaries of a substantial number of discipline-specific capstone courses in our online appendix. Readers may access the summaries at https://osf.io/tg6fa/.

Core Project and Supplemental Activities

In addition to the core activity in the form of completion of a major paper, the course designer may well wish to make some decisions about secondary activities. Should the course instructor or department leaders coordinate with a university librarian to develop a presentation regarding research techniques and information literacy? Should peer review practices be incorporated into the instructional design? If so, at what stages? Should the course instructor coordinate with a university writing center to make a presentation and offer services to capstone students?

The answer to each of these questions is generally yes: activities that inspire interaction within the context of academic pursuits—whether between peers, between students and faculty members, or between students and support staff or specialty faculty—generally contribute to successful academic outcomes (Padgett & Kilgo, 2011; Kuh, 2008). Moreover, supplemental activities like these address academic proficiencies one wishes to achieve and which students will need to master to complete the core task (Carlson et al., 2002). Requiring students to read and summarize senior theses prepared by prior-year students, for example, can contribute to the skill development required for a formal literature review and thereby support acquiring a critical academic proficiency. Like the primary activity, completion of the major project, these activities should be formally built into the course. Many instructors already do so. For example, our western regional survey of sociology and psychology departments showed that 55 percent of respondents used peer review of rough drafts as a regular part of their capstone course. A slightly lower percentage, 48 percent, also used peer review of oral presentations (Hauhart & Grahe, 2010). These and other supplementary activities will support major project completion.

Building activities like these into the formal design of the course can also support consistency among sections and instructors in larger departments. A single framework of shared capstone-based activities can also create a shared sense of morale and engagement among seniors, whether within large departments offering multiple sections or within institutions offering multiple sections of a general education or interdisciplinary capstone course. Moreover, formally requiring students in all sections to engage in these activities does very little to impinge on an instructor's ability to direct his or her own section. Likewise, it does little to undercut academic freedom since the activities can support any theoretical posture or political persuasion.

Other Project Parameters for Typical Capstones

Earlier we summarized the data we collected by describing the typical capstone course (Grahe & Hauhart, 2013; Hauhart & Grahe, 2010, 2012). These common features generally evolve from and reinforce the emphasis on completion of a major project, particularly in the form of a major paper. Other research suggests that the great majority of academic disciplines offer senior capstone courses that follow the major project/major paper model (Henscheid et al., 2000; Schermer & Gray, 2011; Jones et al., 2012). Consequently the structural features we found represented in the typical social science capstone course are supportive of capstone courses from these other disciplines. One reason for adopting this posture is that it supports developing reasonable student expectations for completing the work associated with a major paper. When student expectations are aligned with course requirements, the experience can produce better project outcomes and student success rates (McKinney & Day, 2012). Establishing clear base-line expectations for the major paper therefore is an important way to prepare students for success.

Page Length and Conformed Writing Style

Two features of the typical capstone course are a minimum page require-ment and submission of a paper prepared in conformity with a required writing and citation style. There is substantial research to draw on with respect to the length of senior capstone papers or theses; it is among the elements of the major paper that is commonly required. Our research found that 55 percent of sociology and psychology respondents to our regional survey stated that their capstone did impose a minimum page length (Hauhart & Grahe, 2010). In subsequent research, we reported that the average capstone length requirement in sociology and psychology was eighteen pages (Grahe & Hauhart, 2013). Reports on page length require-ments from individual schools abound in the literature. Jones et al. (2012) report an average page length of twenty to twenty-five pages for history theses at the University of Missouri-Kansas City, a medium-sized public uni-versity, but fifty pages for Yale University, an elite private university. Carlson et al. (2002) write about requiring a "polished, 20-page paper" in the eco-nomics capstone course at Illinois State University. In our regional study of sociology and psychology departments, we found that 88 percent of respon-dents reported page lengths between ten and twenty-five pages (Hauhart & Grahe, 2010).

We strongly recommend adopting a minimum page-length require-ment. We consider this a structural factor that will contribute to a climate for success. Research has suggested that many students respond favorably to highly structured classroom experiences, especially students whose academic preparation is weak (Keogh, Sterling, & Venables, 2007; McKin-ney & Day, 2012). Of course, our recommendation to establish a baseline minimum page length does not answer the question, "What length?" This decision depends on the course designer's assessment of the limits of student preparedness as well as the degree of intellectual ambition and academic rigor the department aspires to instill in its graduating seniors.

While the specific page length minimum one should require does not present an easy open-and-shut answer, the requirement of a writing and citation style that conforms to an accepted standard presents an easier decision. In our study of sociology and psychology departments, 88 percent of respondents stated that their department's capstone course designated a specific writing and citation style for written work. Most academic disciplines long ago committed to an accepted standard. Thus, we recommend both adoption of a designated style and conformity to the professional writing style most representative of the discipline. Invariably psychology department capstones require submission of the major paper in American Psychological Association format, and English departments favor Modern Language Association format. While this advice does not solve the matter definitively for every field, selection of a required format does resolve the matter for students.

Choosing the Topic and Framing the Research Question

An important feature of the senior capstone course that can support student engagement is selection of the topic and framing of the research question or hypothesis. It is an important issue to address, as many analyses of the capstone experience identify poor topic selection and question refinement as one of the most serious deficiencies students exhibit (Bowman, 1989). Bos and Schneider's (2009) surveys of students and faculty members in political science research methods courses identify creating well-stated research questions as one of the significant barriers for students in pursuing research.

There are several approaches to this issue. First, a dichotomous approach conceptualizes the choices available as student chooses versus instructor chooses. Second, there can be a hybrid model where some students choose their own topic and develop it under instructor guidance but some students work on an instructor's research project. Third, a capstone course or section of a capstone course at a larger institution can be exclusively formed around a faculty member's research with research assistant roles available for each student. Finally, a senior seminar or multiple sections of a senior capstone course can be formed around a standardized project that all faculty members support as the major project. Here's our assessment of the strengths and weaknesses of each approach.

The first alternative posed is conceptualized around either extreme in an either-or fashion. The reasons for choosing either extreme can be set out rather quickly. The primary reasons to have students choose their own topic and frame the issue to be investigated are twofold. First, this option forces students to take responsibility for these tasks and complete them; if a student doesn't assume responsibility, he or she will not accomplish the work required for successful completion of the course. Second, a student who does take up his or her responsibility will develop an investment in the project that is arguably greater than where topic assignment and question formation are handled by the faculty member. Where the decision regarding topic selection and issue identification is solely in the discretion of the instructor, the advantages are twofold as well: the likelihood the issue or question will be a good one is heightened, and the indecision, delay, and procrastination otherwise experienced by some students will be eliminated.

Posing the question in this either-or manner, however, misstates the actual range of choices. This first alternative can encompass several subvariations, all of which are arguably better choices than either extreme. One modified model defines the topic selection task as the responsibility of the student but recognizes the faculty member's proper role as mentor. In this model, each student is required to bring forward a proposal. The capstone course instructor can then collaborate with and support the student in forming a good research question within the student's area of interest. Roberts and Pavlak (2002) support this collaborative style.

A second modified model provides both the student and the faculty member an "outlet option" where the student is incapable of helping to identify a serious topic for inquiry. In such a case, the instructor simply chooses due to the student's default; the student, for his or her part, groping for a way to complete the senior experience requirement, may then more readily accept the instructor's selection than otherwise. While this modification undercuts the "student choice" model by relieving the student of what should otherwise be his or her responsibility, it recognizes the wide variation in students' entering behavior and preparation for the capstone experience. Some students are underprepared whether intellectually, academically, or emotionally to assume the full burden associated with a capstone course. This default option is not optimal, but it avoids the unattractive outcome of leaving the weak student stranded.

The hybrid model has a number of qualities that make it an attractive alternative. It shares with the first alternative the retention of student choice as a feature. The hybrid model also has built into it an outlet option in the form of participation in a faculty member's research. The sole weakness to this model consists of the requirement that the instructor would need to have in process or ready for launch a research project suitable to support a number of undergraduates. This may pose a barrier for some instructors, or perhaps even for a department, at a small school with a heavy teaching load or in a field where research is primarily conducted by individuals and where suitable roles as an assistant are difficult to construct within the discipline's standard research methods.

In disciplines where research team projects are common, and especially at larger Research I institutions, a department may choose to build the senior capstone course exclusively around ongoing faculty research. This alternative places substantial reliance on faculty to have ongoing research suitable for the incorporation of senior students in research assistant roles. A variation on this approach not uncommon in engineering and business capstones (Franchetti, Hefzy, Pourazady, & Smallman, 2012; Barry et al., 2011) is to invite volunteer professionals, often alumni, to lead teams of student researchers or act as consultants to student teams. There are many examples of engineering and business capstones in the literature that have successfully followed this model.

Finally, a department or interdisciplinary committee can create and mutually agree to adopt a single major project as the capstone experience for all students. Examples of this type are also common in business and engineering, where students in small teams must each address the same problem. Many "design-build" engineering capstones are of this type. A problem is posed around a single set of requirements, and each team must solve the same problem by designing a feasible solution and then building it.

With respect to topic choice and research question formation, we recommend either a model that incorporates student choice as an intentional design element or a model that entirely eliminates student choice, through either the faculty research option or the department-wide option. The reasons are simple. The most salient feature of failed student capstone experiences is lack of student buy-in or motivation. It is crucial to engage students in the capstone experience. These are the two models that most directly address, and thereby avoid, the hazard of student apathy.

Student choice models ensure that the student has an investment in making a good choice. These can work well when the instructor acts as a mentor and works with students to ensure that topic choice and research question formation not only engage the student's interest but state an important research issue and have some reasonable likelihood of successful completion. "Forced participation models" such as faculty-led research and department-wide projects circumvent the individual student investment dilemma by silently adopting a quasi-military model of motivation. By requiring every graduating student to do the same project, much like requiring every enlistee to complete boot camp, an esprit de corps is established that can carry the cohort successfully through the rite of passage. The key here is creating the atmosphere of shared experience that will permit a cluster of more or less unorganized individuals to form and then cohere into a sociologically meaningful group. When randomly assigned project teams are successful in becoming a true group experience, this model can inspire student motivation and produce good outcomes as well.

A final factor to consider with respect to topic selection and research hypothesis formation is when the process should begin. A number of writers urge that topics should be identified and a decision made prior to the semester in which the capstone course will be completed (Roberts & Pavlak, 2002). This is one advantage of two-semester (one academic year) models like Yale University's history capstone (see Jones et al., 2012): it permits students to begin the early stages of the process in advance of the semester in which they will take the capstone course and complete their major project. Even if a sequenced prerequisite does not precede the capstone course, students should be encouraged to make early decisions. At Saint Martin's University, students enrolled in the Criminal Justice/Legal Studies Senior Seminar are contacted by e-mail as soon as registration for the following semester is complete. Students are invited to meet with their senior seminar advisor at that time, several months in advance of the official start of senior experience, to identify and begin the process of refining suitable questions for their senior thesis. Students who take advantage of the opportunity to engage with the major paper process early typically exhibit better motivation throughout senior seminar and produce better theses.

References, Citations, and Peer-Reviewed Sources

A policy regarding scholarly references warrants consideration. There are two dimensions. First is the question of whether to limit references to those that are peer reviewed or to permit non-peer-reviewed sources. Second, there is the question of whether to set a minimum floor on the number of sources that must be used and referenced.

In many academic disciplines, peer-reviewed sources are considered the gold standard and required as a matter of course. There may be disciplinary areas that are not compatible with this model. For example, it may well be that in emerging fields, there is not yet an established peer review system of creditable publications. In other fields, there may be more or less accepted industry standards but not ones that are reported and governed by true peer review. Examples of emerging fields like these may include studies of Internet business models or research in computer software design and programming. The issue for the capstone course design therefore is to choose a policy that is generally in accord with the contemporary standards of his or her discipline. However, even within disciplines with an established history of peer review, it may be permissible to accept non-peer-reviewed sources for the purpose of establishing an issue that has received public recognition or use of those sources as data. Any policy choice can be adjusted over time should more definite standards emerge within new and innovative areas of study or based purely on pedagogical considerations that emerge through experience.

The limited number of studies available with respect to setting a minimum requirement regarding the number of sources or references suggests that this approach is not as common as setting a minimum page requirement. In either case, the purpose of setting a minimum is to ensure a certain bottom-line degree of effort and minimum academic standards for students who would otherwise be inclined to make less effort and produce a lower-quality product. In our regional study of sociology and psychology departments, 55 percent of respondents stated that they imposed a minimum page requirement, whereas only 41 percent imposed a minimum citation or reference source requirement (Hauhart & Grahe, 2010). As a practical matter, it may be somewhat unnecessary and redundant to set a minimum page requirement and a minimum citation or reference requirement. If the page minimum is set high enough with a general proviso that multiple sources must be cited, most students will produce papers within the range desired with respect to citations in any event. This approach can be supported in a number of ways. In the Criminal Justice/Legal Studies Senior Seminar at Saint Martin's University, students are assigned previously submitted senior theses to read and summarize orally in class early in the term. At the conclusion of each summation, the instructor typically asks about both the length of the paper (all theses must be more than twenty-five pages) and the number of references. Invariably the answer to the latter question is "about two pages worth" (about twenty-five). In this way, the minimum page length required is reinforced and class members see repeatedly that two pages of references constitutes the norm. Moreover, where regular instructor review or periodic student-faculty meetings are required, there will be many opportunities to encourage more research and additional sources, thereby also obviating the need of a strict "minimum citations" policy.

Task Sequencing and Work Completion Time Lines

A critical feature of course syllabi generally is a schedule of readings, assignments, and events for the term or semester. Although capstone courses are decidedly different from other courses within the curriculum, they can also benefit from careful attention to a schedule of activities, task sequencing, and work completion due dates. Carlson et al. (2002) reported that one of the initial problems they encountered with their newly designed capstone course was "keeping students on schedule to complete projects on time." A completion time line is particularly helpful in supporting underprepared students and those who suffer from motivational deficiencies and procrastination.

While a schedule is a useful tool, there are two essential components to developing a good schedule: task sequencing and a related time line for work completion. Task sequencing is the practice of breaking down the core task of completing a major project or major paper into its constituent elements and then placing them in a sequential order that facilitates their completion. We introduced this concept in our illustration of the research continuum in figure 4.3. Thus, by already addressing the selection of a topic for the major project or paper, we have introduced the elementary concept of first things first, which is the essence of task sequencing. The various phases of projection, collection, and reflection that constitute the research continuum simply order the steps of the research process according to this principle. Establishing a task sequence supplies students (especially weak or indolent students) with an order and coherence that they might otherwise lack the ability to establish for themselves. At the same time, this process does detract from the learning challenge that a capstone represents.

The objection can arise that establishing the goals for task completion should be part of the student's responsibility by the time they are seniors. One answer is to merely encourage the instructor to create only a bare-bones guideline for task completion, thereby requiring each student to fill in and complete the task completion plan. This is the method the first author uses at Saint Martin's University, and it works well for most students.

The time line for completing essential phases of the capstone project is a critical feature in the syllabi in our judgment. The best practice is clearly to provide a time line (Roberts & Pavlak, 2002). Few experienced faculty members would, under normal circumstances, fail to place due dates for assignments in a traditional course syllabus. In the typical capstone course, however, there is really only one assignment: complete a major project or major paper within the semester. To have only a single due date that is perhaps fifteen or sixteen weeks out in the future is an invitation to failure for some students. (This can be a daunting challenge even for learned professionals and dedicated scholars.) The upshot for designing a potentially successful senior capstone course is to interweave task sequencing and a detailed project time line for the semester into a logical series of manageable steps that are split by periodic due dates for specific task completions. Students can be involved in establishing the actual dates chosen, thereby increasing investment. Olwell and Delph (2004) describe such a process for the history capstone at Eastern Michigan University, which incorporates a number of supplemental activities leading to sequential completion of phases of the major project.

The research literature supporting these practices has been surfacing regularly over the past few years. Jones et al. (2012) describe task sequencing within the Book Project that is part of the history capstone course at Virginia Tech. They observe that this project "guides senior seminar students" through the process of researching and writing essays that will become chapters in a student book. This terminology defines task sequencing correctly as a functional guide that ensures student effort is directed at sequential tasks that will ultimately build to completion in a final intellectual product. The authors note that they spend class time within the capstone course "explaining the stages historians go through when researching, writing and publishing" their work (Jones et al., 2012, p. 1106). These stages are the task sequences that students will be taught, sometimes implicitly, to follow. The Virginia Tech historians use the phrase "writing a chapter" when discussing the primary activity of this option within their capstone course, and students soon adopt the same conceptualization and language. This language identifies the end stage or final outcome sought in a way that establishes high academic expectations. The phrase distinguishes this particular capstone course goal from being "just another term paper." The authors highlight the importance of task sequencing when they comment directly that the original book project was revised "by introducing more sequencing into the process (by setting manageable, serially completed stages of research and writing)" (Jones et al., 2012, p. 1107). A subsequent statement explains precisely the benefit the Virginia Tech historians observe:

> Each of us also addresses motivation by sequencing the research and writing process. Prior to the senior capstone, few students have had the opportunity to work on a project over an entire semester, and time management difficulties partly explain the substandard quality we saw in their final products. We try to break down the project into more-or-less discrete stages, which include completing a set of common readings,

identifying an appropriate topic, submitting a bibliography, drafting a statement of the thesis, writing drafts of a section of the chapter, and turning in a penultimate draft of the whole. The senior project thus addresses more than the research and writing skills we expect of our majors; the process of writing a chapter provides students with a strategy for undertaking lengthy projects in other contexts, including the workplace. Mastery of the process as well as the product thus counts as "value added" by the course. (Jones et al., 2012, p. 1107)

Similarly, Franchetti et al. (2012) describe their success in an engineering design senior capstone course where task sequencing is given paramount importance. A specific time line requires submission of a proposal by the third week of term, weekly written progress reports, a detailed implementation schedule by the tenth week of the term, a requirement that projects will not be funded until a proposal has been approved and a detailed cost analysis provided and approved, and submission of the final report by the last week of the semester.

Student-Instructor Meetings

An important high-impact practice is to create a high degree of interaction between students and faculty over substantive intellectual matters. A technique that faculty can incorporate into the capstone course to achieve this end is student-instructor one-on-one meetings. Two questions arise. Should the student-instructor meetings be required or optional (that is, student initiated)? Second, how many individual meetings in a regular fifteen-week semester should be expected?

Required student-instructor meetings may seek, and serve, fundamentally different objectives from optional student-initiated meetings. Required meetings that are convened at the behest of the instructor may serve primarily as a means to monitor student progress and ensure reasonably successful student completion of the capstone requirements. Shifting the burden of initiating meetings is a means of creating a student learning experience that compels students to assume responsibility for their own learning. Since one purpose often assigned to the senior experience course is preparation for the transition from higher education to the assumption of adulthood, including transition to the workplace, compelling students to initiate requests for meetings can contribute to this goal of establishing independence through the demonstration of active learning habits. Active learners must chart their own progress on a task, recognize when they need help on an intellectual task, and be willing and able to initiate a request for help that will facilitate their work in completing the task. The goal of fostering qualities of self-governing independence among students within a collaborative educational endeavor cannot be achieved through required meetings. Only by creating a context and opportunity for the display of student initiative can effective student autonomy be supported but also tested. Since the course is by definition for graduating seniors, what better place to force students to relinquish their reliance on passive learning and assume responsibility for moving a project forward?

When the capstone experience is conceived as a classroom course, the instructor will regularly see students and have an opportunity to monitor progress. Still, individual meetings provide further opportunity for interaction between students and faculty members. Out-of-class contact between students and faculty has been linked with greater satisfaction with the overall college experience for students, higher educational aspirations, greater personal and intellectual development, higher academic achievement, and more persistence in college academics (Rodrick & Dickmeyer, 2002).

Roscoe and Strapp (2009) used individual meetings effectively in a career transition capstone in psychology by combining three required meetings with substantive assignments. The first meeting required students to bring their draft application and personal statement letter for graduate school for review. The second one followed up by requiring the student to bring the final drafts of each for review. The third required the student to meet with the instructor to orally evaluate his or her own senior experience at the end of the term and receive feedback from the instructor. Roscoe and Strapp reported that these three required meetings improved the quality of the student work. The meetings also received the highest ratings for student satisfaction on an end-of-course survey.

The Roscoe and Strapp (2009) approach to meetings not only addresses the benefit to be gained from student-instructor interaction but incorporates the more specific practice of prompt feedback. Schermer and Gray (2012) identify "availability and providing timely and constructive feedback" as one of the characteristics of good faculty mentors and an essential good practice for supporting students. In short, high-quality, frequent student-instructor meetings will be beneficial. The question becomes to what extent instructor resources can accommodate individual student meetings. This is the sort of determination each instructor must make.

Peer Review Activities

Schermer and Gray (2011, p. 79) identify as one of the key characteristics of capstone experiences that lead to good outcomes "the opportunity for peer interaction around common problems" or "to give peer reactions/feedback." In our view, peer review should be incorporated as a regular scheduled activity within the capstone course to ensure that peer interaction opportunities focused around substantive work are available.

Woodard (2011) describes the use of peer editing of papers in his discussion of a theology capstone course. It is possible to expand this notion to include a series of peer activities starting within the first weeks. Thus, at Saint Martin's University, the first author requires capstone students to begin reviewing and offering constructive criticism of the written work of their classmates almost from the inception of each student's project. To facilitate the student work, a peer-review sheet is used to guide student reviewers to examine core elements of the papers, including the clarity and suitability of the thesis statement, research methods employed, the quality of the writing exhibited, and so on.

One can also use peer review for oral presentation. Our regional study of sociology and psychology departments found that nearly 70 percent of capstone courses in those disciplines require an oral presentation. The Criminal Justice/Legal Studies senior seminar at Saint Martin's University requires regular oral presentations. An oral presentation review sheet that itemizes a number of important presentation qualities (clarity, speaking voice, posture) as well as substantive criteria (thesis statement or research hypothesis clearly stated, evidence offered) can support peer evaluation. Oral presentations are ideal opportunities for peer engagement through peer assessment in the capstone course.

Conclusion

We have spent a good deal of time on issues related to developing and designing a senior capstone course. We have done so because our reading of the literature on capstone experiences suggests that good design leads to good outcomes. Indeed, while we do not have definitive evidence to offer, we believe, based on the peer-reviewed literature we have analyzed, that good capstone course design matters more than any other factor other than student limitations (Hauhart & Grahe, 2012). This view is perhaps counterintuitive to the belief held by many university and college teachers. Teachers, fond of teaching as they should be, often take personal responsibility for and invest heavily in the outcomes their students achieve. Teachers would like to believe that their efforts in the classroom are the primary factor that instills bright enthusiasm and hones research and writing skills. Maybe this is true. Nevertheless, we recommend that instructors who plan to offer a senior experience adopt our first principle for good capstone teaching: *design the capstone course you intend to offer well.*

CHAPTER SEVEN

TEACHING THE CAPSTONE COURSE

We found in our research that while there does exist what we have characterized as a typical capstone course within sociology and psychology, capstones differ from each other as well. Across the broad range of disciplines found in the modern multiversity, there is variation due to the special requirements of some disciplines and the historical approaches some disciplines have consistently adopted. Moreover, there can be differences between large school and small school senior capstone experiences, and between PhD and other levels of degree-granting institutions. While this chapter will discuss these variations across the university curriculum as a basis for understanding the best practices that have been developed for teaching the undergraduate capstone, we will continue to focus most of our attention on the typical capstone format due to its commonality. The literature suggests many common problems exist that capstone course instructors face regardless of format and regardless of discipline, institutional size, or institutional nature.

The complement to designing a good capstone course is teaching a good capstone course. While we will discuss a number of specific innovative approaches that can support course design, a critical, even foundational, feature of teaching the course is simply delivering the design one has chosen. In this regard, the course design can be analogized to an airline flight plan: having identified where one wishes to go and charted a course to get there, adhering to the plan is perhaps the critical base element for a good outcome. There is more to teaching than sticking with the lesson plan, and some readers will have a broader interest in teaching techniques than our discussion can satisfy. For those readers, we recommend consulting one of the many useful sources that address good teaching more generally.[1]

Our discussion focuses on situations applicable to the capstone where the instructor has delivered on the basic plan and where we believe student outcomes can be improved by using specific practices. For example, actively addressing issues of student motivation and engagement that arise within the capstone course, a common concern among capstone instructors, can improve the capstone experience. Thus, Jones, Barrow, Stephens, and O'Hara (2012, p. 1003) note that "a lack of student motivation is a common refrain" among history professors writing about their capstone experiences. Teaching techniques over and above those embedded within the framework of the course design can be used to inspire better engagement with the course objectives and motivation to complete specific tasks. Viewed broadly, our recommendations are best understood as being either proactive and preventive in nature or, alternatively, mitigating and remedial. The discussion that follows oscillates between these two poles.

Sticking with the Capstone Course Plan

Our discussion of teaching the senior capstone course starts with the assumption that the instructor (as well as colleagues in the department) has invested substantial effort in designing the course. We do not, however, start with the assumption that every capstone course is the same, nor do we assume that all the recommendations put forth in previous chapters have been implemented. We are, after all, realists. We do not need to assume either of these to know that the cardinal principle of teaching a good capstone course is to have confidence in the course you (and others) have designed and set out deliberately to deliver that course to students. Why should this be the paramount principle?

In our view, the answer to that question is relatively simple. You and your codesigners have made a number of conscious choices about the senior capstone course. The likelihood is you have intentionally and collaboratively considered the curricular fit of your capstone course; the course goals; the relation of your capstone course to professional standards in the field; the question of whether alternative capstone projects are available within your curriculum; the prerequisites, course sequences, and capstone course length you wish to require; and the number of students you wish to enroll in each section or offering of the course. Having made these decisions deliberately and thoughtfully, there is no reason to walk away from them. To do so would, among other things, destroy the basis for faculty collaboration and control over curricular matters, as opposed to strengthening those cooperative ties that are the foundational basis for a strong core curriculum that will support a good capstone course (Briggs, 2007). Moreover, even with a carefully developed plan, it would be an unlikely event if the plan was executed as effectively as it might be in the first instance. Thus, giving the plan a chance, with only minor adjustments over time as results suggest, is the better way to proceed (Mastrangeli, 2001).

Flood (2007) discusses the capstone course created for the Northern Michigan University (NMU) nursing program. She observes that one of the cultural gaps NMU nursing students face is preparation for and experience with ethnically diverse patient populations since few are represented in the NMU catchment region. The NMU nursing capstone course was created with this diversity shortcoming in mind; the design was chosen to complement the balance of the curriculum and bring something that would not otherwise be in place. To serve its proper purpose consistent with the overall nursing curriculum then, Flood and her colleagues need to implement the senior capstone experience they have intentionally selected.

The same is true in our judgment for the many specific, discrete activities and the overall nature of the project chosen to designate as the senior capstone experience. Thus, you and your colleagues have defined and described in the college catalogue and elsewhere the core activity and parameters of the major paper or major project in the senior capstone. These structural decisions were made thoughtfully and intentionally. Now, the key initial task for teaching a good capstone course is to communicate effectively the substance of these decisions to students and then to implement the choices you and your colleagues have made for each decision. "Teaching" in this sense means implementing the design plan established.

In 1986 W. Lee Hansen, then a professor of economics as the University of Wisconsin-Madison, introduced a list of "proficiencies" he believed all economics students should master (Carlson, Cohn, & Ramsey, 2002). Many economists were persuaded that Hansen had identified an important list of knowledge-based skills, and many economics departments revised their curricula to incorporate Hansen's proficiencies in their courses, including the capstone course. Carlson et al. (2002) described the incorporation process pursued by their department's curriculum revision at Illinois State University (ISU). They reported, among other things, that it was possible for many of the proficiencies to be subsumed within what they termed "parallel" activities within specific sequenced courses. At the pinnacle of the revised curriculum, the new ISU economics capstone course incorporated the most advanced and sophisticated of Hansen's proficiencies within specified course activities. To ignore some feature of this curricular overhaul would defeat the purpose. If the mastery goal for Hansen's proficiencies is a valid one, then implementing the core capstone course along with supplemental activities that foster one of the proficiencies is the ideal way to proceed.

The scientific basis for proceeding in this way is well established in the literature. One important factor in support of this approach involves the expectations students have built up over time. Students have two types of expectations: general and specific. Generally they expect the faculty to create a classroom framework that facilitates and supports academic work. Students are ready to invest their effort within the confines of the program they encounter so long as it is comprehensible, coherent, and clearly communicated. These positive expectations will likely be fulfilled by the design you and your colleagues have created. There is no reason to deviate from the plan before delivering on it; students expect you, as the faculty member, to come in with a plan, and you need to do so. Although students may growl and grumble at the work required, they will acknowledge the benefit they receive from a structured course experience due to the positive effect it produces on their work (McKinney & Day, 2012). Specific expectations, once established, become even more important. Thus, once an expectation has been established for a course within a major, that expectation should be fulfilled unless very good reasons exist for establishing a new expectation. This ensures that incoming students will find the course the student culture has communicated they can expect to find.

Students who find that their expectations of a course have been fulfilled will complete the course requirements, however rigorous. This is the key to establishing and maintaining a high-achieving academic culture: outgoing students will communicate the high standards to those who they know will follow them, and incoming students, having formed an expectation for a course, will be ready to shoulder the academic burden they anticipate (Brinthaupt, 2004). Thus, the core task for teaching the senior capstone course is to implement the design one has created consistently over time. This will help create a sustainable academic culture of success built on realistic student expectations.

The second skill set for effectively teaching a capstone course is to develop an awareness of the likely problems one will encounter and acquire familiarity with a range of techniques and approaches to mitigate the potential negative impact of anticipated problems. This second agenda constitutes the balance of the discussion in this chapter.

Aligning Student Expectations with Course Requirements

Students entering the senior capstone experience, regardless of how well prepared they are for what is to come, will benefit from clarification by the instructor of the essential nature of the major project or major paper. The transition from traditional classroom courses to the senior capstone model at most schools and within most departments will entail a certain level of disjunction, if not dissonance, due to the changes in the format, course objectives, and general learning experience. In many university courses, students work on what have been termed well-structured problems—problems where all the elements are well constrained and specified explicitly (Juma et al., 2010). An example is a problem in some branch of basic college mathematics: everything a student needs to solve the problem is provided (whether by the textbook for a homework problem or the instructor on an exam). Such a problem has well-defined initial and final states. Typically in well-structured problems, there is a clear solution path from initial defined states to end goal states that the student is expected to master. This is the purpose of this type of problem: to teach students how to achieve the conventionally accepted solution by the most efficacious method. Many students work well within the constraints of well-defined, well-structured problems.

Senior capstone experiences, in contrast, often consist of what have been called ill-structured problems (or nonstructured problems). Problems of this type are characterized as ill defined because some of the elements necessary to state the problem, let alone solve it, are unknown to those charged with the task (Choi & Lee, 2009). Indeed, students in a capstone course are often expected to define the problem for themselves, and to do so, they must also decide what the required elements and parameters of the problem should entail (Juma et al., 2010). This is a radically different form of learning, and the transition from one style to another poses a significant barrier for some students. Those who have intensively studied students faced with solving ill-structured problems note that creating a learning environment to support this effort is not an easy task (Choi & Lee, 2009). The instructor may support this transition by articulating the difference between these two types of problems and acknowledging the difficulty of addressing ill-defined problems.

Research on ill-structured problem solving has suggested that students suffer from situations in which extreme simultaneity forces them to solve too many aspects of an ill-defined problem at the same time (Choi & Lee, 2009). This means that the instructor can facilitate the students' dilemma by helping students define important dimensions of the ill-structured problem incrementally. The instructor might, for example, use an example of how to ask a research question several different ways, debating the pros and cons of each approach until incrementally arriving at a better way to state a thesis or hypothesis. The research methodology might be approached the same way—as a demonstration of a rationally assessed choice process among alternative methods for investigating a particular question. For students who have previously always been shown the proof to a problem and then simply been expected to learn it, this guided, incremental form of pedagogy with respect to the ill-defined task of writing a senior thesis may prove successful.

Another technique that can aid students in addressing ill-structured problems is to illustrate the benefits of asking precisely stated, relevant questions. Generally research has demonstrated that problem resolution is highly correlated with the quality of questions asked during problem formulation and subsequent stages of problem solution (Kochen & Badre, 1974). The instructor could force students to ask questions in an exercise to solve a definitional problem for an ill-structured task where the instructor will answer any question with only yes or no. This exercise can show students that better-formulated questions produce better information and solve the problem more efficiently (Kochen & Badre, 1974). Cross-cultural studies of how young children gain communicative competence demonstrate that where adults force children to reformulate questions until the child gains the information he or she seeks, rather than spoon-feeding the information after a fumbling attempt, produces better linguistic mastery and better problem solving (Corsaro, 2005).

Guiding Student Expectations with Feedback

A faculty member who has never taught a capstone course would be well advised to begin by recognizing that these courses are labor intensive. This is particularly true of the research-based major paper capstone course.

In this format, students are normally expected to present multiple drafts throughout a term. Since papers will be anywhere from twenty to fifty pages, repeated readings within a capstone course section can constitute a substantial workload.[2] Managing that workload is a factor for all capstone instructors.

One way to provide feedback on a periodic basis is to use a standard evaluation instrument. A copy of the evaluation that the first author uses appears in our online appendix (it can be viewed at https://osf.io/tg6fa/). The form recites standard elements that warrant evaluation (quality of the thesis topic and statement, quality of research, quality of writing, seminar contributions, and quality of advising relationship with the instructor). Once the form is prepared for each student's initial draft submission, it can be easily updated for each periodic submission (preserving some of the comments that need reinforcement, editing others, adding comments).

The evaluation form also provides a space for a grade range to be assigned next to each entry if desired. Assigning approximate or estimated letter grades next to substantive comments can be a useful tool for students. Students may attend more closely to the comments that are "downgraded" and may respond with increased motivation when their continued work produces an increase in the grade range. Managing student expectations in this manner is an effective use of feedback that helps direct students to address areas of weakness and move on to pursue work that remains to be accomplished.

Rubrics can be developed to facilitate grading tied to broader learning goals. When considering evaluation rubrics, instructors have a range of resources they can investigate. The rubric chosen should be guided by the goals and learning outcomes the instructor and department have adopted. To that end, any generic rubric should be modified to address the specific purposes of the course. Thus, instructors may rely on one of the sixteen Valid Assessment of Learning in Undergraduate Education (VALUE) rubrics developed by the Association of American Colleges and Universities (www.aacu.org/value/rubrics/index.cfm) but only if course specific adaptations are adopted. The VALUE rubrics consist of ten intellectual and practical skills (inquiry and analysis, critical thinking, creative thinking, written communication, oral communication, reading, quantitative literacy, information literacy, teamwork, and problem solving), five rubrics evaluating personal and social responsibility (civic knowledge and engagement, intercultural knowledge and competence, ethical reasoning, foundations and skills for lifelong learning, and global learning), and one rubric measuring integrative and applied learning. Each rubric is formatted similarly and includes fundamental criteria for each learning outcome. This format includes a single-sentence definition, framing language to connect the learning outcome to the broader curriculum, a glossary of terms and concepts used in the rubric, and a one-page table including each foundational criterion and four rating categories ranging from 1 (benchmark) to capstone (4). Rubrics like these can then also be used as foundational tools for course and program assessment.

Confronting Weak Preparation and Poor Motivation Structurally

In describing their history capstone at Virginia Tech, Jones et al. (2012, p. 1103) touch on one of the common faculty experiences, and sources of frustration, with the capstone course: "Students . . . often tend to see more pain than pleasure in this concluding step to the degree. At VT, those of us teaching the senior seminars routinely face the problem of motivating students to engage fully with the research process. We are not alone: lack of motivation is a common refrain in articles about the history capstone." Mancha and Yoder (2014) found a high degree of agreement between students and faculty regarding the importance of high student motivation for successful completion of psychology capstone at Trinity College. Given that high motivation is needed, its absence will be frustrating for both the student and the faculty member.

Our own research on sociology and psychology capstones also revealed pervasive faculty reference to problems with student engagement with the capstone major project. When we asked our regional survey respondents an open-ended question regarding the dissatisfactions and struggles they experienced in teaching the capstone course, 33 percent described student approaches to the course that reflected an inability or unwillingness to commit fully to the course activity (Hauhart & Grahe, 2010). Our respondents' replies could be separated cleanly into responses that voiced problems with student motivation and responses that commented on insufficient student preparation (Hauhart & Grahe, 2010).

In our subsequent national survey regarding sociology and psychology capstone courses, our data suggested that student limitations such as lack of sufficient preparation and motivation were the primary obstacles to the production and completion of quality senior projects (Hauhart & Grahe, 2012). McKinney and Day's (2012) multi-institutional study of capstone courses also found that while prior courses helped students prepare for the capstone experience, there remained gaps in student preparation that had a negative impact on students' ability to produce successful outcomes in the major project. These findings suggest that one of the paramount teaching tasks of capstone course instructors is devising techniques for minimizing the potential negative impacts of insufficient academic preparation and lack of motivation. Often the two go hand in hand.

Maintaining a Strong Core Curriculum

The obvious antidote to insufficient academic preparation is better academic preparation within the core curriculum, although this is a long-term strategy. As we have already suggested, reliance on prerequisites, course sequencing, and core curriculum research courses can contribute significantly to raising the level of preparedness for students. Research supports this foundational approach. Ishiyama (2005) studied political science department curricula to see whether more structured curricula led to better student learning outcomes. He relied on a twenty-nine-item survey of political science department heads and student test scores. By "structured curricula," Ishiyama meant political science curricula characterized by a sequenced set of courses, the existence of a senior seminar or capstone course, and a required research methodology course taken early in the student's career. Ishiyama concluded there was a strong relationship between the structured nature of a department's curriculum and student learning as measured by the Major Field Aptitude Test II for political science. In earlier research, Ishiyama and Hartlaub (2003) had concluded that more structured political science programs produced graduates who could think more abstractly and critically than less structured curricular programs did. Thus, more structured programs do not simply produce students who test better but students who know more, including how to think about what they know.

Studies by educational psychologists regarding learning also support this view. Svinicki (2004), summarizing research on individual differences that matter, notes that students who have greater depth of knowledge as background learn faster because they can fill in the blanks they are missing with new information and then move forward toward further learning. Svinicki's recommendations mirror ours: students need to master certain broad-based knowledge and skill levels before they will be able to learn what they need to know to complete successively challenging intellectual tasks such as the major paper or major project for the typical capstone course. It would be optimal if the core curriculum achieved this level of student preparedness, but there are ways to do this, to a degree, within the capstone course.

Addressing Lack of Student Preparedness and Motivation in the Capstone Course

One way that Svinicki (2004) and others recommend is to begin the course with some data gathering to establish the degree of depth of knowledge the student cohort possesses. This will help flush out obvious deficiencies in knowledge that may require remedial attention. Some form of pretesting may reveal a limited pattern of underpreparation that can then be addressed. Recall how Jones et al. (2012), who have given this problem a good deal of thought, begin their history capstone course at Virginia Tech by having students prepare a research résumé during the first week of class. Students respond to sixty-seven quantitative and qualitative questions regarding specific research tools and databases and their prior historical research experiences.[3] Completing this set of questions has the effect of reminding students of what they do know as well as what they perhaps should know, while at the same time revealing areas of weakness with regard to what they don't know. The instructor can then use this information to address the research deficiencies they reveal.

Research by McKinney and Busher (2011) supports the idea that prequestionnaires and postquestionnaires to identify specific weaknesses in student preparedness can be an effective tool. Their research on sociology capstone projects suggested that students struggle with applying sociological theory; consequently, both the introduction/literature review and discussion/conclusion sections of major papers correspondingly suffered. Knowing this about one's own student population permits instructors to build in efforts to address this weak link in student preparation and support better student outcomes. Payne, Flynn, and Whitfield (2008) used such an approach effectively in a capstone business course. Capstone courses are premised generally on the assumption that students will retain, and be able to apply successfully, concepts from their prior core courses. However, if there is inadequate initial student learning, the assumption that there will be usable retention is clearly incorrect. As these authors note, citing prior research, inadequate preparedness can thwart the capstone student's acquisition of more advanced knowledge necessary for completion of a major project or paper. One of the ways these authors went about addressing perceived inadequate preparation among their capstone students was to conduct interviews regarding the students' learning goals and the barriers they had experienced in learning new material. The interview, like a research résumé or pretest, can alert capstone instructors to weak areas of preparation. Instructors can then devise solutions that are tailored directly to the deficiencies.

A second means that capstone course instructors can employ to respond to lack of student academic preparation for the challenge that senior seminar represents is to make adjustments to the capstone design. As we have already suggested, a good internal capstone course structure fully implemented is a key to a successful capstone experience. An instructor faced with students whose preparation is substandard can maintain student focus on the project that might otherwise be lost by increasing the structured guideposts and supervision points during the term. Thus, commentators from all disciplines routinely mention student procrastination on capstone major papers or projects as a barrier to successful outcomes (Carlson et al., 2002; Siegfried, 2001; Wallace, 1988). An effective response to the potential for student procrastination is a tighter semester time line. Research suggests that students respond favorably to a highly structured environment for completion of the capstone and a tighter framework will create better outcomes. However, students will acknowledge finding the tighter structure frustrating at the time they are working within its limitations (McKinney & Day, 2012).

A third way in which capstone instructors can modify the course to address a gap in prior preparation is to enlist student engagement as a tool to inspire extra effort. Studies of academic motivation suggest that both intrinsic and extrinsic motivators can support improved learning outcomes (Covington, 2000). However, all students do not respond consistently to intrinsic or extrinsic motivators as the value and meaning students place on either form of reward varies across the setting and the task at hand. If, however, a capstone course instructor can identify what is both discouraging and motivating students facing challenges, then arguably the instructor can change the balance of intrinsic versus extrinsic motivators to inspire more student effort directed at the weaknesses that have been exposed. An instructor might, for example, query capstone students weekly about the difficulties they are facing and the satisfactions they are experiencing, and then use the information to provide some rewards that seem likely to be most successful. The student who is unable to stay on a three-pages-a-week schedule independently can be advised to come in Monday, Wednesday, and Friday with one new page each day. The student who cannot master the required citation style can make a writing center appointment directed at solving that particular problem.

Such an inquiry itself can support student engagement with the task since it produces an effect similar to the Hawthorne effect: lower-status individuals who become the subject of concern and interest by perceived higher-status individuals will often respond in a favorable way to give the higher-status individual what the subjects believe that individual wants (Roethlisberger, Wright, Dickson, & Western Electric Company, 1939). Since it is apparent that the higher-status instructor wants better-quality academic work, many students will respond positively to any form of attention directed toward them from the instructor. In the Hawthorne experiments, researchers found they could improve worker efficiency by increasing the lighting intensity over workers' stations. However, they also found that they could increase worker efficiency by decreasing the ambient light intensity at the workstations (Roethlisberger et al., 1939). In short, it was a researcher effect that produced the outcome. In the context of the senior capstone course, instructor attentiveness to student progress can inspire deeper student engagement—whether the instructor offers positive interactional rewards to students or negative critiques. Many of the best practices used to inspire better learning outcomes, without explicitly saying so, rely on this basic social psychological process.

Forestalling Procrastination

Procrastination is the well-known practice of putting something off until a future date, especially failing to initiate and complete an activity within a prescribed time period when it is expected to be accomplished (Sharma, 1997). Some researchers have argued that there are two distinct variations of procrastination: active and passive (Seo, 2013). Active procrastination is an intentional strategy pursued to create deadline pressure; some students work effectively under such circumstances and produce good outcomes (Seo, 2013). Passive procrastination is an inability to maintain disciplined work habits; passive procrastinators often experience guilt and depression and fail to meet their deadlines, thereby producing poor outcomes (Seo, 2013). The latter is the form of motivational problem experienced by most students (and some faculty members!). Students faced with an ill-structured problem in a capstone course may be especially prone to procrastination. There are indications in the research literature that procrastination increases when frustration rises due to facing a complex task for which the subject is ill prepared (Sharma, 1997). Some studies have also suggested that personal situational factors (e.g., depression) and personality traits may influence procrastination behavior, but the results of this research have been mixed (Sharma, 1997). The problem is difficult to address because the short-term benefits of stress reduction and better health in the early stages of procrastination are so appealing (Tice & Baumeister, 1997).

With respect to forestalling and preventing student procrastination within the capstone, the solution is, within limits, not to permit it. This is accomplished by two interrelated strategies: strict adherence to a series of graduated deadlines imposed on all students within the capstone course and application of a more intensive review process to procrastinators and increasingly dire warnings if those reviews are not heeded. Thus, the student who has fallen behind the timeline by week 4 of a standard semester should receive weekly reviews, preferably in writing, for the following four weeks. These should include increasingly cautionary warnings regarding the consequences for noncompletion or poor completion. The advantage of written reviews is that each succeeding review can refer back to the failure to take the action assigned in the previous week's review. Indeed, computers make it exceedingly simple to revise each week's review the following week, quoting liberally the directions given to the student to bring his or her work up to par or on deadline and then reciting the failure to do so. Oral presentations can also be used to inspire action from procrastinators: students will recoil from required weekly demands to update their peers orally on what they have accomplished in the past week when they have done nothing. The embarrassment that unprepared students will experience when facing their peers with nothing to say can constitute a substantial incentive to complete assigned work by the due date. Eventually most procrastinators will begin to complete their work when subjected to techniques like these.

Life Development as an Impediment

A factor that may influence a student's motivation and performance within the capstone course is his or her developmental life stage. It is apparent that students vary in their maturity just as they vary along other dimensions. A student who has not resolved some developmental issues may engage in behaviors and make choices that are baffling to mentors. Why, for example, do excellent students miss deadlines and exhibit low effort? Why do students sometimes misdirect their efforts to low-priority tasks rather than focus on substantive issues?

Americans between ages eighteen and twenty-five are passing through a stage of life that Jeffrey Arnett (2001) dubbed "emerging adulthood," a modern phenomenon where youth transition between childhood with little or no responsibility and adulthood with full responsibility. Skipper (2012) has reviewed this stage of life as it relates to student transitions in the senior year of college. The concept usefully describes "a range of developmental tasks that coincide with the transition out of college (e.g., critical thinking, identity development, career decision making, emotional maturity, self-sufficiency)" (p. 29). As we have discussed, the capstone course provides a vehicle for some of this transition. Thus, it is useful to understand the ways that students' thinking may be distinct from those of their instructors because of their age and maturity.

Skipper (2012) discussed the concept of emerging adulthood in light of Patricia King and Karen Kitchener's reflective judgment model (1994), which considers stages of understanding knowledge identified as prereflective, quasi-reflective, and reflective. At its simplest, prereflective refers to seeing the world concretely by categorizing decisions as right and wrong. Transitioning into reflexive thinking means understanding that abstraction exists and that knowledge is affected by the context within which a question has been asked. Skipper reminds us that students are often in the quasi-reflexive stage: they understand that uncertainty exists but struggle with full integration and synthesis of contradictory and competing aspects of reality. Naturally this tension can be exacerbated by the ill-structured problem that students often must address in their capstone experience.

As students grapple with the ill-defined problem their capstone course presents, they are also forming adult identities as they make the transition from college. Three developmental vectors from Chickering and Reisser's (1993) theory of psychosocial development may be heightened for transitioning students: "(a) establishing identity, (b) developing purpose, and (c) developing integrity" (Skipper, 2012, p. 34). Skipper (2012) concludes that the developmental literature suggests three principles to help students more effectively move through these stages: "(a) validating learners as knowers, (b) situating learning in learners' [life] experiences, and (c) defining learning as mutually constructing meaning" (p. 44). She suggests that too many college programs fail to encourage students to achieve "self-authorship" using these principles. The capstone course can, and should be, one place to do so.

Not every student will experience difficulties from the life stage transition. For those who do, teaching techniques that address Skipper's three principles can be developed to help them. For example, the instructor can orally validate the portions of a learner's class presentation that show knowledge by repeating points that are well made in front of the learner's peers. The instructor could also query capstone class members regarding their interest in a topic early in the semester to permit them to situate their work in their own life experience through their responses. Instructors can help students become "research learners" by describing their own research work and explaining its importance. This approach joins the instructor with the students in a process of learning through research that can make the capstone meaningful. Finally, instructors can seek outside help from other department members, advisors, or campus life staff who can act as mentors or simply offer reminders regarding the importance of capstone completion generally.

Using Peer Review Effectively

One of the techniques we recommend that faculty build into the senior course is peer review. Peer review forces participation and engagement; consequently, it is a generalized cure-all to individual student isolation, ennui, overwork, malingering, and stasis. Used liberally, it prevents conditions like these from developing.

There are several ways to use peer review in the typical major paper capstone course. First, class members may offer reviews of each other's drafts (Badger, 2010). Second, they may offer evaluations of their peers' oral presentations. Third, they may review their classmates' final drafts the week prior to submission at the end of term. All three reviews are conducted purely for the constructive benefit that students receive from the reviewer and reviewed/subject roles. Peers typically do not have authority to award grades but merely offer observations and suggestions for improvement. All three approaches provide substantial benefits.

Initially we should remind ourselves that any activity that increases student interaction regarding the substantive issues that form the intellectual core of the senior project generally contributes to successful course outcomes. This is true whether the substantive interaction is with other students, with faculty instructors and mentors, or with outside evaluators or audiences, although there are differences in the degree of benefit received from different interaction settings and partners. Peer review is one means of increasing interaction over the substantive work that students are pursuing.

Research has demonstrated that peer review is an active learning technique that can increase student engagement and satisfaction and improve the quality of work. Reuse-Durham (2005) organized nineteen students to engage in peer review of partial research papers in an Applied Research in Education course she had taught previously. She sought to find out whether students would view the activity as positive and meaningful, whether peer evaluators would report learning something from the activity, and whether better papers would result. In response to a survey, all of the student researchers agreed that the peer feedback was helpful, constructive, and understandable and that the experience was positive. Student researchers reported overall that the exercise demonstrated to them that they needed to provide more substantial information from sources in the literature review section of their papers. They also agreed that peer review during the final paper revision process was helpful in improving the final draft. Reuse-Dunham concluded that the papers subjected to review were significantly higher in quality than papers that had not been subjected to peer review.

There are better and worse ways to conduct peer review. Orsmond, Merry, and Reiling (1996) considered whether the use of marking criteria (a modest rubric or marking guide) was helpful to students in assessing their peers' work. Seventy-eight first-year biology students participated in pairs in developing posters regarding an issue of their own choice within comparative animal physiology. They initially were just given verbal instructions regarding marking standards; later they were given written guidelines; finally, they were given marking forms. Once the students had completed marking their forms for the posters, tutors independently conducted blind evaluations with the same form. The results clearly demonstrated that students discriminated more carefully between good and bad work when using the marking forms.

Badger (2010) developed a model plan for peer review in the context of her social work capstone course. Her approach employed a detailed rubric that students were directed to use in four peer reviews over the term. The instructor also gave explanations of the review process early in the semester and provided specific examples of how to give feedback. In self-assessments before and after the feedback, the data suggested that the peer reviews improved students' written work. An end-of-term survey also elicited a generally favorable response to the peer review exercises.

Several students noted in open-ended response that the experience made them less defensive to receiving feedback. They also noted the benefit of feedback from multiple sources, a research finding that has been confirmed in other studies (Badger, 2010). In sum, guidance in the form of written evaluation criteria for papers and presentations will secure the best peer review experience from students and for students.

Other studies of peer review suggest the benefits of organizing peer groups around demonstrated academic competence. Generally studies suggest that better students receive better peer ratings because, in part, they contribute more to cooperative learning when working with other students. This means that good students should be paired with as many other students as possible in using peer review over a term so that all students receive the "good student bump" from working with those students. Persons (1998) examined factors that can affect peer evaluation within student learning groups in an introductory financial accounting course. Persons found that accounting majors and students with higher grade point averages received higher peer evaluations and concluded that these students possessed both higher motivation to participate and better understanding of the accounting tasks. This contributed to creating a better learning environment for other students. Persons further found that higher group performance ratings were associated with higher group homework grades and higher instructor-awarded participation grades. This too suggested that distributing higher-performing students among groups raised the quality of group work. Davies (2006) reached much the same conclusion.

Davies (2006) wanted to evaluate whether judging the quality of students' work could be achieved by using students' peer review comments rather than by relying on final grades given by student reviewers. Generally Davies found high agreement between student comments about quality and the actual grade students awarded peer work. Davies also concluded that better students tended to be more critical of their peers overall in the marking process. However, within that finding, top students tended to "overmark" and "overcomment" (i.e., be less critical) compared to weaker students. Both tendencies tend to make better students highly influential in the peer review process, and because they are such good students, this tends to raise the quality profile of those they review and grade. Better students have more influence on other better students because other better students are willing to listen to them. Better students have more influence on weaker students because their comments and grades are not unkind to them while at the same time conveying quality comments.

Identifying More Specific Learning Outcomes

We have already suggested that a more highly structured capstone experience can support student success, especially for academically unprepared students. A related way of achieving such a structure is to increase the number and specificity of learning goals for the capstone paper. While it may be entirely sufficient for some students to say, "Complete a major paper on a significant question of scholarly merit," other students will benefit from a detailed list of discrete objectives that they should fulfill. This will help students recognize that they can break down the larger project into more manageable tasks corresponding to specific learning goals.

Thambyah (2011) reports on using this approach within an undergraduate engineering capstone course. Initially Thambyah notes that the engineering capstone is a research-based course with an open-ended format. It consists of what we have termed an ill-structured problem format where there is not a discrete, well-defined problem to solve with all elements of the problem provided. Thambyah adopted Anderson and Krathwohl's (2001) revision of Bloom's taxonomy to design the learning outcomes. The goal was to establish well-defined learning objectives so that students could mark their progress across these goals as they proceeded to solve the otherwise open-ended engineering research problem.

Thambyah integrated the engineering students' general learning goals and expectations so they coincided with the six cognitive processes and four knowledge dimensions of Bloom's revised taxonomy table. This produced twenty-four discrete learning outcomes that the students (and the instructor) could use for assessing student progress. For example, discrete learning objectives specific to the student's project could be identified along the six forms of cognition on the continuum: remember, understand, apply, analyze, evaluate, and create. As the student displays each conceptual skill in the course of solving the problem, the success can be marked by the assignment of grades or simply by acknowledgement. The use of more closely specified learning objectives does not tell the student in an open-ended, nonstructured research project how to do the research; it does, however, offer learning guideposts in an otherwise ambiguous environment. Thambyah concludes that more research on the use of carefully defined learning objectives will demonstrate that students benefit from their use and improves the quality of their engineering research.

Increased Support from Information Literacy and Writing Centers

Lack of academic preparedness can be partially remedied in the senior capstone course by increased use of library and writing center resources. Studies have suggested that increases in student learning and retention arise from both high-impact practices like the senior capstone when combined with information literacy goals, thereby leading to increased skill levels (Riehle & Weiner, 2013). In effect, the two work in tandem to produce better outcomes. A social work professor and a librarian collaborated in a case study to try to understand why students could not complete library tasks in a capstone course (Plionis, Thompson, & Eisenhower, 2005). They found that student needs in understanding an increasingly complex set of sources on the Internet and students' misperceptions about the research process contributed to their inability to complete library research successfully. The authors' solution was to separate the capstone paper into ten assignments focused on distinct phases of the research process. They also required, and offered, more feedback about student progress. While this improved student task completion success, it also increased time commitments from librarians because students were more likely to seek out further guidance (Plionis et al., 2005).

Basic deficiencies in writing ability will have a negative impact on students' ability to produce a major paper or report. One can envision, for example, the situation of students who may be described as finding themselves in the worst-case scenario: having to prepare a capstone thesis in English without the level of skills and capacities needed to do so because they are being asked to write in a nonnative second language (Li & Vandermensbrugghe, 2011). University writing centers offer a range of services that can be used to support senior capstone students whose basic writing skills, like those of nonnative, second-language speakers, do not rise to the level required for proficient preparation of a major paper or senior thesis. As one example, writing groups have been shown to be quite effective in raising the level of writing ability while conserving instructor resources (Li & Vandermensbrugghe, 2011).

Letting Students Decide

We have addressed the question of whether the student, the instructor, or some combination of the two should select the research topic and formulate the research question or thesis statement. In considering the three alternatives, we noted the primary advantage of the student choice option: students will be more invested in researching a topic or question of their own choosing and hence be willing to commit more time, effort, and resources to a project that engages them. This important principle can also be used to create other practices to address issues of motivation within the capstone course.

Vander Schee (2011) wanted to explore ways in which conventional approaches to grading could be used to improve students' sense of control and, consequently, their academic performance. Reviewing the literature, Vander Schee noted that grading schemes have often been used to motivate students to complete assignments. An obvious example is to award a certain percentage of a course grade for participation to encourage students to engage with the class and instructor. Vander Schee found, however, that few studies had investigated permitting students to select the weighted percentages for the assignments that lead to a final course grade. He therefore permitted students to select their own personal percentage weight distribution among assignments, noted the grades achieved compared to the previous year's grades, and queried students using a survey regarding their opinions about the self-selection process. While Vander Schee states there was only a marginal improvement in grades, the survey results suggested to him that students were responding to the increased sense of control over their work and their destiny that self-selection produced. Thus, students perceived they could influence the outcome of their learning experience due to their control over the percentage grading distribution. Consequently, they were more likely to believe the system was fair and were encouraged to put out their best effort. This is the same principle underlying topic self-selection: an increase in feelings of autonomy and control can inspire motivation, which leads to better effort and a better outcome.

While Vander Schee's (2011) research related to achieving control over the percentage weight distribution in grades, if the principle holds, then giving students more choice, within limits, on any number of dimensions within the capstone course can act to improve motivation. For example, one might give students a choice at the end of the term as to how they would like to present their major paper or project: as an oral presentation to their classmates in senior seminar or as a poster presentation at a campuswide scholars' conference. Research shows that giving students a choice on an issue that affects their lives within the senior capstone experience can favorably influence their engagement, commitment, motivation, and outcomes. Thus, we favor empowering students with opportunities to exercise choice whenever possible.

Maintaining Effective Role Relationships in Internship Capstones

Increasingly, internship and practicum-based capstone courses constitute common formats within some disciplines. Perhaps engineering and business departments select this model most frequently. Although they are popular, Johari and Bradshaw (2008) note that it is not uncommon for these capstones to produce less-than-satisfactory outcomes. They found, among other dissatisfactions, that internship capstone projects are regularly described as "boring and wasteful, or going out of control" (p. 330). More serious concerns leading to poor outcomes can also develop. Fernald et al. (1982, p. 158) received complaints regarding sexual advances from two of twelve female students in private industry practicum placements over a two-year period. While it can be that the core plan for the internship is faulty, Johari and Bradshaw (2008) take the view that the constituent elements of project-based internship capstones are fluid since they are relationship based. In their view, this means that regular evaluation of the role performances within the internship setting will be necessary to ensure alignment between the various role relationships, the task orientation of the project, the satisfaction derived from the project, and the project outcomes. To explore the manner in which a problem-based learning experience in an information technology internship actually works, Johari and Bradshaw conducted tape-recorded intern interviews, kept status review notes, examined e-portfolios, completed mentor interviews, and reviewed mentor evaluations of the student interns.

The results of Johari and Bradshaw's (2008) qualitative investigation suggested that internship capstones fail when student interns, mentors, or instructors do not enact the performance behaviors called for by their roles. The results suggested that the projects needed to be manageable but challenging and, most important, collaborative in nature. A project that requires collaboration by its design will invite that cooperation, and this is a start. Nevertheless, collaborative relationships can fail, and one of the primary role requirements of the instructor's job in such a capstone is to monitor regularly the role performances and adjust role relationships to maintain an optimal learning environment. The authors note that the various means they used to study the internship were all suitable to monitoring progress of a project so that role guidance can be offered, whether to student interns, mentors, or themselves. Durso (1997) described a corporate-sponsored capstone course in psychology where he used in-class time to monitor the progress and collaborative quality of projects through regular student reports. The instructor can intervene when a student report suggests a less-than-optimal collaborative relationship is developing and mediate the student-practitioner relationship.

Research by Pascual (2010) supports these findings: internship-based problem-oriented learning programs need to include communities of practice (a set of relations among persons with a common interest— engineering students with practicing engineers, for example) around a project with "open spaces for relatedness" (a collaborative potential). When these conditions are maintained, participants will cooperate effectively and create a successful outcome. The key for the instructor is to maintain the open collaborative environment, encourage dynamic interaction around the core project, and ensure effective relatedness. Dougherty and Parfitt (2013) describe one innovative approach to solving this problem. They created a space for dedicated and controlled collaborative discussion forums online where students could pose questions and practitioners could respond to those questions within the context of an architectural engineering capstone course. This approach created a space for relatedness around common professional interests but controlled the interaction between students and practitioners otherwise.

Incentivizing Better Students

The ideal environment for the senior capstone experience is a combination of intellectual challenge, academic support, and collaborative opportunity. It is apparent to anyone who has taught at the university level that students demonstrate a range of entering behaviors. One feature of a successful capstone course will be whether it poses a challenge for students of different ability levels. While we have discussed problems posed by underprepared students, gifted students too may pose a challenge when they are not motivated to perform at the level at which they are capable. Studies have suggested that gifted students may possess more intrinsic motivation than less gifted students (Clinkenbeard, 2012). This is both good and bad. On the one hand, gifted students are often inherently motivated and may not require further incentives to perform well. On the other hand, if that motivation is not activated, it may be difficult to spur motivation by extrinsic means since these students are less responsive to external incentives.

Research has identified a strong framework as helpful for underprepared students who sometimes flounder when faced with the responsibility that independent work in a capstone course entails (Keogh, Sterling, & Venables, 2007). Gifted students, however, respond positively beyond minimum requirements to a combination of increases in autonomy and control, opportunities to receive meaningful feedback, and mentor contact that produces feelings of relatedness (Clickenbeard, 2012). One way to expand the range and difficulty of challenges to gifted students is to broaden the opportunities to display their senior project or papers to diverse audiences. Giving good students' intellectual work greater visibility can contribute substantially to student motivation for better students, whose interest may lag if new challenges and opportunities are not available at each successive stage. When gifted students have a series of choices available and then increasing opportunities for independence, feedback, and mentor contact, they will respond positively to increased intellectual demands and excel to the full extent of their capability (Clickenbeard, 2012).

Jones et al. (2012) offer the most comprehensive statement of how a postcapstone presentation opportunity can be effectively used to incentivize and reward students for successful work. In a section entitled "After the Capstone," Jones et al. describe three models for increasing public display and recognition: the portfolio, an undergraduate research journal, and presentation at a campus or conference event. As these authors suggest, these are incentives that by and large can be used to "motivate the few, [but] do not serve as a tool to overcome the apathy and apprehension of the many" (p. 1105).

Portfolios permit students to collect their best work for presentation to the faculty as a display of their competence. Portfolio review by the faculty to meet graduation requirements is, in itself, not a high-visibility practice. (One exception may be an art portfolio, which can be put on public display to coincide with faculty review.) Yet portfolios can be combined with opportunities for more public recognition. For example, portfolios can be collectively displayed in a department office, display case, or library foyer. It also is rather easy to develop a website that displays seniors' portfolios in PDF form. In addition to temporary display, senior theses or portfolios could be permanently retained in a university library archive, whether in paper format (library space limitations permitting) or in some form of cybercatalogue. Academically elite institutions, Oberlin and Harvard University among them, often offer this sort of recognition and opportunity (Jones et al., 2012). Typically the senior thesis or major paper is the central element of most students' portfolios, so limiting the archive to these papers may be optimal. Either the portfolio or the senior paper can also function as a writing sample for seniors ready to enter the job market.

A second option is the collection of major papers or senior theses in an undergraduate research publication. This approach provides substantially greater potential for public visibility and formal recognition. Moreover, the publication process provides students one more opportunity to review and edit their work and thereby learn again the value of rewriting and revision that scholarly work regularly entails. Undergraduate research journals may be department or campus based. Campuswide undergraduate research journals provide the widest possible potential audience for students' work but are more administratively unwieldy unless there is broad support among a number of departments and faculty. Department or discipline-based undergraduate research journals appear to be more common, and perhaps for precisely this reason. There are undergraduate history journals supported by departments at Indiana University (*Primary Source*) and Virginia Tech (*Virginia Tech Undergraduate Historical Review*), for example. There have been suggestions that this trend is growing, although the sustainability of undergraduate research journals has been questioned (Jones et al., 2012).

Virginia Tech's history department has offered a variation on the undergraduate research journal for a number of years: the Book Project. The project is a version of the capstone course: each student writes a major paper on a historical topic that will then constitute one "chapter" in a book (Jones et al., 2012; Stephens, Jones, & Barrow, 2011). The book is professionally bound, distributed to students, assigned an ISBN number, and deposited in the university library. Such a project is made possible in part by the size of the university, the size of enrollment in the history major, and the number of history faculty able to support the project at Virginia Tech.

Some type of presentation in a public forum is perhaps the most common form of display used to recognize student work in the capstone course. As we have suggested, oral presentations within the context of the course are an important opportunity to engage students, permit peer review, and enable instructor assessment. Presentations beyond the classroom can continue to contribute to students' verbal communication skills while offering students a different audience for their work. The elevation of presentations from within a class to an outside audience changes students' perception of the experience and can act as a strong incentive to present one's very best work.

Presentation at public forums can take many forms. Some departments require participation in a public presentation on campus. The University of Nevada, Reno, history department requires mandatory participation in a public research colloquium on campus for students who have written a senior thesis (Jones et al., 2012). At Manhattanville College, students in the dance and theater program must combine a traditional academic research paper in fall term with performance of an original creative piece in spring term (Posnick, 2014). It is perhaps more common for public presentation opportunities beyond the senior capstone course to be voluntary. Within history departments, Carleton College, Hope College, Northwestern University, and Virginia Tech reportedly follow some variation on this model by hosting a campus presentation (Jones et al., 2012). These can take the form of a department-sponsored seniors' presentation day or, as at Hope College, an invitation to the college-wide Celebration of Undergraduate Research (Jones et al., 2012).

Public presentation at local or national conferences is another option. The conference may be specifically intended for undergraduate research, or it may be a professional conference with undergraduate research panels or sessions. Off-campus presentations like these offer students an opportunity to step beyond their local comfort zone dominated by faculty, friends, and family and display their work on a wider stage. Presentation at forums like these are typically voluntary but permit the ongoing collaboration of students with faculty in the course of preparing student work for public exhibit to an increasingly sophisticated audience of peers and professionals. There is an assumption that only the very best student work will be put forward at conferences of this nature. Still, students whose work achieves the highest standards of academic excellence need motivation to sustain their own intellectual aspirations and local, regional, or national conferences can contribute significantly to that end.

Jones et al. (2012) do not discuss a final form of intellectual challenge and achievement after the capstone: revision and submission for publication of the student's major paper or senior thesis to a professional journal. There are understandable reasons for such an omission. First, very few undergraduate students can approach the quality of intellectual and scholarly work that publication in a peer-reviewed journal requires. Second, very few colleges or universities can support faculty efforts to work one-one-one with even the most promising undergraduates to achieve this goal. It is, however, worth commenting on because it provides the best students the opportunity to continue their work after completion of the capstone, and it offers faculty mentors a satisfying continuation of their work with serious young protégés. Moreover, with the right student and good professional guidance, professional publication can be achieved by undergraduates, as my own work with Courtney Choi (BA, 2011) attests (Hauhart & Choi, 2012).

As our discussion here suggests, there are innumerable ways for instructors to leverage opportunities beyond the capstone course to enhance that experience for the best students. It is even possible to scaffold a sequence of opportunities that integrates such experiences more intimately with the senior course. The course design for Saint Martin's University's Criminal Justice and Legal Studies capstone course is one example. Saint Martin's has for a number of years sponsored a campus-wide Scholar's Day each April. Participation is voluntary. Students submit a one-page application form and statement of their research or thesis work, and a committee of faculty chooses participants. One way to employ a scholar's day to the benefit of seniors working on their capstone project would be to simply encourage students to complete an application. This is not how I approach it, however.

While Saint Martin's Scholar's Day is voluntary, submission of an application to participate is required for completion of the course requirements for the senior seminar in criminal justice. This requirement is written into the course syllabus. Moreover, the syllabus states that participation in Scholar's Day is required if a class member is selected (although no one has ever been truly required to participate since virtually everyone ever selected has wanted to present their work). Finally, students know that the senior seminar advisor routinely works with seniors to prepare and present their work beyond graduation, including professional publication (Hauhart & Choi, 2012). Many seniors now look forward to this opportunity, a rare privilege.

This scaffolding technique permits the instructor to leverage outside opportunities to offer capstone students additional incentives at several levels of achievement. Making Scholar's Day applications mandatory has pleasantly surprised any number of average students when their senior work has been selected for presentation to a campuswide audience. Moreover, every senior in criminal justice or legal studies has been asked to raise the bar by making one more small effort (submitting the Scholar's Day application) to demonstrate competence. The consequence is a student culture that now routinely accepts the fact that capstone course work is not simply the final hurdle to graduation. Rather, it is an opportunity for any student to achieve a level of success he or she might not otherwise experience. More effort has been exerted, leading to better student outcomes and, occasionally, academic work of distinction.

Conclusion

Teaching the capstone course is different from teaching any other course. Its content is frequently amorphous, the intellectual demands rigorous and challenging, the time resources limited, and the outcome more dependent on student resources, limitations, and initiative than any other course. The effect, as Jones et al. (2012) commented, is that some students may experience the course as "more pain than pleasure" and the transformative experience sought may not materialize. This means that one feature of successfully teaching the senior capstone course is establishing a solid narrative of expectation from the first day of the term.

Durel (1993), among others, has observed that the senior capstone course is a rite of passage. From one perspective, it is a ritual celebration that announces a person's transition from one social status to another, as in a graduation ceremony or wedding. Another view emphasizes the subjection of a person to an ordeal, or initiation rite, that is a core cultural requirement for the status transition. In many cultures, ritual body scarification is used as an ordeal marking, quite literally, the passage from childhood to adulthood. Roberts and Pavlak (2002, p. 179) characterize the capstone rite of passage as an "experiential and symbolic test" that both affirms and challenges the learner. While one may resist the experience, one cannot truly make the transition from the status of child to the status of adult in any culture without undergoing the ordained cultural ordeal along with one's peers. Looked at in this manner, it is clear that a senior capstone course constitutes a rite of passage for American undergraduates. Teaching a successful capstone course requires conveying this narrative to students in a way that socializes them to the meaning of the experience.

Separation and Transition

An important feature of all rites of passage is separation from the current status (Durel, 1993). Seniors are at the culminating terminus of their undergraduate career. They must become ready to relinquish their undergraduate status and accept their status as graduates. To do so, however, seniors must be ready to give up the immature ways of many undergraduates. In the context of the capstone course, for example, students must accept responsibility for their senior project or major paper and carry out the ordeal without any guarantee of its ultimate success. They can, of course, find support for this transition in many quarters: from the instructor, university librarians, the campus writing center, and others. In the final analysis, however, they alone must expose themselves to the experience of completing the course requirements and shoulder the burden of presenting themselves as ready for initiation into the next status.

This is the narrative that the instructor needs to articulate to enable graduating seniors to understand that the course will be rigorous and demanding because it is a necessary experience that caps their under-graduate years. They must accept that it is an experience they must pass through to become full-fledged graduates. In order to achieve this new status, students should be told, and they must learn, that they need to relinquish evasion, avoidance, and procrastination behaviors and assume the active, engaged, responsible behaviors of a qualified university grad-uate. As in other cultures, the inevitable transition to adulthood cannot be avoided successfully. Seniors will demonstrate their capacity to make this transition by what they do and what they do not do. The instructor's responsibility is to communicate this to them.

Acceptance and Incorporation

The complementary behaviors that round out the senior capstone experi-ence rite of passage are acceptance and incorporation. Just as graduating seniors must forgo the luxury of acting like freshmen, they must acquire and demonstrate their mastery of behaviors that will mark them as ready to be college graduates. Thus, they must accept the fact that completion of the senior capstone course will require performing the necessary steps to complete the major project or paper core task by exhibiting their adop-tion of the research, writing, and style standards of the discipline they wish to enter. No longer can graduating students act as if it is someone else's responsibility to organize society for their benefit, prepare assignments to give them, stand patiently waiting to receive their papers, diligently review and correct those papers, and provide every other form of support they need. Rather, graduating students must accept that it has now become their responsibility to weave together in a meaningful synthesis their educational experience. Their actions must simply announce: *I've learned what you've taught me, and I am ready to carry the culture of the discipline forward.*

The capstone instructor can facilitate this acceptance by articulating the inevitable: there is only one way out of the senior capstone experience:

to run the gauntlet. Thus, students should be given as much information about what the capstone experience will be like as early in the term as possible. They should, for example, be told that it will be part of their job to integrate and exhibit what they have learned from their major; that they will be held to high academic standards and expectations; that the course is academically challenging; yet there are active and cooperative learning activities to assist them but they must avail themselves of these opportunities; that they are not alone in their quest, but that their peers and the instructor are there to assist them if they will take advantage of the assistance; that they will need to spend substantial time on their project; but once they have done so, they can expect prompt, professional feedback. Communicating these points in a persuasive manner will encourage students to take up a commitment to the senior capstone experience. This attitude alone will make every phase of the capstone course more enjoyable, more productive, and more effective. The activities that constitute their senior experience will then work their magic, for as Padgett and Kilgo (2012) found, these are the high-impact practices that will produce a successful outcome.

CHAPTER EIGHT

USING THE CAPSTONE COURSE FOR ASSESSMENT

A significant portion of departmental assessment often is conducted based on the capstone course. This raises a number of important questions regarding the use of the senior course for course and program evaluation that faculty and administrators will need to address. What is the nature of the assessment required, and what are the methods used to make judgments about courses and programs? How much of a department's assessment protocol is regularly attributed to the capstone course across the disciplines? How meaningful and effective is assessment that derives from examining the senior capstone course? What approaches are commonly used for assessing the capstone course, and which are most valid? These and other important questions regarding use of the senior experience for programmatic evaluation should be carefully considered before adopting the capstone course as the principal arena for assessment.

Assessment in higher education serves multiple purposes. Among them, one can list providing data about student learning, evaluating student progress through a major program, evaluating the quality of instruction, providing a review directed at appraising program and institutional effectiveness, and establishing accountability to external constituencies. There are, however, varying attitudes toward course and program assessment, and these differing perspectives can have a significant impact on the manner in which assessment evaluations are gathered and used. The inherent difficulties produced by different perspectives are often compounded by a lack of clarity regarding the meaning of assessment and its value to students, faculty, and administrators. Initially assessment should be distinguished from student evaluation or, as we more commonly say, grading. Assessment, whether of student learning or program effectiveness, has a relationship to, but is not merely the same as, issuing grades to students that reflect in some gross manner the symbolic quality of their work in a course. Grading is not assessment. We discussed grading student performance in the capstone course briefly in previous chapters. Here, we are interested in evaluating the capstone course, not the student. There are a number of ways in which to evaluate a course, including the capstone course.

The Assessment Movement in Higher Education

The contemporary focus on assessment arose from reports that high-lighted variation in the quality of academic preparation among college graduates in the 1980s (Wang & Hurley, 2012). Over time, many state and regional accrediting associations have required colleges and universities to implement assessment protocols, whether for general education curricula, major academic programs, or institution-wide. Although it is widely acknowledged that assessment serves many useful purposes, the notion that externally imposed assessment is a wholly salutary and beneficent initiative has not been universally embraced. Because this is a book about capstones, we do not trace the full development of the assessment movement or provide a thorough discussion of assessment protocols and measures.[1]

Assessment is a topic that seldom initially inspires enthusiasm among rank-and-file faculty. The literature is rife with such expressions. Berheide (2007, p. 27) notes, "I have never met a faculty member who was excited about doing assessment." She goes on to divide faculty attitudinally regarding assessment between those who are "resistant" and those who are "downright hostile." Catchings (2004, p. 6), part of this latter group at one time, calls *assessment* the "A" word, presumably equating it with the "F" word, thereby addressing it as a profanity. Many similar published refrains from faculty besieged by demands to "assess their courses" can be found (Chin, Senter, & Spalter-Roth, 2011). Even those who are supportive of assessment recognize the substantial faculty resistance that can arise in response to demands for assessment (Weiss, Crosbey, Habel, Hanson, & Larsen, 2002).

This history of resistance to assessment on the part of many faculty members is understandable, if not explained well in many instances. The basis for the resistance appears to be twofold. On the one hand, faculty members are understandably leery of any initiative that has the potential for limiting freedom of academic expression, inquiry, and scholarship. Historically it is worth pointing out that many attempts have been made by both internal and external constituencies to control academics and limit their freedom of thought and speech (Schrecker, 2009, 2012). Even many well-meaning defenders of academic freedom often suggest, however implicitly, that there should be limits to academic freedom of speech and thought (Bromwich, 2012). This gives many faculty members pause and concern when contemplating the imposition of requirements and standards by anyone other than themselves. For example, Metz (2010) has considered the seemingly quite reasonable expectation that universities, especially publicly funded ones, should be responsive to calls from the society that supports them to be accountable, including preparing graduates to assume occupational positions within society or embrace the society's central values. Metz points out that any obligation along these lines potentially runs afoul of and even contrary to a scholar's obligation to follow wherever the search for truth leads. This might include, for example, criticizing the idea that a college or university should have any accountability for training students to fit into an unjust society or measuring the effectiveness of an education by standards others have developed. The fear is that assessment is simply a way for administrators and external entities like legislators to control what goes on in the academy.

A second concern of faculty, although one not always effectively articulated, is that already overburdened faculty members are being asked to do yet more without any reasonable adjustment in their salary or benefits. These are, at many colleges and universities, proportionally more meager than twenty or forty years ago. According to national survey data, faculty members work on average more hours per week than most other occupations, and that figure grew during the 1990s (Jacobs, 2004). Consider in this context the nontenured faculty member who must teach a 4/4 sequence of classes, often with high enrollments, participate on university committees, and conduct research and publish. Unless the faculty member has an interest in publishing on assessment itself, the requirement to do more assessment is an uninviting one since it can reduce time for other scholarly activities and reduce professional autonomy (Cummings, Maddux, & Richmond, 2008), More to the point, consider the vastly underpaid adjunct instructor who shuttles among three institutions to cobble together a living, without benefits, and then is asked to contribute to a department's assessment. It is not difficult to grasp the nature and source of faculty reluctance to fully embrace assessment under these scenarios.

Using the Senior Capstone Course for Program Assessment

While these concerns are real and cannot simply be wished away by those committed to the value of assessment, it is undeniable that the assessment movement continues to grow (Wang & Hurley, 2012). Assessment today, like senior capstone courses, is nearly omnipresent. Virtually every review of contemporary higher educational practice one reads confirms capstones have grown in scope and importance (Rowles, Koch, Hundley, & Hamilton, 2004) or that assessment is a vital part of the contemporary academic learning environment (Cortes, 2012) or both (Christ & Moore, 1994). Given the tension between legitimate faculty interests and the continuing calls for assessment, the question of the role for assessment regarding the capstone course is an important one. Berheide (2007) argues that the senior capstone course is an excellent vehicle for assessment purposes because assessment there is "easier" than in other options that exist. Moreover, Berheide (2007) suggests that the capstone course provides a better setting for evaluating student learning than other courses within an academic program. Catchings (2004), after his own institution conducted a self-study and his department of communications adopted a new capstone course as the basis for its own assessment, overcame his antipathy to the process. Ultimately he agrees with Berheide (2007) that the senior capstone is suitable, and perhaps optimal, for program assessment.

Berheide's twin rationales of suitability and efficacy for using the senior experience as a basis for assessment possess some force. Many authors report that assessment has been an integral component of the capstone courses at their institution for many years (Kerrigan & Jhaj, 2007; Rhodes & Agre-Kippenhan, 2004). Indeed, a theme within both the capstone literature and the assessment literature is their mutual suitability for each other. If, then, an assessment must be performed, is there a reason that it should not be conducted in the most academically efficient and productive manner possible? And if we are going to conduct a program assessment, wouldn't we wish to do so within a context where student learning may be most effectively evaluated? Finally, if the capstone course is held forth as the crowning achievement of the undergraduate experience, shouldn't that experience rightfully be evaluated for the benefit it provides graduating seniors? The rather obvious answer to each of these questions should suggest that the capstone course is highly suitable for use for assessment purposes.

Assessment over the years has become a topic bedeviled by technical requirements and academic jargon, but in essence, the term denotes the rather mundane task of evaluation of the value of a program or course, or indeed the university itself. Alfred North Whitehead observed that assessment at the most basic level tried to discover whether an entity served the function it was intended to serve—whether, in the case of the university, it united students and faculty in "imaginative learning" (Brooks, Benton-Kupper, & Slayton, 2004, p. 275). The same can be said of program assessment or course assessment. Each tries to determine whether evidence supports their respective reasons for existence and whether the current iteration suggests the important objectives sought are actually being achieved (Brooks et al., 2004). Since learning is the ostensible objective of every course, a simple way to think about assessment for the capstone course is whether students learn more than they knew previously about a particular subject, process, or realm of knowledge and to analyze to what extent they gained breadth and depth in their understanding after the capstone experience (Gruenther, Bailey, Wilson, Plucker, & Hashmi, 2009). Capstone courses are often employed as proxies for the entire program they represent on the ground that the learning goals embodied in the capstone experience are effectively the program goals imported into the culminating course. Thus, the argument goes, an evaluation of the success of the senior capstone course will offer a fair measure of whether the entire program is achieving the goals it has set for itself.

While rationales for assessment apply equally to most disciplines in the arts and sciences, published discussions of assessment practices are almost nonexistent in some fields. Our approach to this book has been determined in part by the relative paucity of published materials regarding capstones in music, art, theater, drama, and performance courses. Published discussions of assessment protocols within these disciplines are equally rare, although occasional articles addressing program evaluation in these fields have appeared (Johnson, McGuinness, McCorkendale, & Laney, 2007). We also approach the topic in the same manner we have followed throughout the book generally: since the typical capstone course is a semester-long seminar directed at producing a major project or major paper, we focus most of our discussion on this format. Many of our observations, however, are equally applicable to other capstone formats, including internship or practicum-based capstone courses and senior capstones that rely on production of a portfolio. Given the limitations inherent in writing and publishing a book, we believe this is the most productive and beneficial way to proceed for most readers.

Capstone Assessment: Externally Driven, Internally Desired, or Both?

The source of the impetus for conducting assessment is one distinguishing feature that has a bearing on what type of assessment one elects to conduct. Historically, assessment arose as a response to concerns that educational institutions were not ensuring that their programs prepared students satisfactorily to assume their roles as productive citizens in a free, democratic society. There was a demand for accountability that is still a significant force behind the assessment movement. Increasingly, this concern has taken the form that college graduates are not prepared to enter the contemporary workforce, as many studies have suggested (Gardner & Perry, 2012). In the wake of these concerns, disciplines with professional associations often developed standards for certification, or accreditation, intended to ensure that graduates of programs within the discipline meet some minimum levels of competency prior to graduation. Durant's (2002) description of the accreditation-driven assessment process at the University of Baltimore's graduate program in public administration is representative.

The National Association of Schools of Public Affairs and Administration (NASPAA) is a membership-supported organization whose goal is to ensure excellence in graduate education for public service professions. It arose from a predecessor organization that was formed in the early 1950s. As Durant (2002) recounts, the NASPAA began requiring graduate programs in public administration to perform "mission-driven and outcomes-oriented assessments" in the early 1990s. Durant's account of assessment at the University of Baltimore's School of Public Affairs MPA program during the 1993–1994 and 1994–1995 academic years makes clear that it was the demand for accountability from the outside—from NASPAA—that solely inspired the program's evaluation effort. Indeed, Durant states the program developed its capstone course as a mission-driven and outcomes-oriented addition to the curriculum directly "in response to NASPAA's guidelines" (p. 194). This has been a common theme in capstone course development as Rowles et al. (2004, p. 14) discuss in their division of capstones into three styles:

"mountaintops, magnets, and mandates." Many professional associations, such as the Accreditation Board for Engineering and Technology (ABET) and the Association to Advance Collegiate Schools of Business, as well as the six regional higher education accrediting organizations, require that program assessments meet certain standards. Durant argues, as many others have, that assessment has benefits beyond pleasing accreditors, yet it is instructive to note how the goals of accreditors often take precedence over other goals favored by faculty, students, and even administrators.

The alternative to capstones created to satisfy an external constituency or mandate are capstones developed to integrate learning across a program or permit students to engage in a culminating experience that has the potential to imbue students with attitudes and skills needed for transition beyond the academic setting. While it is unfair to characterize externally inspired capstones as driven purely by adherence to the itemized requirements of a professional association or state licensing exam protocol, it is sometimes difficult to flexibly integrate externally imposed standards with other goals. Within those capstone courses primarily designed to meet institutional or departmental goals, Rowles et al. (2004) identify two obvious forms: interdisciplinary or multidisciplinary versus discipline-specific capstones. They refer to these as mountaintops and magnets, respectively.[2]

While one can argue that assessment should be a process that is relatively similar regardless of the impetus for its pursuit, such a view would ignore the critical difference between externally imposed and internally chosen inspirations for course and program evaluation. Clearly, where there exists an external agency with enforcement authority over a given realm of professional knowledge and a corresponding certification and accreditation regime it has developed, this is a quite different situation from one in which educators, relying on their best professional judgment, develop some standards they wish to apply to judge their effectiveness. For that reason, we address the assessment process for each style of capstone separately.

Using the Capstone Course to Meet External Certification Requirements

Engineering is one of several academic fields in which an outside accrediting agency has established a professional certification regime whose mandates strongly influence both the reliance on capstone courses and their use in assessment. The Accreditation Board for Engineering and Technology

2000 requires that students engage in a major design experience prior to graduation. A common response to this certification requirement is to develop a senior design capstone course, and many can now be found discussed in the literature (Thambyah, 2011; Tickles, Yadong, & Walters, 2013; Todd & Magleby, 2005). A series of survey studies of engineering programs in American universities beginning in the late 1990s confirmed the popularity of senior design capstone courses and attributed their increased use directly to criterion 4 of the ABET 2000 requirement (Gnanapragasam, 2008). Indeed, an increase in the use of teamwork projects in these senior design capstone courses between 1995 and 2005 has been attributed to criterion 3 of the ABET 2000 mandates (Gnanapragasam, 2008). In short, engineering is one of several disciplines where the nature of the capstone course may be located in the planners' objective to satisfy the external demands of accreditors. As such, engineering may be used to illustrate the reciprocal, even circular, nature of capstone course configuration and course and program assessment within this mandate style.

Briefly, one can summarize the relationship as one in which faculty analyze the external agency's requirements, embed those requirements in its program, and, most particularly in the capstone course, rely on assessment of the capstone course to assess the program; and then report back to the external agency that the program did or did not fulfill its mandate. A loop can be used to symbolically represent this interrelationship (figure 8.1).

FIGURE 8.1. The Flow of Influence in External Driven Assessment

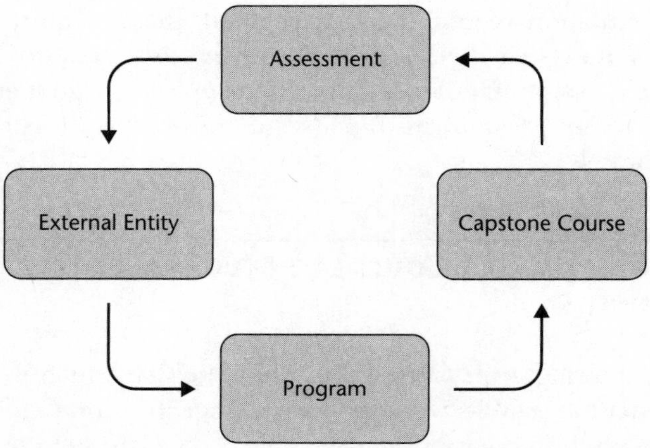

Note the causal direction in figure 8.1. Assessment in a capstone course of this type addresses directly the external entity's specific mandates, which typically are reflected quite closely in desired program outcomes. For example, Gnanapragasam (2008) describes the various assessment tools used for the Seattle University civil engineering capstone as specifically chosen to evaluate the criteria 3 a-k ABET 2000 outcomes. A table that Gnanapragasm (2008, p. 260) presents shows that "all program outcomes, except *b* and *j* are assessed through the capstone course." In short, ABET's criteria are embedded in the capstone course, and the capstone course goals are nearly synonymous with the program goals, which are nearly synonymous with ABET requirements. This is the common loop configuration of externally mandated assessment requirements that are relied on to design a program's capstone course and then provide feedback in the form of assessment.

Objectives for General Education Capstone Assessment

The nature of assessment for interdisciplinary or multidisciplinary capstone courses is considerably different from the model described for assessment driven by external agency mandates. Although there are likely to be some minor differences among the interdisciplinary or multidisciplinary programs offered, the differences that exist do not seem to us dissimilarities that warrant a notably distinct or special treatment. As a consequence, we will focus our discussion on what appears to be the most common type of interdisciplinary or multidisciplinary capstone course in the curriculum: the general education–based senior capstone experience.

Several initial considerations establish the point of departure for assessing the capstone course that is tied to a general education or university-wide program. First and foremost, a valid capstone course assessment must include a review of the capstone's learning goals and determine to what extent those goals align with the general program goals sought (Catchings, 2004). To the extent there is substantial alignment between the senior capstone experience goals and the wider program goals, an assessment of the course may reasonably stand in as a proxy for an assessment for the program. Rhodes and Agre-Kippenhan (2004) address the importance of this point with respect to Portland State University's interdisciplinary general education capstone experience, a required component of every graduating senior's academic program.

Portland State University (PSU) is a large public institution (it had more than twenty-three thousand students in 2001–2002 and nearly thirty thousand students today) with 120 degree programs (undergraduate and graduate combined). In fall 1994 the faculty revised its undergraduate general education program to, among other things, include a six-credit interdisciplinary capstone course as the culminating experience (Rhodes & Agre-Kippenhan, 2004). The capstone courses at PSU are intended to accentuate community-based learning that arguably allow students to gain academic and professional skills while establishing connections with the wider Portland, Oregon, community. In 2002–2003 the university reported more than 150 capstone courses in its undergraduate curriculum.

As Rhodes and Kippenhan (2004) note, capstone course assessment at Portland State presents a significant challenge due to the number and variety of complex multidimensional projects that constitute capstone courses there. This makes the task of just determining whether the overall general education program goals and individual course objectives align an essential but difficult one. The result has been a multipronged assessment effort intended to approach the task from a range of perspectives; ultimately, the process inspired the adoption of a common assignment for the university capstone courses. The primary purpose of the common assignment is the need to impose a certain level of consistency and uniformity on the capstone experience, which can then be used as a standard for evaluation across the program (Rhodes & Kippenhan, 2004).

For the common assignment, each student writes a three- to five-page analysis of his or her senior experience with a specific focus on one of the four university studies (i.e., general education) goals: communication, critical thinking, variety of human experience, or social/ethical responsibility. After an initial pilot year and external review, general agreement emerged that the common student assignment was a valid way to assess student learning outcomes for a diverse program of the type conducted at Portland State, although a number of revised approaches to the assessment process were proposed and adopted. In essence, the faculty at Portland State found that the nature of assessment had to be adjusted to fit the nature of the beast: while there was a sensitivity to the needs of individual instructors and individual courses, a consistency of language across the university about the goals for student learning and the goals sought as course objectives was needed if there was going to be any meaningful review across the entire curriculum. This meant that the assessment tools, such as rubrics, had to incorporate standards applicable to the diversity of course approaches while imposing some consistent standards for comparison (Rhodes & Kippenhan, 2004). In short, there needed to be a dynamic interrelationship between the nature of the program, the nature of the capstone course, and the nature of the assessment methods designed to offer a credible evaluation of either or both.

The PSU interdisciplinary general education capstone program has incorporated one other feature of assessment that deserves note: continual review, evaluation, and revision. In a recent publicly reported configuration, for example, assessment at PSU now uses three data-gathering strategies: (1) midterm qualitative assessments through peer observation for 20 percent of the capstones offered; (2) an end-of-term quantitative course evaluation survey for students that addresses how well the course engaged the four curriculum goals of the university studies program; and (3) a qualitative section of the end-of-term evaluation instrument that asks for student feedback regarding how the course facilitated learning and community engagement, what could be changed about the course, and how those proposed changes might be developed and incorporated (Kerrigan & Jhaj, 2007).

The amount of data gathered from these reviews annually is truly staggering given that three thousand seniors were graduating each year when Kerrigan and Jhaj wrote in 2007. The mechanisms set up for annual review were extensive and elaborate, and thus not without opposition and controversy. Still, as they conclude their discussion, Kerrigan and Jhaj (2007) note that the university's future assessment plan includes an initiative to assess students' final work products from their capstone experiences and their written reflections on that experience. A faculty group has been assembled for these purposes, and Kerrigan and Jhaj (2007) report that an initial qualitative study of the students' reflections on their capstone experience has already contributed to a deeper understanding of how students interpret their final-year culminating experience at Portland State. In short, the university conceived of assessment as an ongoing program of review that is itself subject to review, reconfiguration, and renewal.

General education assessment protocols at other universities share many similar qualities to those developed at PSU (Blattner & Frazier, 2004). At Southeast Missouri State University (SMSU), a midsized public institution, an interdisciplinary faculty group like the group at PSU initially met to discuss evaluating the general education program on three criteria: the ability to locate and gather information; the ability to think, reason, and analyze critically; and the ability to communicate effectively. The committee then developed guidelines to measure the prevalence and effectiveness in achieving these objectives in student work.

The following year, sixteen faculty members reviewed three hundred pieces of student work from capstone courses for evidence addressing the three criteria. As at PSU, SMSU continued to expand its general education assessment process. Ultimately representative samples from all freshman seminars and student work from all students in the senior seminars (capstones) were collected and evaluated at the end of each semester. Results from these assessments were communicated more broadly in faculty workshops and also fed back into teaching since many faculty began to use the measurement rubrics as guides to their own statement of learning objectives. As at PSU, SMSU reports a process of anticipated continual revision in the life of its general education assessment protocol.

A number of other extended descriptions of general education assessment practices that rely on capstone courses as a significant feature of the evaluation protocol may be found in the literature: University of Louisiana at Monroe, Oxford College of Emory University, and Southern Polytechnic State University (Galle & Galle, 2011); California State Polytechnic University at Pomona (Fernandez, 2006); Millikin University (Brooks, Benton-Kupper, & Slayton, 2004); Indiana University–Purdue University Indianapolis (Rowles et al., 2004); DePaul University (Carlson, 2001); and Southwest Missouri State University (Matthews & Cattau, 2001).

Capstone Course Assessment within an Academic Discipline

While a number of institutions offering university-wide capstone programs in addition to PSU have developed complex plans for assessing those courses across the breadth of the curriculum, it is important to recall that only 10 to 20 percent of capstone courses are interdisciplinary in nature or embedded in a general education program: 12.9 percent interdisciplinary (Padgett & Kilgo, 2012), 21 percent integration of material between a discipline and general education (Hauhart & Grahe, 2010), and 16.3 percent of respondents who identified capstone courses as interdisciplinary (Henscheid et al., 2001). This is another way of reminding ourselves that the vast majority of capstone courses are discipline specific in nature. In Henscheid et al. (2001), 70.3 percent of all respondents reported having a discipline- or department-based course. Consequently, we turn our attention now to assessments related to those courses.

Eder (2004), in his perceptive paper on conducting general education assessment, argues that universities have made more progress in constructing direct assessments of student learning within the disciplines than they have in doing the same for general education programs. By "direct assessment," Eder means using evidence- or outcome-based measures of student learning (i.e., exams, projects, logs, portfolios, direct observations, senior theses, or major papers) as compared to methods that focus on ascertaining student perceptions of their learning through surveys, questionnaires, interviews, focus groups, or reflective essays. It is difficult to know what Eder bases his judgment on with respect to the frequency and effectiveness of the use of direct methods between general education or interdisciplinary assessment and discipline-specific assessment, but his discussion does focus on the difference between the two primary modes of assessment activities: direct and indirect. The fact is that both modes are used throughout the assessment movement and nowhere more or less than in assessing capstone courses, whether for their own effectiveness or as proxies for an entire program. Hence, one way of discussing assessment in capstone courses is to examine some of the more common specific forms of direct and indirect assessment that have been devised.

There is, however, one intervening condition that merits discussion first. While the division between interdisciplinary/general education and discipline-specific capstones is an important one, it is equally important to consider that there are multiple formats for senior capstone courses that can be characterized as discipline specific. Among the most common are internship or practicum-based capstone courses; traditional classroom-based courses that do not involve a major paper, thesis, or project; courses designed as transitional preparations for entry into a profession or career; and senior capstone courses that involve disciplinary research leading to completion of a major paper, major project, or senior thesis. While these different iterations of the discipline-specific capstone course share the core curriculum they arise from, each also presents a quite different environment and set of learning objectives. It will therefore be beneficial to make an initial examination of the peculiarities of these formats before reviewing the assessment methods that may be employed.

Assessing the Internship or Practicum-Based Capstone Course

One form of discipline-specific capstone course common to some areas of study is the senior experience tied to an internship or field practicum. These capstone courses commonly include a project orientation, sometimes referred to as problem-based learning, or characterize their educational focus as community-based learning. Regardless of the terminology employed, these are senior courses that entail some form of engagement with an entity outside the university structure, whether business, professional, social, or community related. They typically ask students to address some real-world issue endemic to the field site and offer quite a different senior experience from other discipline-specific models. Arguably, capstone courses of this type may benefit from methods of assessment that take into account the peculiarities of both the field-based, real-world nature of these courses and the particular nature of the outside entity acting as a partner in the senior experience with the student and the academic department.

While there are many qualities and elements of the internship-based senior capstone that warrant consideration with respect to assessment, one of the more obvious that must be addressed is the addition of a new stakeholder in the process: the outside partner. A review of several capstones of this type demonstrates the centrality of the outside partner in creating and sustaining a successful field-based experience. Campbell and Lambright (2011) note the importance of the outside stakeholder in their graduate MPA capstone program at Binghamton University. Although a graduate rather than undergraduate capstone, Campbell and Lambright's description of the course illustrates the commonalities between community-based capstone courses regardless of the academic level. They observe that the views of supervisors and other representatives of cooperating community organizations are important to MPA programs for two reasons. First, since training for public service is the goal of MPA programs, the degree to which representatives of groups acting on behalf of the public are satisfied with the work of graduating seniors will tell their academic programs whether their curriculum has been effective in training students. Second, MPA programs wish to develop close ties with community organizations for many reasons. Consequently, it is important for these organizations to be pleased with their academic program partners (Campbell & Lambright, 2011). The same can easily be said for undergraduate field placement capstone experiences.

To determine whether the Binghamton University MPA capstone program has been successful, the authors surveyed representatives of fifty-six community organizations cooperating with the capstone course experience over a four-year period. The final-year capstone MPA course at Binghamton is a one-semester course required of all graduating MPA candidates. The authors note that these capstone projects may generally be characterized as service-learning projects. Generally students must identify a social or public policy issue that confronts a community organization, research that issue, and complete a substantial, professional-quality paper in the form of a report that assists the organization in addressing that issue in its work (Campbell & Lambright 2011). The authors comment that while service-learning projects can provide nonpaid labor to pursue projects, the student interns can also be a drain on organizational resources since they are often unfamiliar with the organization (as are their academic advisors) and require start-up time to acquire basic information. Naturally, some students are higher achieving, possess better entering skill sets, and are more highly motivated than others. The question becomes whether the benefits students deliver outweigh the resource costs involved in hosting them.

The researchers determined that sixty-four individual community organization representatives acted as field capstone supervisors for sixty-nine students from 2005 to 2009. Survey questions were primarily closed-ended and relied on a five-point Likert-style scale. Multiple regression analysis was used to differentiate the impact of various factors. From among the survey population the researchers conducted interviews with ten randomly selected respondents. Generally the authors found that close working relationships between the organization supervisor and the student resulted in successful capstone experiences, while capstones characterized by a lack of connection or insufficient connection between the community organization supervisor and the student produced less successful outcomes. The quantitative analysis showed that three factors were related to successful capstone outcomes: faculty contact, supervisor engagement, and Binghamton location in relation to the university. However, the interviews suggested that factors related to supervisor engagement and the degree to which the community organization prioritized the capstone project were most determinative of success or lack of success (Campbell & Lambright, 2011). In sum, the research showed that for an internship or practicum-based capstone experience to be successful, there must be an engaged, positive connection between the student and the organization supervisor. Other studies reach the same conclusion (Dougherty & Parfitt, 2013).

Assessment of a Discipline-Specific, Integrating Capstone Course

Some departments choose to rely on an integrative culminating course for their discipline-specific senior experience. Psychology departments often use a history of psychology course (often identified as a "history and systems" course) as an integrative capstone course (Milar, 1987). As of 1997, for example, Perlman and McCann (1999a) reported that based on their survey of American university psychology departments, more than half of all departments, regardless of size or terminal degree awarded, offered a history and systems course. In another published article, Perlman and McCann (1999b) reported that with respect to capstone courses, 23 percent of psychology departments required a history and systems classroom-based capstone, while another 16 percent required an integrative history and systems course of majors but one not necessarily limited to seniors or identified as a senior capstone. Courses of this nature are more closely akin to other core courses within a major curriculum than any of the other forms of discipline-specific capstones. Thus, these courses are classroom based, but unlike the more common major paper or major project capstone course, they include more traditional classroom activities such as lectures. They also typically include more and varied graded assignments than a single-major, semester-long paper or project. The upshot for assessment purposes is that capstones like these are assessed in much the same way as other courses within the curriculum. This means that many indirect methods, such as end-of-term student evaluations, are often used. Those direct methods tied to grading of student assignments or tests are also frequently adopted as forms of assessment. External forms of assessment that are labor intensive, such as student interviews, are seldom used for capstone courses of this type. Some external indirect forms of assessment that are labor conserving such as focus groups are occasionally incorporated (Morgan & Johnson, 1997). Here, the range of routine means of assessment predominates, with few unique demands for innovation since the capstone course mirrors the format of many standard courses. Since the primary justification for courses of this type is often the integrative, synthesizing objective of uniting the disparate coursework that forms the core curriculum, direct tests of knowledge mastery (i.e., testing and grading) are likely sufficient when supported by at least one measure of student perception.

Assessment of a Discipline-Specific Thesis or Research-Based Capstone Course

As our own research and the research of many others suggests, the discipline-specific thesis or research-based capstone course is the most common format. This is the capstone form that faculty are most commonly called on to assess (Hauhart & Grahe, 2012). There are innumerable individual modes of assessment that have been developed (Ishiyama & Breuning, 2008), but this recognition is not a very helpful starting point for determining which may constitute the best practice. Initially one can distinguish between evaluations of student learning based on activities that faculty already engage in within the classroom setting and strategies over and above in class assessment. The in-class methods include analysis of grades, review of completed course work assignments for indications of student learning, reviews of course syllabi, or reliance on standard end-of-term student course evaluations. These traditional means of classroom-based materials review are sometimes referred to as forms of internal assessment (Ishiyama & Breuning, 2008). Methods that are over and above these, and thus external to traditional classroom methods, include comprehensive examinations, exit interviews, pre- and posttests, portfolio analyses, evaluation of the senior thesis or research paper, or surveys of graduating seniors (Ishiyama & Breuning, 2008). This latter group generally requires additional faculty effort beyond what teaching a course involves.

Generally there is an inverse correlation between the quality of measurement provided by an assessment method and its expediency: the best methods for assessing learning usually take longer (more faculty time is expended) and, hence, cost more (Ishiyama & Breuning, 2008). This last observation has inspired many faculty members to look for assessment methods that limit their time investment while maximizing the quality of review. This is one factor that has drawn faculty across the disciplines to select the senior capstone course and its primary outcome, the major paper or major project, as a suitable subject for assessment. The senior experience arguably best represents the goals and outcomes sought by a department and does so conveniently within a single course offering. As we observed at the start of this chapter, Berheide (2007) persuasively argues that this combination of qualities makes the capstone course a natural object for selection as a proxy for program review.

Generally discipline-specific capstone courses have become popular for program assessment (Berheide, 2007; Catchings, 2004). National surveys reveal that a number of disciplines, sociology (Spalter-Roth & Erskine, 2003) and political science (Kelly & Klunk, 2003) among them, rely on senior capstone courses as the most common site for program assessment. This may be true in part because a key question within assessment circles is how to best evaluate complex skills, such as advanced writing, research, and information literacy capabilities or the acquisition of nebulous qualities like values and dispositions (Wright, 2005). The typical capstone course may offer the best environment for assessment of these more complex forms of learning. Ishiyama and Breuning's (2008) examination of the assessment plans at fifty political science departments illustrates this point well: each of the seven most frequently mentioned learning outcomes is typical of the senior capstone course: knowledge of theories, knowledge of political institutions and processes, knowledge of subfields, critical thinking, methods and research skills, writing skills, and speaking skills.

The identification of the senior capstone course as suitable for assessment does not resolve the question of the most practicable means for assessment or identify the methods that will best reveal the breadth and depth of learning in its various dimensions. There are those formative assessment methods that can be used in any classroom setting and embrace important learning principles by emphasizing active student involvement, continuous feedback between teacher and student, and opportunities for teacher-student interaction (Angelo & Cross, 1993; Eisenbach, Golich, & Curry, 1998). There are also summative assessment formats that rely primarily on end-of-term evaluations of learning processes and product outcomes. Among the more popular are graduating senior student surveys, comprehensive exams, evaluation of the senior capstone course or senior thesis, a portfolio review, and capstone course and senior exit interviews (Ishiyama & Breuning, 2008). Many rubrics available can include evaluation criteria keyed to the specific learning objectives identified for a capstone course. These rubrics can be used to inform both grading and course or program assessment.

Although there is not a single study or set of national surveys that definitively confirms that reliance on evaluating the major paper or capstone project is the most common manner in which discipline-specific capstone courses are assessed, the cumulative circumstantial evidence suggests that this is likely the case. Berheide (2007), for example, begins with the premise that the senior capstone course is suitable for assessing just how well the major has achieved its educational goals. She then discusses some of the many departments that have used capstone products to assess their overall programs. (By "capstone product," Berheide means the major paper, a poster, an oral presentation before a faculty committee or at a campuswide conference, or the report on a major capstone project.) Moreover, she discusses evaluation of the capstone end product as though this was the only viable approach to assessing a senior capstone course. Berheide's assumption in this regard does not quite seem to be borne out as a practical matter by other commentators, although evaluating capstone products is an important means of direct assessment.

In our regional survey of sociology and psychology departments, we asked our sample population whether "student progress in the capstone course or senior thesis [was used] as a form of assessment" (Hauhart &

Grahe, 2010, p. 11). Sixty-one percent of those who responded answered that they used the capstone course for assessment; another 10 percent responded that they planned to do so. In response to an open-ended follow-up question regarding how the capstone course or senior thesis was used for assessment purposes, many respondents stated that the major paper (or a sample of capstone papers) was evaluated according to learning outcomes, either separately or as part of an overall student portfolio (Hauhart & Grahe, 2010). Respondents also reported they used student evaluations of their capstone courses (86 percent) as an assessment method.

The primary advantage in using the major paper or major project as a means of assessment is that it constitutes the most direct method of analyzing what the capstone course contributes to learning outcomes related to research, writing, and presenting. A second advantage is that as a "product" (rather than a perception) it displays, in easily recognizable fashion, the extent to which more amorphous goals, such as acculturation in professional norms and attitudes, have been incorporated directly into a novice piece of professional work. The direct nature of both of these approaches arguably makes capstone course product assessment superior to other means, such as student evaluation surveys at the end of the semester. At Augustana College, students completing Senior Inquiry appear at the campuswide Celebration of Learning each spring and present their work as oral presentations or posters. The presentations are used to assess the student and the course. All faculty members attend and grade the presentations using a common rubric. Those evaluations are also used to review the senior experience and make changes regarding how it is taught (Schermer & Gray, 2010).

The capstone major paper is also an excellent source for assessing intangible learning such as critical thinking. Hummer (1997) describes a method developed at the University of Detroit-Mercy for operationalizing the concept so that critical thinking can be more reliably and consistently judged. The process requires faculty members to familiarize themselves with the language of critical thinking found in the literature (interpret, criticize, discriminate, summarize, justify, and so forth); define critical thinking as it relates to a specific discipline; denote the skills required for the display of critical thinking; and make a list of the major paper content areas and specify linkages to critical thinking that can, and should, be found there. This chart can then be used to assess the major paper for instances of critical thinking, much like a more comprehensive rubric can be used to evaluate a paper across many value dimensions. The careful delineation of what constitutes critical thinking is perhaps the core requirement for successfully using this approach. Other higher-order cognitive skills can also be addressed in the same manner by operationalizing the key elements of the skill, placing those in a meaningful context, and developing a rubric to measure the skill in the capstone paper.

Using Rubrics to Evaluate the Major Paper or Senior Thesis

The example above raises once more the general topic of adopting comprehensive rubrics to assess capstone courses. A rubric is simply a standard of performance summarized in a format that permits easy comparison to the paper, project, or presentation that is subject to review. While rubrics may be developed to evaluate capstone courses built around an internship experience or submission of a portfolio of work, we will limit our discussion here to the more typical capstone course that requires a major project or paper. The use of rubrics for evaluating papers has become increasingly common as a means of ensuring academic accountability. This procedure has been extended to the senior capstone course by a number of institutions. The College of Wooster's capstone course, called the Senior Independent Study, is evaluated by a rubric. Creating the rubric was one of the first steps taken by faculty charged with implementing the course (Schermer & Gray, 2012) as adoption of a rubric may be more complex than it sounds. While it is possible to rely to a degree on rubrics developed by other disciplines and institutions, a rubric does need to reflect the goals that an instructor or department seeks, or discordant measures will be introduced into the assessment process. The following factors should be taken into account in the process of developing a suitable rubric for use in a capstone course.

A meaningful distinction arises between capstone courses that require only a major paper that constitutes a simple review of the literature as compared to those that require investigation of a hypothesis through the collection, by one method or another, of original empirical data. Correspondingly, the qualities of mind and skill sought to be measured by a rubric should be quite distinguishable for each approach. It would be entirely unsuitable to use a rubric that sought to measure theoretical innovation, for example, for a simple literature review where no theoretical innovation will occur. This means that the choice of a rubric must be carefully matched to the actual projects that students will be asked to complete. This presents a problem for instructors whose senior experience embraces a wider range of projects since the rubric will need to have the flexibility to evaluate projects that vary across several dimensions.

Peat (2006) discusses the development of a rubric that would be suitable for use where a paper in the form of a literature review is the core task. She created the rubric for a research methods class for public affairs majors, most of whom were concentrating their studies in criminal justice. The literature review constituted the primary assignment within the class, similar to a capstone course requiring only a literature review of secondary materials. As Peat observes, the nature of the project dictates that assessment should focus solely on content, organization and structure, appearance, and correctness. In other words, since the project in Peat's course is not expected to produce theoretical innovation, sophisticated data manipulation, critical thinking, or a host of other more complex cognitive tasks, the rubric should reflect only the objectives that are anticipated outcomes and not pretend to measure qualities of mind or skills that the project is not intended to elicit.

Peat's (2006) discussion of the development of her rubric is of interest for another reason. She recounts how the first version of a rubric she produced to assess literature reviews was so lengthy and complex that she and her colleagues determined it was likely to defeat some of the purposes sought. This can be a common pitfall of rubrics where the complexity of the instrument overwhelms the level of evaluation that would produce an optimal assessment instrument. Overly complex rubrics can over time actually discourage their own use, especially where several faculty members within a department or institution teach separate sections of a capstone course and are obligated to apply the rubric (even though they may not have helped develop it). Peat's reduction of twenty-two criteria for scoring student papers to a much more manageable five criteria is a cautionary tale for those creating a rubric for the first time.

What we might identify as the personalized nature of assessment tools can be illustrated by reference to Sum and Light's (2010) discussion of the assessment methods they designed for their political science capstone course. They begin by explaining that their design started with an exploration of the goals they wished to achieve. These can be divided into three broad themes: overarching goals of critical thinking and effective communication for student learning, departmental goals for political science majors that include exposing students to a holistic view of the discipline and facilitating student reflection on major themes and concepts with an eye toward future democratic citizenship, and using the capstone course as a vehicle for departmental and institutional assessment.

Only after identifying their goals did the authors decide on the major activities that would form their senior capstone experience.

The capstone course Sum and Light (2010) devised was formed around a simulated academic conference where students present papers to one another. Students are directed to resurrect a paper written for one of their previous political science courses. The instructor reviews the topics and organizes the students into panels. The panel presentations occupy four of the eight weeks of the course. The instructor evaluates the oral presentations according to a rubric developed for that purpose at the university level. Students submit three copies of their papers. The instructor and two students review the papers for critical thinking and effective written communication according to a second rubric, also developed at the university level. This process provides an opportunity for direct peer and instructor assessment of two student artifacts, which is useful for student learning as well as to assess learning and the course itself.

Sum and Light's (2010) political science capstone course also includes three additional activities that allow indirect assessment. The course mapping exercise requires students to rate the ten courses that constitute the political science curriculum across four key learning goals on a Likert scale: critical thinking, written and oral communication, and understanding the discipline. This helps faculty members identify weaknesses in core courses. Students are also given an open-ended exit survey that asks them to anonymously evaluate the strengths and weaknesses of the program and the faculty. Finally, a learning-through-teaching activity organizes students into teaching teams that must leave the comfort zone of their own classroom and offer a group teaching presentation to small groups of 100-level students in an introduction to government course. The student audience assesses these presentations according to the university's oral presentation rubric.

The discussion of Sum and Light's (2010) approach is intended to reinforce our principal point in this chapter: the assessment methods chosen must be suitable to both the departmental goals and the nature of the capstone course being assessed. Clearly the course mapping exercise would not fit within an assessment plan that was more directed at evaluating student learning solely within the capstone course. Similarly, the rubrics designed for use in reviewing nonexperimental, nonempirical undergraduate papers, such as a portfolio of papers submitted for a capstone course in the English major (McDaniels, 2009), might not be suitable for assessing a senior research project that involves multiple stages from conception to data gathering and manipulation to written and oral presentation. Sum and Light (2010) devised their assessment "glove" to fit the "hand" it was intended to measure.

Where higher-order cognitive skills are expected to produce a major paper that displays more sophisticated methods, data collection, data manipulation, and results, the rubric cannot limit the criteria it intends to measure quite so easily. At the same time, the rubric should strive for succinctness. McKinney and Busher (2011) report on their direct assessment of a major paper research-based capstone course through use of a comprehensive rubric at three Illinois institutions. Their assessment of these courses involved multiple protocols including review of syllabi, pre- and postcourse questionnaires to students, student reports of class features, and analysis of the course outcomes revealed in major papers and theses. With respect to the capstone paper reviews, a 20 percent random sample of eighteen students across eight sections of research-based capstones at the three institutions was drawn and a forty-one-item coding scheme was used (based generally on Pyrczak, 1999). The skills and qualities assessed mirrored the goals of typical capstone courses with respect to research, writing, presentation, critical thinking, high-impact deep learning, and other similar values. As McKinney and Busher (2011) note (echoing Berheide, 2007), assessing capstone course final products is perhaps the most meaningful method for securing direct assessment of student learning.

Assessing the Professional Issues and Senior Transition Capstone Course

Finally, some senior capstone courses are designed to primarily facilitate the preparation of graduating seniors for their transition beyond the undergraduate setting. Courses of this nature tend to focus on developing seniors' awareness and realistic perception of the nature of graduate education and academic careers and the nature of careers and job opportunities for students who plan to enter the workforce directly after completion of their degree. Nauta (2002) describes such a course in psychology at Illinois State University.

Assessment of a course of this nature should primarily focus on students' perceptions of the usefulness of the classroom activities for achieving the major course objective of familiarizing students with the realistic career options open to them as college graduates as compared to the nature of graduate education and career paths that extend beyond the bachelor's degree. Nauta (1997) bases her evaluation of the success of her professional careers course on carefully reviewing student feedback. Roscoe and Strapp (2009) offer a similar capstone course, Professional Issues in Psychology, at Western Oregon University. They also focus their assessment on eliciting students' views regarding the benefit, or "helpfulness," of the various course activities. More generally, the authors attempted to measure students' increased feelings of efficacy (i.e., competence or preparedness for transition). Such a measure, if positive, would presumably indicate an increased felt readiness to move beyond the status of student and into the adult workforce or adult roles. Since this is a primary goal of transitions capstones, assessing course success on this objective is naturally of signal importance.

Conclusion

Berheide (2007) identifies the capstone course as an especially suitable course for assessment of student learning and the achievement of departmental and institutional goals. There are many good reasons to share this view, as many departments have come to realize. The key to developing useful assessment tools lies in carefully defining the goals sought within the senior capstone experience and tailoring the assessment methods to optimally reflect those goals. Direct evaluation methods have the advantage of exhibiting students' acquisition of knowledge and skills in the context of artifacts that can be objectively rated. Rubrics for both written and oral communication can be developed and used effectively in this way. Indirect methods, on the other hand, are especially effective at revealing students' perceptions and attitudes regarding their learning experience. Together, the two can be used effectively in the capstone course to assess student learning, course quality, and departmental and institutional objectives.

CHAPTER NINE

CONCLUSION: AN IDEAL CAPSTONE COURSE

In this chapter we offer our recommendations for designing and conducting the ideal capstone course for student learning. We do so in light of the existing structure of American higher education with a focus on maximizing faculty and institutional resources. Chapter references after each entry refer the reader back to discussions of each subtopic.

In 1998 John N. Gardner and Gretchen Van der Veer published a collection of essays expressing what was then considered the ideal picture of the senior-year experience. Included in the book was an essay by Sax and Astin that addressed the goal of developing citizenship among college graduates, often expressed in college catalogues and voiced by college presidents in public speeches. Acknowledging that the development of civic virtue among college students was a challenging task, Sax and Astin reported the results of their own study, which suggested students could gain in citizenship qualities over the course of their college career. Their detailed analysis of the sort of college-based activities that might contribute to acquiring citizenship behavior included socializing with someone of a different race/ethnicity, engaging in volunteer work, and leaving home to attend college.

In 2008 we began our study of capstone courses in sociology and psychology departments across the western region of the United States by canvassing the literature to develop a list of the stated purposes or routinely sought goals announced for the senior capstone course. When we distributed our survey, we asked respondents to indicate from a list of eight objectives those that their capstone course embraced. The most common goals reported were "to review and integrate learned material" and "help students extend and apply learned material." More than 80 percent of all respondents with capstone courses selected these goals. The least likely purposes to be chosen were "help students become more active as citizens" and "it socializes students as active citizens," with fewer than 30 percent of respondents with capstone courses selecting either (Hauhart & Grahe, 2010).

The juxtaposition of these two very different commentaries on the goals sought for the senior college experience likely reflect different historical influences. Assuming that Sax and Astin (1998) identified correctly three discrete behaviors (diversity socializing experiences, volunteer activities, and attending college away from home) that can increase interest in civic identity, the typical capstone course offered within a traditional academic discipline today may have little influence in developing citizenship qualities in graduating seniors. The sociologists and psychologists who responded to our study, having recognized the limited potential for the capstone course to accomplish this goal, may have very consciously minimized efforts to achieve what is less achievable within that context. Perhaps less ideally, sociologists and psychologists may have simply shifted their purposes with the tenor of the times and focused their energies on students' acquisition of disciplinary knowledge when the culture as a whole shows less interest in civic virtue and citizenship.

These two very different study outcomes with regard to fostering citizenship remind us that while the senior capstone is an important part of the college curriculum, it can never achieve every positive outcome that might be envisioned for it. We must recognize that the goals sought by the senior experience are subject to change over time—in priority, if not complete substitution. Although we offer a set of recommendations we believe can help create the ideal capstone course, we express humility in the face of this task. We remind ourselves, and you, that the principles we have chosen to accentuate and the objectives we believe the capstone can and should pursue may not include the goals you might select nor will the goals set out today be especially suitable goals for tomorrow's curricula. Therefore, we urge you to adopt our suggestions only after critical reflection and encourage you to engage in continual, realistic reassessment of the choices you have made, the objectives you are pursuing, and the practices you have adopted.

Interdisciplinary or Disciplinary?

This initial choice in many instances will be resolved for you. To the extent a cross-campus committee has decided that the institution should offer or require an interdisciplinary senior experience, perhaps tied to the general education program, your core choice as a course designer will be made for you. The same may be true for many of the details of the campuswide interdisciplinary capstone course. For that reason, we are not going to offer a detailed proposal for this format. Rather, we suggest that many of the principles we identify next with respect to the discipline-specific, research-based capstone course remain applicable.

The Ideal Capstone Course

In our view, the research literature suggests the ideal discipline-specific capstone course is a research-based course one semester long, scaffolded in sequence by one or more required undergraduate research courses, and offered in either a classroom-based seminar format or an internship/practicum format. The senior capstone experience should also include the following features. (Chapter references for our prior discussions of each topic appear in parentheses after each entry.)

Recommendations for Course Design Best Practices

- Be intentional. Develop the senior capstone course only after a collaborative effort to review the existing curriculum, one's shared objectives, and the degree to which national professional standards should be incorporated into the senior course. Analyze and take into account the interests of various stakeholders. (Chapter 6)
- Ensure the external and internal framework of the course is fully delineated, clearly observable and communicated, and designed to support optimal student learning. The structure created may be the most important factor in establishing realistic student expectations, importing learning objectives into the course, and producing positive outcomes. (Chapter 6)
- Choose to create a senior capstone experience for all students, whether in the major or across the campus (interdisciplinary/general education). Mutual participation and engagement in shared academic experience creates student cohesion, supports morale, and contributes

to the creation of a positive learning environment for all students. (Chapter 6)

- Create one or more prerequisite undergraduate research courses in a sequence leading to the capstone course. This will substantially reduce the number of underprepared students who stumble when encountering a thesis or research-based capstone. (Chapters 4 and 6)
- Cap enrollment at the level for optimal achievement of learning objectives and that institutional resources will permit. Advocate for reasonable enrollments to support high levels of instructor-student interaction within the senior capstone course. (Chapter 6)
- Provide a meaningful course description that will help create realistic expectations regarding the requirements, core task, and rigor of the capstone experience. Have instructors of prerequisite core curriculum research courses explain the role of the course to students. (Chapter 6)

Recommendations for Capstone Major Project Best Practices

- Continue to build a framework of sound expectations for the capstone course by erecting clear parameters for a number of basic course requirements. Early, clear communication of the nature of the capstone experience and early efforts to familiarize students with the core task and sequential steps that the major paper or major project will entail can contribute to aligning student expectations for the course with the standards students will be asked to meet. Alignment between student expectations and the nature of the course will produce stronger commitment to the course activities that lead to successful course completion. (Chapters 5 and 6)
- Define the major paper or project in concrete terms; be candid about the open-ended, ill-defined nature of the issue to be solved if defining that issue is part of the students' task in a student choice model. Will a simple review of the literature regarding an issue in the field be satisfactory for completion of the capstone course? Is data collection required? Will students have the chance to work on data collection on a faculty-designed project? Is the only acceptable standard a full research model developed by the student? Clarify each of these issues. (Chapter 6)
- Incorporate appropriate supplemental activities into the capstone course. Although the major paper or major project may be the goal, use suitable supplemental activities to permit students to work toward that goal in stages. (Chapter 6)

- Select a suitable minimum page length for the major paper or research report. Specify clearly whether the minimum page length is exclusive of all front and back matter, such as the abstract, table of contents, charts, tables, appendixes, and references. Select a suitable writing and citation style. Provide access to a style guide through library reserve or other means. (Chapter 6)

Recommendations for Capstone Teaching Best Practices

- When resources permit, favor the student choice model, or a guided student choice model, for selecting the topic, issue, or research question to be pursued. Student motivation is an important element of the successful senior experience, and empowering students to investigate questions that they themselves identify and form contributes measurably to maintaining student motivation. (Chapter 6)
- In senior capstone courses where there is the potential for multiple graded phases or activities within the course model, consider using a "let them decide" framework for weighting the value of some intermediate phases of the paper or project. Giving students power to decide issues of importance, including where a degree of emphasis in evaluation should lie, increases investment and creates feelings of ownership that contribute to student motivation. Adopt practices that encourage initiative and self-direction so that the senior experience will foster autonomy and prepare students generally for life beyond college. (Chapter 7)
- Make a clear decision about requiring peer-reviewed sources, and communicate the proper use of such sources. Have an explicit written policy regarding plagiarism, provide it to students, and place it on a course website (if one is available). Make a decision about whether a minimum number of sources or a minimum number of citations is required. (Generally we do not favor a minimum number of citations or sources because the requirement induces some students to artificially and unnecessarily introduce cites for the sake of meeting the quota.) (Chapter 6)
- Use task sequencing and task timelines to support student completion of the major paper or project. Create regular, periodic due dates for completion of project phases to thwart procrastination and maintain progress toward project completion. Build in more specific learning outcomes throughout the major paper or project where possible. By increasing the number and specificity of learning outcomes articulated and sequencing them properly along a time line, students who would

otherwise be tempted to float and procrastinate can be guided through the series of steps necessary to achieve project completion. While this approach relieves the student of full responsibility for exercising the initiative, it helps those students to complete a satisfactory project who might not otherwise be able to do so. (Chapter 6)

- Create a mechanism for maintaining regular student-instructor inter-action and project review. In a small-seminar format, this can include routine oral progress reports and presentations. It can, and should, involve periodic one-on-one student-instructor meetings as faculty resources permit. Where a value is placed on student initiative, the framework and requirements of the course can be designed to require that students take the initiative for at least some meetings and be evaluated accordingly for any failure to handle this responsibility. An important quality of successful capstone courses is the degree of instructor-student interaction on substantive issues regarding completion of the major paper or project. (Chapter 6)

- Build in frequent, regular opportunities for peer review. Student-student interaction on substantive issues related to the major paper or project is not as crucial as student-instructor contact, but it can benefit students when organized properly. It also has the distinct benefit of conserving faculty resources for one-on-one meetings and other critical activities only the instructor can perform. (Chapter 6)

- Use peer review for several discrete activities: periodic assessment of writ-ten drafts, routine assessment of oral presentations, and peer assessment of final drafts immediately prior to revision for submission. In using peer review, adopt two practices supported by the literature: (1) provide a modest rubric for either written or oral presentation reviews and explain the assessment guide to class members, and (2) use the better students to maximum effectiveness by rotating them throughout the class as often and as widely as possible. Better students are more critical of their peers and raise the standards for discourse about substantive issues. They also maintain high standards for good writing and proper style. (Chapter 7)

- Build into the capstone course early opportunities for students to meet with library staff for a research refresher and with writing center staff for an introduction to the resources available for peer review and writing guidance. Clearly communicate, with regular reminders, that research and writing support are available from these sources and that class members should avail themselves of the opportunity to use and benefit from these resources. (Chapter 7)

- Plan on addressing instances of weak preparation and poor motivation aggressively when they arise. In a perfect world you will not have any weak or poorly motivated students because you have a cohort of mature, self-directed seniors. However, you likely do not live in a perfect world and therefore must prepare to address the actual student audience that populates your college or university. Have a strategic plan for guiding academically weak students to all available resources. Ensure that poorly prepared students follow through with guidance and referrals. Confront procrastinators, laggards, slackers, and underachievers with early, candid, and pointed evaluations of their lack of initiative, poor work, and poor engagement with the senior experience. Cite deficient work in regular written evaluations presented to students who are not meeting the minimum academic standards. Keep all students hewed to the project time line. (Chapter 7)

Recommendations for Capstone Course Support Best Practices

- Adopt methods that incentivize better students to reach beyond the minimum requirements of successful course completion. Consider forming a hierarchical tier of activities that challenge better students to excel. These can include final presentation of capstone projects to a departmental faculty panel; participation in a campuswide scholar's day; creation of posters of project results for display in departmental offices and hallways; presentation at an undergraduate research conference; contribution to a special campus publication for undergraduate research or a department-supported book project; or preparation of a manuscript for submission to a disciplinary journal under the guidance or coauthorship with a faculty mentor. (Chapters 5 and 7)
- Develop simple but regular reporting mechanisms that permit constant monitoring of professional supervisor-student relationships in senior experiences that involve internships or practicums. These can be informal, instructor-initiated, periodic telephone calls to the off-campus supervisors, or the use of simple evaluation forms submitted regularly by the professional project mentor. Successful senior experiences in an internship or practicum model depend on sustained, highly interactive relationships between students and their professional mentors. The capstone course instructor needs to ensure the relationships are positive, engaged, and successful. (Chapter 7)
- Communicate to students that completion of the rigorous challenge that the senior experience presents is a rite of passage that every

graduating major and every graduating senior must complete. Model for class members a combination of support and inevitability. Consider having past students attend early semester class meetings and recount their passage through the senior experience, culminating in their successful completion of the major project. (Chapter 7)

- Establish shared protocols and standards for student evaluation and the award of grades and for course and program assessment. Adopt measures and indexes that are tailored to the nature of the capstone you have designed and the goals you and your colleagues have selected. Ensure that student feedback regarding the course is collected through surveys, interviews, or reflective papers. Use the student feedback you receive along with faculty or instructor feedback to revise and fine-tune your course periodically. (Chapter 8)

Final Recommendation: Deliver the Course; Then Reassess

- Having developed a thoughtful approach to the senior experience that is compatible with departmental, disciplinary, and institutional goals, *stick to the plan.* Communicate the expectations, standards, and requirements to the capstone students. Monitor their efforts at achieving the course goals. Redirect students' energy as necessary. Implement the course design. *Stick to the plan.* (Chapter 7). Only then should you assess, and periodically revise based on your assessments, your plan for the course. (Chapter 8)

Conclusion

Our review of the literature suggests to us that a senior capstone course developed and implemented along the lines that we have recommended will produce successful student outcomes for the overwhelming majority of students. Such a design will also achieve departmental and institutional goals, permit a sound platform for course and program assessment, and permit faculty to guide students on the major paper or project effectively within the limits of their time and resources. In our view, creating a sound design within the parameters we have suggested is the best practice for teaching the senior capstone course that one can find.

In sum, we agree with Upson-Saia (2013) who offers the following three suggestions for best practices in designing and delivering capstone courses:

- Think locally: Judiciously prioritize learning outcomes for majors and honestly assess departmental constraints.
- Think holistically: Assess institutional expectations and resources and fashion your capstone course to maximize—not ignore—the very real limitations these will impose on the senior experience.
- Reassess periodically but otherwise deliver the course chosen.

These generally provide a good summary of three critical facets of course construction and review that will ensure your capstone course is suitable, feasible, and optimal in design.

NOTES

Chapter 1: Overview of the Capstone Course

1. We found many comparable examples of confusion or frustration in both the sessions we hosted at the 2008 Pacific Sociological Association annual meeting in Portland, Oregon, and in our conversations with our colleagues at our own institutions.

Chapter 2: The Role of the Capstone Course in the Curriculum

1. There was consistency between other high-priority items between types of courses. For instance, whether disciplinary or interdisciplinary, critical thinking was the most frequently listed course objective. Similarly, discipline-based courses and project-based experiences reported nearly identical objectives. Other desired skills included oral/written communication proficiency and ability to perform independently, along with teamwork and group work, although the use of different modalities here too varied across institutional type. Public institutions were three times more likely to use teamwork or group work within

the capstone experience as private institutions. Private schools were nearly twice as likely as public institutions to incorporate writing skills (Padgett & Kilgo, 2012).

2. Briefly, the LEAP initiative of the Association of American Colleges and Universities emphasizes reliance on essential learning outcomes; introduction of high-impact educational practices; authentic assessments that promote applying knowledge to real-world problems; and the goal of "inclusive excellence," where every student has the opportunity to benefit from a liberal education.

Chapter 3: Characteristics of the Capstone Course

1. For detailed reviews of discipline-specific capstone courses, summaries of relevant peer-reviewed studies regarding individual capstones are on our companion website page: https://osf.io/tg6fa/. The website for an Australian project, "Capstone Curriculum across Disciplines," also provides access to relevant materials: www.capstonecurriculum.com.au. The director for the Australian project, Nicolette Lee at Victoria University, Melbourne, Australia, has organized a growing network of educators worldwide interested in capstone studies. She may be contacted at Nicollete.Lee@vu.edu.au.

2. There are slight differences in the conceptualization of the capstone course across the four institutions Schermer and Gray (2012) studied. In Allegheny College's capstone, the Senior Comprehensive Project, every graduating senior completes "a sustained independent act of inquiry or creativity consistent, in methodology and focus, with the nature of such work in that student's academic major" (p. 5). Augustana College's course, Senior Inquiry, "include[s] a variety of models, such as traditional independent research, internships, literature reviews and analysis, civic engagement projects, and student teaching" (p. 12). At Washington College, there is even greater variability. Its senior capstone was (until recently) termed "Senior Obligation" and, according to the institution, "The exact nature of the capstone has always varied across departments, largely as a reflection of the many different modes of inquiry existing at a liberal arts institution" (p. 15). Finally, students at the College of Wooster complete a capstone as part of the independent studies program. Wooster's capstone lasts longer: "Over two semesters, each senior works individually with a faculty advisor (the 'first reader') on a topic agreed upon between the student and the advisor, culminating in a thesis

or creative project, and defended in an oral presentation" (p. 19). In short, Schermer and Gray's (2012) study provides some comparative data across institutions and disciplines but also reveals distinctly different capstone experiences as well.

3. Other formats for the senior experience that were listed included interdisciplinary courses (16.3 percent), career planning courses (3 percent), and transition courses with a focus on preparation for life after college (5.8 percent). This range of courses does not fully reflect the complete continuum of alternatives, however, because another 4.6 percent were identified as "other" (Henscheid et al., 2000).

4. Padgett and Kilgo (2012) did not pursue precisely the same range of capstone options named by Henscheid, so further comparisons were limited. They did not present data on a career planning course or a transition course, but did offer specific data on three new alternatives: the internship (3.9 percent), comprehensive exam (2.4 percent), and performance/exhibition (1.2 percent) capstone courses. The two missing formats for senior courses from the Henscheid et al. (2000) study could be included in the slightly larger "other" category (7.1 percent) that Padgett and Kilgo (2012) reported. Alternatively, the results could reflect a substantial diminishment, almost to the statistical zero point, with respect to career planning and transition-style capstones over the decade between the two studies. Further research is required to resolve this issue.

5. What Padgett and Kilgo (2012) provide uniquely relative to the other multi-institutional studies is an analysis of preferred class objectives, topics, and practices. In keeping with a trend in assessment that we will discuss in a later chapter, the National Survey of Senior Capstone Experiences (NSSCE) measured targeted objectives rather than the more global purposes and goals we discussed in chapter 2. However, the NSSCE also asked respondents to "select the three most important objectives" rather than "check all that apply." The authors list seventeen discrete capstone goals to choose from. These include some of the general objectives often pursued (critical thinking, oral communication), but also discipline-specific topics and skills such as teamwork, writing skills, research, and career development. The results show that none of these objectives are ranked with predominance. Critical thinking approaches a dominant ranking at 49.6 percent, but many objectives receive response rates between only 1 and 5 percent. These include preparation for transition to graduate school, certificate preparation, life skills, development of out-of-class student-instructor interaction,

and satisfaction with academic discipline. Moreover, another five are below 1 percent (increased connections with peers, satisfaction with the institution, satisfaction with the instructor, increased use of campus services, and persistence to graduation). Naturally these are goals within many capstone courses, but are not among the three most important cited by survey respondents. Objectives that received responses between 10 and 30 percent represent common and critical capstone course objectives, although not among the three most important identified by these survey respondents. These include the ability to conduct scholarly research, 27.6 percent; ability to perform independently, 18.7 percent; appreciation of the discipline, 17.5 percent; career preparation, 25 percent; professional development, 23.5 percent; proficiency in oral communication, 14.9 percent; proficiency in written communication, 22.8 percent; and a residual category of other, 10.4 percent. From a methodological point of view, one may wonder which of these would have increased in importance if the NSSCE had asked respondents to choose the five most important outcomes. While interesting, Padgett and Kilgo's (2012) survey results may be influenced by the manner in which they posed their question.

6. When comparing the importance of various capstone experiences among the different studies in table 3.2, only the internship response is markedly different. This does not suggest that these institutions do not engage in internships, but rather their descriptions of the capstone experience do not include internships as a critical component. As Schermer and Gray (2013) state regarding the overall percentage of capstone components, "one would expect significant variation if the results were broken down by academic division" (p. 35). This theme is consistent with earlier conclusions. Thus, internships may be limited in popularity to very specific fields that are not highly represented in the survey populations examined and not featured in catalogue descriptions. More generally, the results show that most students at these institutions in all majors can expect to complete a written paper with a literature review and a reflective analysis with some oral presentation (all above 50 percent). In comparison, the likelihood that a student will collect data through experiments or questionnaires in the field or laboratory, statistically analyze those data, and present a poster (all between 25 and 50 percent) are all more likely to occur in social or natural sciences. Correspondingly, creating or contributing to artistic expression (33 percent) will more likely be a format and objective pursued in the creative arts programs.

7. There was only one response for ten meetings and another for fifteen meetings; these responses likely reflect meetings that occurred weekly through a quarter or semester system. We did not publish these data in our paper as the reviewers believed it added confusion, not clarity, to our results. We have had personal experience with such a system where students work with faculty mentors or consultants, however, and recognize this pattern as one that some departments and institutions follow.

8. The most fully developed procedure is from the College of Wooster, where mentors are assigned based on considerations of student topic and the need to distribute faculty load across the department. They further report that some departments use a system where each student submits an order preference and the department matches student preferences for specific faculty mentors where possible. Other departments employ a first-come, first-serve approach. While this is the most flexible approach, all four institutions discuss the need to assign a mentor through a process that considers student topic, faculty strengths, and faculty workload.

9. An interesting note from our national survey was that higher minimum paper standards (more pages, more references) were associated with increased likelihood to submit the paper for publication, although minimum paper standards were not related to less prestigious professional formats (oral presentation on campus or conference presentations). It is not possible to assign causation to this finding, but it does suggest better outcomes are associated with increased expectations.

Chapter 4: The Role and Design of Research Projects Leading to the Capstone Experience

1. Biology may represent a discipline at an academic crossroads: research experiences are already present within biology, so it is now a question of how to best use them within the context of undergraduate education. Cheesman, French, Cheesman, Swails, and Thomas (2007) completed a survey of over four hundred biology department chairs to examine the impact of the National Research Council report (2003) and determine commonalities in major requirements. The researchers found that only 18 percent of chairs had read the report and only 12 percent of those who read it were planning curriculum changes because "the focus of Bio2010 is too narrow to affect their

undergraduate curriculum" (p. 517). Cheesman et al. did note a large increase in the number of departments requiring research methods and statistics relative to the results of another major study of the discipline conducted fifteen years earlier.

2. Another resource for undergraduate research program development is a book edited by Roman Taraban and Richard Blanton (2008), *Creating Effective Undergraduate Research Programs in Science.* Taraban and Blanton argue that building such programs is justified by the benefits they supply to undergraduate education. Primary chapters describe model programs, while other chapters document the benefits of research experiences for faculty members and for students. This book can provide guidance to individuals seeking to build strong undergraduate research programs in sciences, or it can be used to compare the effectiveness of existing programs through established findings.

3. Davis and Sandifer-Stech (2006) also noticed that not all cohorts showed similar improvement. This finding raised the possibility that there is a further instructor effect where "style and expectations between their instructors may have negatively impacted students' confidence during their senior year" (p. 64). This highlights the importance of developing a consistent set of expectations within a department for a motivated and well-prepared instructor.

4. The limited nature of these single-university survey results notwithstanding, the longitudinal findings are particularly interesting because they mark potential changes as a consequence of participation in undergraduate research opportunities. The researchers wanted to investigate the impact of research participation on cognitive processes, critical thinking, and personality differences between high, medium, and no research levels. Examining the data from the longitudinal study suggests that in an examination of academic and intellectual gains, individuals in the moderate-research and high-research groups both showed more gains than those in the no-research group. These gains were consistent in science and technology skills, but there were no effects of research in personal-social activities or vocal preparation. The study also revealed that the high-research group displayed better critical thinking in year 4 but not year 1, compared to the no-research group. And finally, there were statistically significant differences in SAT math and verbal scores between high- and no-research groups (Webber-Bauer & Bennett, 2003). Because the study is not experimental, causation cannot be inferred or persuasively determined; rather, the differences in critical thinking revealed can be used to suggest

that this is beneficial. Webber-Bauer and Bennett (2003) first included personality as an intended covariate, but because the means differed between research groups, they examined it as a dependent measure. Although neuroticism decreased for all students, they found that the high-research group compared to the no-research group reported higher neuroticism in both years 1 and 4. Similarly, the high-research group reported lower extraversion than the other groups during both years, though all groups showed greater extraversion overall. This lack of difference may suggest that those with certain traits are more likely to seek out, or be sought for, research experiences. One notable change was that high-research groups had higher "openness" in year 4 but not in year 1. Agreeableness and conscientiousness were not different across years or research groups. There were no reported differences between majors or gender. While the purely correlational nature of the data prevents an attribution of causation, this finding suggests that undergraduate research opportunities can lead to more openness as a personality trait characteristic.

5. These types of examples abound in the Healey and Jenkins (2009) text and can be found in our online appendix as well. Schroeder et al. (2009) use open-ended questions in electromagnetic engineering to spur student innovation. Barry, Drnevich, Irfanoglu, and Bullock (2012) describe the capstone for civil engineering capstones at Purdue University where students work in, and faculty members teach on, real-world proposals prepared for local clients with budgets ranging up to $10 million. Burnette and Wessler (2013) describe a course in dynamic genomics where students learn to sequence DNA from known samples and then work on unknown samples for a group capstone project. And Levia and Quiring (2008) encourage their students to complete capstone projects focused on real-world problems in geography. In each case, students received support to help find an authentic question and worked to complete a project that could potentially build on and extend existing knowledge while addressing a problem outside the classroom.

6. These decisions are affected by the size of the institution or department. Smaller schools might experience limited fiscal or laboratory resources, but they often have more faculty time available for contact with students. In a large PhD-granting institution, there might not be enough laboratory space or time in the semester to allow undergraduate students to complete major projects since there will be competition from graduate students. Perhaps the medium-sized MA-granting department

will fare best where suitable laboratory facilities exist: PhD candidates are not present to dominate their use, and the faculty-student ratio is sufficiently reasonable to free up some faculty time for mentoring undergraduate projects. In the end, the department will likely encourage those undergraduate student research projects that it can afford to offer within the limits of available resources.

7. Rowland et al. (2012) examined this topic of student interest and skill diversity when considering research methods curriculum development. Their research focuses on early-stage learning rather than capstone, but it highlights the challenges that departments and instructors must address. First, they discuss the challenges that underprepared students face in an active research laboratory, noting that "some academics are unwilling to take undergraduate students into the laboratory until they know the student has some prior research experience" (p. 47). For students with minimal interest or with no prior experience, they designed their laboratory course for second-year students with two "parallel and equivalent laboratory streams" (p. 49). Students self-selected into the research group, with most choosing the track where they could "focus on developing core understanding and improving their laboratory techniques" (p. 49) and a small core group participating in a standard undergraduate research experience that "allowed undergraduate students to work during their regular time-tabled BIOC2000 laboratory hours with the aim of obtaining useful results for an extant research project at our institution" (p. 50). Although they found challenges implementing the distinct streams, students were generally satisfied, and the authors concluded that "a bifurcated laboratory stream is a viable mechanism for providing challenge for more motivated students, while maintaining a similar overall increase in skills for students in the two streams" (p. 61).

8. The argument against offering alternative capstone courses is analogous to the argument against tracking in education: creating one experience that the "elite" are encouraged to pursue and other experiences that the "ordinary" student is offered tends to create self-fulfilling prophecies where students are negatively labeled by their early academic experiences and discouraged from reaching beyond expectations. Consequently some students earn a second-class degree and are condemned to the limits which that degree imposes.

9. At Pacific Lutheran University, all senior capstone students are required to make a public presentation of their capstone project. In psychology, this takes the form of a poster conference. Capstone students, as

well as research methods students, present their projects to interested attendees, including other students, their professors, other faculty or administrators, their friends, and family members. In multiple sessions, students take turns standing in front of their posters and speaking about what they learned. While the posters are often focused on the research findings, the conversations also include discussions about what it was like to complete the project.

10. While the Thomas and Hodges (2010) text is designed specifically for social and health sciences, similar products can be found in other disciplines. Reynolds et al. (2009) developed BioTAP to foster increased participation in undergraduate research experiences. Though developed specifically for biology at Duke University and not explicitly designed for capstone projects, their rubric was intended to "serve as a model for other STEM departments" (p. 897) and is applicable to undergraduate research generally. Full details of the program are available online (www.science-writing.org/biotap.html). There are four sections: higher-order thinking, mid- and lower-order writing, accuracy and appropriateness of the research, and qualifications for awards and honors. The rubric follows an academic publishing template with drafts, reviews, and revision.

Chapter 5: Research Project Impediments and Possibilities

1. Lest we inadvertently convey the appearance that it is only scientific research that is prone to acts of academic dishonesty, recent commentaries from disciplines across the academic spectrum have identified fraud and plagiarism as a cause for concern. Disciplines as dissimilar as nursing (Burns, 2009), geography (Griffith, 2008), economics (Frey, Frey, & Eichenberger, 1999), and African literature (Hitchcott, 2006) experienced their own crises, episodes, and calls for action related to academic dishonesty. Pierce (2004), writing in *History Today*, recounts one of the more brazen literary forgeries of Shakespeare's work. Although a compelling example, Pierce's story is not a contemporary one: it was in 1794 when William-Henry Ireland concocted an elaborate scheme to create a trove of "Shakespeare papers," including a purported new play. In short, there is little to suggest that concerns over authenticity and integrity are limited to any single field or particular era.

2. Faculty at large public universities experience even further pressures on their time such as higher teaching loads and increased class

preparation demands. Yet faculty at Research I universities are still expected to produce publications, leading Sharobeam and Howard (2002) to question whether Research I science and mathematics faculty can manage to be productive given these conditions. In a survey of faculty from large, publicly funded research universities, most respondents reported pursuing their research in the summer or during holidays. They reported receiving insufficient financial support for travel or release time for these activities. When asked to list the five factors that limited their research productivity, respondents predominantly identified time constraints as the primary factor. Other commonly listed factors were teaching load, money (equipment and facilities), lack of motivated students, and family.

3. In January 2013, Brian Nosek and Jeffrey Spies founded the Center for Open Science (COS). The COS and its accompanying Open Science Framework (OSF) software were designed to change science by making it easier to store relevant scientific materials (log books, research plans, stimuli, data, analyses, reports) online and share them publicly. They hope this will radically change the scientific enterprise (Brian Nosek, COS progress report, July 2013). OSF allows researchers to share or hide their materials with the click of a "make it public" button. OSF anticipates that normative pressures among the scientific community will ultimately bring about widespread change. The COS's most recent initiative is to advertise publication "badges" where authors can highlight that their methods are open (all materials are archived publicly), their data are open (data are archived publicly), or their project was registered (the hypotheses and analysis plan are time-stamped so that the results are known not to be affected by data manipulation).

4. Capstone students are encouraged to choose theoretically inspired moderating variables and measure them after the completion of the direct effect. The nine studies were determined by identifying the three most cited articles from nine psychology subfields and then coding them for feasibility. Information and materials provided by authors of the original studies are shared publicly on a free homepage using Open Science Framework software (https://osf.io/wfc6u/). The CREP received funding from both Psi Chi and the Center for Open Science to offer small research awards to students who conducted direct replications of one of nine studies. As of January 2014, over twenty-five student researchers are working on CREP replications, and about five of them are doing so for a capstone or senior research project.

5. Karukstis and Hensel (2010), and their collaborators, focus their efforts
    on helping faculty at primarily undergraduate institutions engage in
    this type of research because these institutions face unique resource
    challenges that must be overcome. They argue that if faculty limita-
    tions cannot be minimized and faculty cannot be properly supported,
    the likelihood is that appreciable undergraduate research opportuni-
    ties will not occur. They list potential barriers to effective faculty support
    for research at primarily undergraduate institutions that reflect what
    we and others have noted: "a lack of time brought on by relatively high
    teaching loads and substantial advising expectations" (p. vii). They also
    note difficulties that result from [primarily undergraduate institutions]
    focusing on teaching support rather than research infrastructure and
    that undergraduates are by definition more inexperienced than gradu-
    ate students as collaborators.

    In his chapter, "Multiple Approaches to Transformative Research,"
    Karukstis (2010) includes numerous specific examples of research activ-
    ities that have created a role for undergraduate students in completing
    the research. For instance, Michael McCormick collected data related
    to an Antarctic ecosystem. Though students did not accompany him
    on the Antarctic field trip, he intends to have senior thesis students
    help complete subsequent analyses. In another chapter, Withers and
    Detweiler-Bedell (2010) suggest ways that using transformative research
    projects can improve experiential learning across the science curricu-
    lum. They highlight reasons that engaging in meaningful research is
    beneficial relative to typical learning practices. Faculty benefit by stay-
    ing more active in current science advances within their discipline and
    integrating teaching and scholarship activities. Students benefit from
    actively experiencing science rather than passively learning about it.
    The authors point to the active learning stance that is supported by any
    hands-on research activities as productive of actual student learning.
    They also note the added benefits of "developing skills in creativity and
    practice in generating new knowledge," which prepares students to be
    more creative and excited "to generate the next set of transformative
    ideas" (Withers & Detweiler-Bedell 2010, p. 39).

Chapter 6: Designing the Capstone Course

1. The final step in Todd and Magleby's (2005) approach is to analyze the
    constraints that the proposed course will face if it is to be implemented.

They offer a long list of considerations that they analyzed with respect to their proposed externally sponsored, engineering design capstone course. We return to other points raised in their discussion of externally supported capstones in chapter 8.

2. We note that "others" may include accrediting bodies or professional associations whose standards, good opinion, and ultimate review may warrant consideration as important stakeholders.

3. Todd and Magleby (2005) point out that the e-portfolio can then be used for program assessment, since the competencies were chosen based on their agreement with the Council on Social Work Education's standards.

4. Saint Martin's University, a private Benedictine liberal arts college, has a main campus enrollment of approximately fourteen hundred students. Its Senior Seminar in criminal justice and legal studies enrolls between six and thirteen students each semester and is offered in both fall and spring semesters. Typically about twenty students graduate with criminal justice degrees each year at the main campus.

5. Courtney's senior thesis is arguably one of the most successful in seminar history at Saint Martin's University: a revised version was accepted for publication within weeks of submission to a highly regarded national law journal (Hauhart & Choi, 2012).

6. Kim reported her results to the police commander in a 102-page report, which was edited to a 60-page senior thesis. With her advisor's assistance, her thesis was later edited to a 40-page paper for submission to a professional journal. The paper has been accepted for publication at a peer-reviewed journal pending revision in light of the peer reviewers' comments.

Chapter 7: Teaching the Capstone Course

1. Sources that discuss the principles of good teaching more generally include Biggs (2003), Chickering and Gamson (1987), Kuh and Associates (2005), Ramsden (2003), and Weimer (2002).

2. Hillary Rodham Clinton submitted a ninety-two page undergraduate honors thesis on Saul Alinsky in political science at Wellesley College in 1969. Fortunately, most of the major papers you receive will not be as long.

3. Jones et al. (2012) also administered the same sixty-seven-item protocol at the end of the course as one means of assessment. See chapter 8.

Chapter 8: Using the Capstone Course for Assessment

1. Among the many sources available on assessment generally, we recommend beginning with Banta and Associates (2002); Brown, Bull, and Pendlebury (1997); Maki (2004); Webber (2012); Fletcher, Meyer, Andersen, Johnston, and Rees (2012); Cummings, Maddux, and Richmond (2008); and Wang and Hurley (2012).

2. Rowles et al. (2004) use the term *mountaintops* to symbolize what they see as the interdisciplinary capstone's tendency to draw students to the pinnacle of two or more disciplinary peaks where they can then survey the whole terrain of learning they have experienced across a broad curriculum. Rowles et al. use the term *magnets* for discipline-specific capstones because they view them as pulling together through a force of central attraction the various strands of a discipline, leaving the student with a unified experience of the major as a whole.

REFERENCES

Allard, S. W., & Straussman, J. D. (2003). Managing intensive student consulting capstone projects: The Maxwell School experience. *Journal of Policy Analysis and Management, 22*(4), 689–701. http://dx.doi.org /10.1002/pam.10165

American Chemical Society. (2008). *Undergraduate professional education in chemistry: American Chemical Society guidelines and evaluation procedures for bachelor's degree programs.* Washington, DC: American Chemical Society.

American Political Science Association. (1951). *Goals for political science: Report of the Committee for the Advancement of Teaching.* New York: Sloane.

American Psychological Association. (2013). *APA guidelines for the undergraduate psychology major: Version 2.0.* Retrieved from http://www.apa.org /ed/precollege/undergrad/index.aspx

American Sociological Association. (1991). *Liberal learning and the sociology major: A report to the profession.* Washington, DC: American Sociological Association.

Anderson, L., & Krathwohl, D. (2001). *A taxonomy for learning and teaching: A revision of Bloom's taxonomy of educational objectives.* New York: Addison Wesley Longman.

Angelo, T. A., & Cross, K. P. (1993). *Classroom assessment techniques: A handbook for college teachers.* San Francisco: Jossey-Bass.

Arnett, J. J. (2001). Conceptions of the transition to adulthood: Perspectives from adolescence through midlife. *Journal of Adult Development*, *8*(2), 133–143. http://dx.doi.org/10.1023/A:1026450103225

Association of American Colleges. (1985). Project on redefining the meaning and purpose of baccalaureate degrees. In *Integrity in the college curriculum: A report to the academic community: The findings and recommendations of the Project on Redefining the Meaning and Purpose of Baccalaureate Degrees*. Washington, DC: The Association.

Association of American Colleges. (1991). *The challenge of connecting learning: Project on liberal learning, study-in-depth, and the arts and sciences major*. Washington, DC: The Association.

Atchison, P. (1993). Creating the capstone connection. *Teaching Sociology*, *21*(3), 226–228. http://dx.doi.org/10.2307/1319015

Auchincloss, L., Laursen, S., Branchaw, J., Eagan, K., Graham, M., Hanauer, D., . . . Dolan, E. (2014). Assessment of course-based undergraduate research experiences: A meeting report. *CBE Life Sciences Education*, *13*(1), 29–40. doi:10.1187/cbe.14–01–0004

Ault, R. L., & Multhaup, K. S. (2003). An issues-oriented capstone course. *Teaching of Psychology*, *30*(1), 46–48.

Badger, K. (2010). Peer teaching and review: A model for writing development and knowledge synthesis. *Social Work Education*, *29*(1), 6–17. http://dx.doi.org/10.1080/02615470902810850

Banta, T., and Associates. (2002). *Building a scholarship of assessment*. San Francisco: Jossey-Bass.

Barry, B. E., Drnevich, V. P., Irfanoglu, A., & Bullock, D. (2012). Summary of developments in the civil engineering capstone course at Purdue University. *Journal of Professional Issues in Engineering Education and Practice*, *138*(1), 95–98. http://dx.doi.org/10.1061/(ASCE)EI.1943–5541.000 0084

Bauer, K. W., & Bennett, J. S. (2003). Alumni perceptions used to assess undergraduate research experience. *Journal of Higher Education*, *74*(2), 210–230. http://dx.doi.org/10.1353/jhe.2003.0011

Berheide, C. W. (2007). Doing less work, collecting better data: Using capstone courses to assess learning. *Peer Review*, *9*(2), 27–30.

Berkson, J., & Harrison, A.-L. (2001). An integrative capstone course for the conservation biology curriculum. *Conservation Biology*, *15*(5), 1461–1463. http://dx.doi.org/10.1111/j.1523–1739.2001.00343.x

Biggs, T. (2003). *Teaching for quality learning at university*. Buckingham, UK: Society for Research into Higher Education/Open University Press.

Blattner, N. H., & Frazier, C. L. (2004). Assessing general education core objectives. *Assessment Update, 16*(4), 4–6.

Bos, A. L., & Schneider, M. C. (2009). Stepping around the brick wall: Overcoming student obstacles in methods courses. *PS: Political Science and Politics, 42*(2), 375–383. http://dx.doi.org/10.1017/S1049096509090519

Bowman, J. S. (1989). The MPA capstone experience: The essence of analysis is surprise. *Policy Studies Review, 8*(4), 920–928. http://dx.doi.org/10.1111/j.1541–1338.1989.tb01012.x

Boyer Commission on Educating Undergraduates in the Research University. (1998). *Reinventing undergraduate education: A blueprint for America's research university.* Stanford, CA: Carnegie Foundation for the Advancement of Teaching.

Boysen, G. A. (2010). An integrative undergraduate capstone course on the unconscious. *Teaching of Psychology, 37*(4), 237–245. http://dx.doi.org/10.1080/00986283.2010.510972

Briggs, C. L. (2007). Curriculum collaboration: A key to continuous program renewal. *Journal of Higher Education, 78*(6), 676–711. http://dx.doi.org/10.1353/jhe.2007.0036

Brinthaupt, T. M. (2004). Providing a realistic course preview to students. *Teaching of Psychology, 31*(2), 104–106.

Bromwich, D. (2012). Academic freedom and its opponents. *Raritan, 31*(3), 19–33.

Brooks, R., Benton-Kupper, J., & Slayton, D. (2004). Curricular aims: Assessment of a university capstone course. *Journal of General Education, 53*(3/4), 275–287.

Brown, G., Bull J., & Pendlebury, M. (1997). *Assessing student learning in higher education.* London, UK: Routledge.

Brown, J. N., Pegg, S., & Shively, J. W. (2006). Consensus and divergence in international studies: Survey evidence from 140 international studies curriculum programs. *International Studies Perspectives, 7*(3), 267–286. http://dx.doi.org/10.1111/j.1528–3585.2006.00251.x

Brownell, J. E., & Swaner, L. E. (2010). *Five high-impact practices: Research on learning outcomes, completion and quality.* Washington, DC: Association of American Colleges and Universities.

Burnette, J. M. III, & Wessler, S. R. (2013). Transposing from the laboratory to the classroom to generate authentic research experiences for undergraduates. *Genetics, 193*(2), 367–375. http://dx.doi.org/10.1534/genetics.112.147355

Burns, D. (2009). Cut out the plagiarism. *Nursing Standard, 23*(25), 61.

Campbell, D. A., & Lambright, K. T. (2011). How valuable are capstone projects for community organizations? Lessons from a program assessment. *Journal of Public Affairs Education, 17*(1), 61–87.

Campbell, H., & Tatro, B. J. (1998). Teaching program evaluation to public administration students in a single course: An experiential solution. *Journal of Public Affairs Education, 4*(2), 101–122.

Carlson, J. (2001). Caring about more: An integrative capstone course connecting religious studies with general education. *Teaching Theology and Religion, 4*(2), 81–88. http://dx.doi.org/10.1111/1467–9647.00098

Carlson, J. L., Cohn, R. L., & Ramsey, D. D. (2002). Implementing Hansen's proficiencies. *Journal of Economic Education, 33*(2), 180–191. http://dx.doi.org/10.1080/00220480209596466

Carter, J. L., Heppner, F., Saigo, R. H., Twitty, G., & Walker, D. (1990). The state of the biology major. *BioScience, 40*(9), 678–683. http://dx.doi.org/10.2307/1311436

Carlson, M., & Youngblut, L. H. (1998). Where the wild papers are: Producing a student portfolio in the undergraduate seminar. *History Teacher, 52*(1), 43–56.

Catalano, G. D. (2004). Senior capstone design and ethics: A bridge to the professional world. *Science and Engineering Ethics, 10*(2), 409–415. http://dx.doi.org/10.1007/s11948–004–0037–1

Catchings, B. (2004). Capstones and quality: The culminating experience as assessment. *Assessment Update, 16*(1), 6–7.

Cavanagh, S. T., Quarmby, K. A., & Unwin, S. (2014). Infinite variety: Undergraduate research in theatre studies. In I. Crawford, S. Orel, & J. O. Shanahan (Eds.), *Initiating and sustaining research and creative inquiry in undergraduate education: A practical guide for faculty in the arts and humanities* (pp. 74–81). Washington, DC: Council for Undergraduate Research.

Chamely-Wilk, D., Dunn, K., Heydelt-Kirsch, P., Holman, M., Meeroff, D., & Peluso, J. (2014). Scaffolding the development of students' research skills for capstone experiences: A multi-disciplinary approach. *CUR Quarterly, 34*, 18–25.

Cheesman, K., French, D., Cheesman, I., Swails, N., & Thomas, J. (2007). Is there any common curriculum for undergraduate biology majors in the 21st century? *BioScience, 57*(6), 516–522.

Chickering, A. W., & Gamson, Z. (1987). Seven principles for good practice in undergraduate education. *American Association for Higher Education Bulletin, 39*(7), 3–7.

Chickering, A. W., & Reisser, L. (1993). *Education and identity*. San Francisco: Jossey-Bass.

Chin, J., Senter, M. S., & Spalter-Roth, R. (2011). Love to teach, but hate assessment? *Teaching Sociology, 39*(2), 120–126. http://dx.doi.org/10.1177/0092055X11401562

Choi, I., & Lee, K. (2009). Designing and implementing a case-based learning environment for enhancing ill-structured problem solving: Classroom management problems for prospective teachers. *Educational Technology Research and Development, 57*(1), 99–129. http://dx.doi.org/10.1007/s11423–008–9089–2

Christ, W. G., Malinauskas, M. J., & Hunt, G. T. (1994). Assessment in theatre programs. In W. G. Christ (Ed.), *Assessing communication education: A handbook for media, speech, and theatre educators* (pp. 311–332). Hillsdale, NJ: Erlbaum.

Christ, W. G., & Moore, R. C. (1994). The capstone course. In W. G. Christ (Ed.), *Assessing communication education: A handbook for media, speech, and theatre educators* (pp. 155–179). Hillsdale, NJ: Erlbaum.

Clinkenbeard, P. R. (2012). Motivation and gifted students: Implications of theory and research. *Psychology in the Schools, 49*(7), 622–630. http://dx.doi.org/10.1002/pits.21628

Cooper, H. (2010). *Research synthesis and meta-analysis: A step-by-step approach*. Thousand Oaks, CA: Sage.

Corley, C. R. (2013). From mentoring to collaborating: Fostering undergraduate research in history. *History Teacher, 46*(3), 397–414.

Corsaro, W. A. (2005). *The sociology of childhood*. Thousand Oaks, CA: Pine Forge Press.

Cortes, B. S. (2012). Assessing the undergraduate business research paper: The capstone course in economics revisited. *National Social Science Journal, 38*(1), 11–17.

Council on Undergraduate Research. (2013). *Fact sheet*. from http://www.cur.org/about_cur/fact_sheet/

Covington, M. V. (2000). Intrinsic versus extrinsic motivation in schools: A reconciliation. *Current Directions in Psychological Science, 9*(1), 22–25. http://dx.doi.org/10.1111/1467–8721.00052

Crawford, I., Orel, S., & Shanahan, J. O. (2014). *Initiating and sustaining research and creative inquiry in undergraduate education: A practical guide for faculty in the arts and humanities*. Washington, DC: Council for Undergraduate Research.

Crawford, I., & Shanahan, J. O. (2014). Undergraduate research and creative activities in the arts and humanities: Challenges, opportunities, and rewards. In I. Crawford, S. Orel, & J. O. Shanahan (Eds.), *Initiating and sustaining research and creative inquiry in undergraduate education: A practical guide for faculty in the arts and humanities* (pp. 1–11). Washington, DC: Council for Undergraduate Research.

Cummings, R., Maddux, C. D., & Richmond, A. (2008). Curriculum-embedded performance assessment in higher education: Maximum efficiency and minimum disruption. *Assessment and Evaluation in Higher Education, 33*(6), 599–605. http://dx.doi.org/10.1080/026029307017 73067

Cuseo, J. B. (1998). Objectives and benefits of senior year programs. In J. N. Gardner & G. Van der Veer (Eds.), *The senior year experience: Facilitating integration, reflection, closure, and transition.* San Francisco: Jossey-Bass.

Cutucache, C. E., Chen, H., Conroy, B., Madden, C., Peterson, D., Strathman, L., . . . Kolok, A. S. (2014). Culturing undergraduate research among the Nebraska Watershed Network, microbiology students, and the community. *CUR Quarterly, 34,* 33–37.

Davies, P. (2006). Peer assessment: Judging the quality of students' work by comments rather than marks. *Innovations in Education and Teaching International, 43*(1), 69–82.

Davis, J. C., & Sandifer-Stech, D. M. (2006). Wade into the water: Preparing students for successful quantitative research. *Family Relations, 55*(1), 56–66. http://dx.doi.org/10.1111/j.1741–3729.2006.00356.x

Davis, N. J. (1993). Bringing it all together: The sociological imagination. *Teaching Sociology, 21*(3), 233–238. http://dx.doi.org/10.2307/1319017

Dickinson, J. (1993). The senior seminar at Rider College. *Teaching Sociology, 21*(3), 215–218. http://dx.doi.org/10.2307/1319012

Dougherty, J. U., & Parfitt, M. K. (2009). Framework for teaching engineering capstone design courses with emphasis on application of internet-based technologies. *Journal of Architectural Engineering, 15*(1), 4–9. http://dx.doi.org/10.1061/(ASCE)1076–0431(2009)15:1(4)

Dougherty, J. U., & Parfitt, M. K. (2013). Student and practitioner collaboration in an online knowledge community: Best practices from a capstone course implementation. *Journal of Architectural Engineering, 19*(1), 12–20. http://dx.doi.org/10.1061/(ASCE)AE.1943–5568.000 0100

Durant, R. R. (2002). Toward becoming a learning organization: Outcomes assessment, NASPAA accreditation, and mission-based capstone courses. *Journal of Public Affairs Education, 8*(3), 193–208.

Durel, R. J. (1993). The capstone course: A rite of passage. *Teaching Sociology, 21*(3), 223–225. http://dx.doi.org/10.2307/1319014

Durso, F. T. (1997). Corporate-sponsored undergraduate research as a capstone experience. *Teaching of Psychology, 24*(1), 54–56. http://dx .doi.org/10.1207/s15328023top2401_15

Eder, D. J. (2004). General education assessment within the disciplines. *Journal of General Education, 53*(2), 135–157. http://dx.doi.org/10.1353 /jge.2004.0026

Eisenbach, R., Golich, V., & Curry, R. (1998). Classroom assessment across the disciplines. *New Directions for Teaching and Learning, 75*, 59–66. http://dx.doi.org/10.1002/tl.7506

Elrod, S., Husic, D., & Kinzie, J. (2010). Research and discovery across the curriculum. *Peer Review, 12*(2), 4–8.

Fanelli, D. (2010). "Positive" results increase down the hierarchy of the sciences. *PloS One, 5*(4), e10068–e10068. http://dx.doi.org/10.1371 /journal.pone.0010068

Fernandez, N. P. (2006). Integration, reflection, interpretation: Realizing the goals of a general education capstone course. *About Campus, 11*(2), 23–26. http://dx.doi.org/10.1002/abc.163

Fernald, C. D., Tedeschi, R. G., Siegfried, D., Gimore, D. C., Grimsely, D. L., & Chipley, B. (1982). Designing and managing an undergraduate practicum course in psychology. *Teaching of Psychology, 9*, 155–160.

Fletcher, R. B., Meyer, L. H., Andersen, H., Johnston, P., & Rees, M. (2012). Faculty and students' conceptions of assessment in higher education. *Higher Education, 64*(1), 119–133.

Flint, W. (1993). Ideological contradiction and the problem of closure in the sociology capstone course. *Teaching Sociology, 21*(3), 254–257. http://dx.doi.org/10.2307/1319023

Flood, L. (2007). Using a capstone cultural diversity paper for program outcomes evaluation. *Nursing Education Perspectives, 28*(3), 130–135.

Franchetti, M., Hefzy, M. S., Pourazady, M., & Smallman, C. (2012). Framework for implementing engineering senior design capstone courses and design clinics. *Journal of STEM Education: Innovations and Research, 13*(3), 30–45.

Frank, M. C., & Saxe, R. (2012). Teaching replication. *Perspectives on Psychological Science, 7*, 595–599.

Freedman, S. M., & Phillips, J. S. (1985). The effects of situational performance constraints on intrinsic motivation and satisfaction: The role of perceived competence and self-determination. *Organizational Behavior and Human Decision Processes, 35*(3), 397–416. http://dx.doi .org/10.1016/0749-5978(85)90030-5

Frey, R. L., Frey, B. S., & Eichenberger, R. (1999). A case of plagiarism. *Kyklos*, *52*(3), 311. http://dx.doi.org/10.1111/j.1467–6435.1999.tb00219.x

Galle, J. K., & Galle, J. (2010). Building an integrated student learning outcomes assessment for general education: Three case studies. *New Directions for Teaching and Learning*, *2010*(121), 79–87. http://dx.doi.org/10.1002/tl.390

Galvan, J. L. (2004). *Writing literature reviews: A guide for students of the social and behavioral sciences* (2nd ed.). Glendale, CA: Pyrczak Publishing.

Gardner, J. N., & Van der Veer, G. (1998). *The senior year experience: Facilitating integration, reflection, closure, and transition.* San Francisco: Jossey-Bass.

Gardner, P., & Perry, A. L. (2012). Transitioning into the 21st century workplace: Will seniors be ready? In *The senior year: Culminating experiences and transitions* (pp. 135–154). Columbia: University of South Carolina, The National Resource Center for the First Year Experience and Students in Transition.

Garfinkel, H., & Tierney, J. F. (1957). Teaching note: A coordinating course in the political science major. *American Political Science Review*, *51*(4), 1178–1182. http://dx.doi.org/10.2307/1952481

Gnanapragasam, N. (2008). Industrially sponsored senior capstone experience: Program implementation and assessment. *Journal of Professional Issues in Engineering Education and Practice*, *134*(3), 257–262. http://dx.doi.org/10.1061/(ASCE)1052–3928(2008)134:3(257)

Goldstein, G., & Fernald, P. (2009). Humanistic education in a capstone course. *College Teaching*, *57*(1), 27–36. http://dx.doi.org/10.3200/CTCH.57.1.27–36

Gorman, M. F. (2010). The University of Dayton operations management capstone course: Undergraduate student field consulting applies theory to practice. *Interfaces*, *40*(6), 432–443. http://dx.doi.org/10.1287/inte.1100.0530

Grahe, J. E., Brandt, M. J., IJzerman, H., Cohoon, J., Aarts, A. A., Peng, C., . . . van Emden, R. (2014). *Collaborative Replications and Education Project (CREP).* https://osf.io/wfc6u/

Grahe, J. E., Guillaume, E., & Rudmann, J. (2014). Students collaborate to advance science: The International Situations Project. *CUR Quarterly-Online*, *34*(2), 4–9.

Grahe, J. E., & Hauhart, R. C. (2013). Describing typical capstone course experiences from a national random sample. *Teaching of Psychology*, *40*(4), 281–287. http://dx.doi.org/10.1177/0098628313501040

Grahe, J. E., Reifman, A., Hermann, A. D., Walker, M., Oleson, K. C., Nario-Redmond, M., & Wiebe, R. P. (2012). Harnessing the undiscovered resource of student research projects. *Perspectives on Psychological Science*, 7(6), 605–607. http://dx.doi.org/10.1177/1745691612459057

Griffith, D. A. (2008). Ethical considerations in geographic research: What especially graduate students need to know. *Ethics, Place and Environment*, 11(3), 237–252. http://dx.doi.org/10.1080/13668790802559650

Gruenther, K., Bailey, R., Wilson, J., Plucker, C., & Hashmi, H. (2009). The influence of prior industry experience and multidisciplinary teamwork on student design learning in a capstone design course. *Design Studies*, 30(6), 721–736. http://dx.doi.org/10.1016/j.destud.2009.06.001

Guillaume, E., & Funder, D. (2012). *Summary of the International Situations Project.* http://rap.ucr.edu/ISP.html

Hagen, B., Awosoga, O., Kellett, P., & Dei, S., O. (2013). Evaluation of undergraduate nursing students' attitudes towards statistics courses, before and after a course in applied statistics. *Nurse Education Today*, 33(9), 949–955. http://dx.doi.org/10.1016/j.nedt.2012.11.005

Harrison, A. M. (1994). A career-oriented capstone course for chemistry undergraduates. *Journal of Chemical Education*, 71(8), 659–660. http://dx.doi.org/10.1021/ed071p659

Hartmann, D. J. (1993). Program assessment in sociology: The case for the bachelor's paper. *Teaching Sociology*, 20(2), 253–254. http://dx.doi.org/10.2307/1317395

Hartmann, J. Q., Widner, S. C., & Carrick, C. (2013). Strong faculty relationship and academic motivation as potential outcomes of undergraduate research. *North American Journal of Psychology*, 15, 215–234.

Hathaway, D. K., & Atkinson, D. (2001). The senior seminar: Preparation for life after college. *Primus*, 11(4), 326–336. http://dx.doi.org/0.1080/10511970108984008

Hauhart, R. C., & Choi, C. C. (2012). The good faith exception to the exclusionary rule. *Criminal Law Bulletin*, 48(2), 316–346.

Hauhart, R. C., & Grahe, J. E. (2010). The undergraduate capstone course in the social sciences: Results from a regional survey. *Teaching Sociology*, 38(1), 4–17. http://dx.doi.org/10.1177/0092055X09353884

Hauhart, R. C., & Grahe, J. E. (2012). A national survey of American higher education capstone practices in sociology and psychology. *Teaching Sociology*, 40(3), 227–241. http://dx.doi.org/10.1177/0092055X12441715

Hay, E., Snowball, D., Varallo, S., Hilton-Morrow, W., & Klein, S. (2014). Research-methods modules: Preparing students for the capstone in communication studies. *CUR Quarterly*, 34, 6–10.

Healey, M. (2014). Integrating undergraduate research into the curriculum: International perspectives on capstones and final-year projects. *CUR Quarterly*, *34*(4), 26–32.

Healey, M., & Jenkins, A. (2009). *Developing undergraduate research and inquiry.* Heslington, York, England: Higher Education Academy.

Hefferan, K. P., Heywood, N. C., & Ritter, M. E. (2002). Integrating field trips and classroom learning into a capstone undergraduate research experience. *Journal of Geography*, *101*(5), 183–190. http://dx.doi.org /10.1080/00221340208978498

Heise, G. A. (1992). Bridging the gap: A seminar in psychology and public policy issues. *Teaching of Psychology*, *19*(4), 228–230. http://dx.doi .org/10.1207/s15328023top1904_8

Henscheid, J. M. (2012). Senior seminars and capstone courses. In M. S. Hunter, J. R. Keup, J. Kinzie, & H. Maietta (Eds.), *The senior year: Culminating experiences and transitions* (pp. 25–28). Columbia: National Resource Center for the First-Year Experience and Students in Transition, University of South Carolina.

Henscheid, J. M., & Barnicoat, L. R. (2003). Capstones in higher education. In J. W. Guthrie (Ed.), *Encyclopedia of Education* (Vol. 1, pp. 239–241). New York: Macmillan.

Henscheid, J. M., Breitmeyer, J. E., & Mercer, J. L. (2000). *Professing the disciplines: An analysis of senior seminars and capstone courses*. Columbia, SC: National Resource Center for the First-Year Experience and Students in Transition, University of South Carolina.

Herner-Patnode, L. M., & Lee, H.-J. (2009). A capstone experience for preservice teachers: Building a web-based portfolio. *Journal of Educational Technology and Society*, *12*(2), 101–110.

Hitchcott, N. (2006). Calixthe Beyala: Prizes, plagiarism, and "authenticity." *Research in African Literatures*, *37*(1), 100–109.

Hora, M. T., & Ferrare, J. J. (2013). Instructional systems of practice: A multidimensional analysis of math and science undergraduate course planning and classroom teaching. *Journal of the Learning Sciences*, *22*(2), 212–257. http://dx.doi.org/10.1080/10508406.2012.729767

Hummer, A. (1997). Measuring critical thinking outcomes via the capstone course paper. *Assessment Update*, *9*(3), 8–9.

Hunter, A., Laursen, S. L., & Seymour, E. (2008). Benefits of participating in undergraduate research in science: Comparing faculty and student perceptions. In R. Taraban & R. L. Blanton (Eds.), *Creating effective undergraduate research programs in science* (pp. 135–169). New York: Teachers College Press.

Ioannidis, J.P.A. (2005). Why most published research findings are false. *PLoS Medicine, 2*(8), 696–701.

Ishiyama, J. (2005). The structure of an undergraduate major and student learning: A cross-institutional study of political science programs at thirty-two colleges and universities. *Social Science Journal, 42*(3), 359–366. http://dx.doi.org/10.1016/j.soscij.2005.06.011

Ishiyama, J., & Breuning, M. (2004). A survey of international studies programs at liberal arts colleges and universities in the Midwest: Characteristics and correlates. *International Studies Perspectives, 5*(2), 134–146. http://dx.doi.org/10.1111/j.1528–3577.2004.00163.x

Ishiyama, J., & Breuning, M. (2008). Assessing assessment: Examining the assessment plans at 50 political science departments. *PS: Political Science and Politics, 41*(1), 167–170. http://dx.doi.org/10.1017/S104909650808
80220

Ishiyama, J., & Hartlaub, S. (2003). Sequential or flexible? The impact of differently structured political science majors on the development of student reasoning. *PS: Political Science and Politics, 36*(1), 83–86. http://dx.doi.org/10.1017/S1049096503001744

Jacobs, J. A. (2004). The faculty time divide. *Sociological Forum, 19*(1), 3–27. http://dx.doi.org/10.1023/B:SOFO.0000019646.82538.cc

Johari, A., & Bradshaw, A. C. (2008). Project-based learning in an internship program: A qualitative study of related roles and their motivational attributes. *Educational Technology Research and Development, 56*(3), 329–359. http://dx.doi.org/10.1007/s11423–006–9009–2

Johnson, G. F., & Halabi, A. K. (2011). The accounting undergraduate capstone: Promoting synthesis, reflection, transition, and competencies. *Journal of Education for Business, 86*(5), 266–273. http://dx.doi.org/10.1080/08832323.2010.514013

Johnson, R. L., McGuinness, C., McCorkendale, S. C., & Laney, M. A. (2007). Teaching program evaluation in the visual and performing arts. *American Journal of Evaluation, 28*(4), 546–557. http://dx.doi.org/10.1177/1098214007308156

Jones, K. N., & Haywick, D. W. (2010). Size doesn't matter: Designing undergraduate research projects on the basis of student ability and availability. *Abstracts with Programs—Geological Society of America, 42*(1), 75–75.

Jones, K. W., Barrow, M. V., Stephens, R. P., & O'Hara, S. (2012). Romancing the capstone: National trends, local practice, and student motivation in the history curriculum. *Journal of American History, 98*(4), 1095–1113. http://dx.doi.org/10.1093/jahist/jar538

Juma, N. M., Gire, E., Corwin, K., Washburn, B., & Rebello, N. S. (2010). Students' and instructor's impressions of ill-structured capstone projects in an advanced electronics lab. *AIP Conference Proceedings*, *1289*(1), 181–184. http://dx.doi.org/10.1063/1.3515193

Karukstis, K. K. (2004). Creating time for research: Recommendations from faculty at predominantly undergraduate institutions. *Journal of Chemical Education*, *81*(11), 1550–1551. http://dx.doi.org/10.1021/ed081p1550

Karukstis, K. K. (2010). Multiple approaches to transformative research. In K. K. Karukstis & N. H. Hensel (Eds.), *Transformative research at predominately undergraduate institutions* (pp. 21–34). Washington, DC: Council on Undergraduate Research.

Karukstis, K. K., & Hensel, N. H. (2010). *Transformative research at predominately undergraduate institutions*. Washington, DC: Council on Undergraduate Research.

Kelly, M., & Klunk, B. E. (2003). Learning assessment in political science departments: Survey results. *PS: Political Science and Politics*, *36*(3), 451–455.

Kenny, R. W., Boyer Commission on Educating Undergraduates in the Research University, & Carnegie Foundation for the Advancement of Teaching. (1998). *Reinventing undergraduate education: A blueprint for America's research universities*. Stony Brook: State University of New York at Stony Brook.

Keogh, K., Sterling, L., & Venables, A. (2007). A scalable and portable structure for conducting successful year-long undergraduate software team projects. *Journal of Information Technology Education*, *6*, 515–540.

Kerrigan, S., & Jhaj, S. (2007). Assessing general education capstone courses: An in-depth look at a nationally recognized capstone assessment mode. *Peer Review*, *9*(2), 13–16.

Kindelan, N. (2010). Demystifying experiential learning in the performing arts. *New Directions for Teaching and Learning*, *124*, 31–37. http://dx.doi.org/10.1002/tl.418

King, P. M., & Kitchener, K. S. (1994). *Developing reflective judgment: Understanding and promoting intellectual growth and critical thinking in adolescents and adults*. San Francisco: Jossey-Bass.

Kinzie, J. (2012). Optimizing high-impact practices in the senior year. In M. S. Hunter, J. R. Keup, J. Kinzie, & H. Maietta (Eds.), *The senior year: Culminating experiences and transitions* (pp. 25–28). Columbia: National Resource Center for the First-Year Experience and Students in Transition, University of South Carolina.

Klos, N. Y., Shanahan, J. O., & Young, G. (2011). *Creative inquiry in the arts and humanities: Models of undergraduate research.* Washington, DC: Council for Undergraduate Research.

Kochen, M., & Badre, A. N. (1974). Questions and shifts of representation in problem solving. *American Journal of Psychology, 87*(3), 369–383. http://dx.doi.org/10.2307/1421379

Kuh, G. D. (2008). Why integration and engagement are essential to effective educational practice in the twenty-first century. *Peer Review, 10*(4), 27–28.

Kuh, G. D., Kinzie, J., Schuh, J. H., Whitt, E. J., & Associates. (2005). *Student success in college: Creating conditions that matter.* San Francisco: Jossey-Bass.

Landrum, R. E. (2012). *Undergraduate writing in psychology: Learning to tell the scientific story.* Washington, DC: American Psychological Association.

Langford, J. (2014). Antiquity for undergraduate researchers. In I. Crawford, S. Orel, & J. O. Shanahan (Eds.), *Initiating and sustaining research and creative inquiry in undergraduate education: A practical guide for faculty in the arts and humanities* (pp. 12–22). Washington, DC: Council for Undergraduate Research.

Lee, M. A. (2012). Teaching strategic management: Moving from case analysis to applied research. *Review of Business Research, 12*(2), 69–77.

Levia, D. F., Jr., & Quiring, S. M. (2008). Assessment of student learning in a hybrid PBL capstone seminar. *Journal of Geography in Higher Education, 32*(2), 217–231. http://dx.doi.org/10.1080/03098260701514041

Levine, A. (1998). A president's personal and historical perspective. In J. N. Gardner & G. Van der Veer (Eds.), *The senior year experience: Facilitating integration, reflection, closure, and transition* (pp. 51–58). San Francisco: Jossey-Bass.

Levine, A., & Carnegie Council on Policy Studies in Higher Education. (1978). *Handbook on undergraduate curriculum.* San Francisco: Jossey-Bass.

Levy, P. (2009). *Inquiry-based learning: A conceptual framework (version 4).* Sheffield: Centre for Inquiry-Based Learning in the Arts and Social Sciences, University of Sheffield.

Li, L. Y., & Vandermensbrugghe, J. (2011). Supporting the thesis writing process of international research students through an ongoing writing group. *Innovations in Education and Teaching International, 48*(2), 195–205. http://dx.doi.org/10.1080/14703297.2011.564014

Lightfoot, T., Sand, A., & Wilbur, W. (2014). Visual arts departments as sites of undergraduate research. In I. Crawford, S. Orel, & J. O. Shanahan (Eds.), *Initiating and sustaining research and creative inquiry in undergraduate education: A practical guide for faculty in the arts and humanities* (pp. 61–68). Washington, DC: Council for Undergraduate Research.

Lipson, C. (2005). *How to write a BA thesis*. Chicago: University of Chicago Press.

Locks, A. M., & Gregerman, S. R. (2008). Undergraduate research as an institutional retention strategy: The University of Michigan model. In R. Taraban & R. L. Blanton (Eds.), *Creating effective undergraduate research programs in science: The transformation from student to scientist* (pp. 53–80). New York: Teachers College Press.

Lopatto, D. (2008). Exploring the benefits of undergraduate research experiences: The SURE survey. In R. Taraban & R. L. Blanton (Eds.), *Creating effective undergraduate research programs in science* (pp. 112–132). New York: Teachers College Press.

Lucas, C. (2006). *American higher education: A history*. New York: Palgrave.

Maki, P. (2004). *Assessing for learning: Building a sustainable commitment across the institution*. Sterling, VA: Stylus.

Mancha, R., & Yoder, C. Y. (2014). Factors critical to successful undergraduate research. *CUR Quarterly, 34*, 38–45.

Masiello, L., & Skipper, T. L. (2013). *Writing in the senior capstone: Theory and practice*. Columbia: University of South Carolina National Resource Center for the First-Year Experience and Students in Transition.

Mastrangeli, J. (2001). Practice makes almost perfect: A seminar experience. *Primus, 11*(4), 337–346. http://dx.doi.org/10.1080/1051197010 8984009

Matthews, V. H., & Catau, J. C. (2001). Reshaping general education for the twenty-first century: The interdisciplinary capstone class at Southwest Missouri State University. *Journal of Public Affairs, 5*, 79–94.

McDaniels, P.E.W. (2009). Adjusting the mark: Utilizing a portfolio assessment tool in the English capstone course. *Researcher: An Interdisciplinary Journal, 22*(4), 1–19.

McGaw, D., & Weschler, L. (1999). Romancing the capstone: The jewel of public value. *Journal of Public Affairs Education, 5*(2), 89–105.

McGoldrick, K. (2008). Writing requirements and economic research opportunities in the undergraduate curriculum: Results from a survey of departmental practices. *Journal of Economic Education, 39*(3), 287–296. http://dx.doi.org/10.3200/JECE.39.3.287–296

McKinney, K., & Busher, M. (2011). The sociology research experience capstone course at three institutions. *Teaching Sociology, 39*(3), 290–302. http://dx.doi.org/10.1177/0092055X11407349

McKinney, K., & Day, M. D. (2012). A multi-institutional study of students' perceptions and experiences in the research-based capstone course in sociology. *Teaching Sociology, 40*(2), 142–157. http://dx.doi.org/10.1177/0092055X12437970

McNair, T. B., & Albertine, S. (2012). Seeking high-quality, high-impact learning: The imperative of faculty development and curricular intentionality. *Peer Review, 14*(3), 4–5.

McNary-Zak, B., & Peters, R. T. (2014). Developing undergraduate research in religious studies: Thinking across the curriculum. In I. Crawford, S. Orel, & J. O. Shanahan (Eds.), *Initiating and sustaining research and creative inquiry in undergraduate education: A practical guide for faculty in the arts and humanities* (pp. 42–51). Washington, DC: Council for Undergraduate Research.

Merkel, C. A. (2003). Undergraduate research at the research universities. *New Directions for Teaching and Learning, 93*, 39–53.

Metz, T. (2010). A dilemma regarding academic freedom and public accountability in higher education. *Journal of Philosophy of Education, 44*(4), 529–549. http://dx.doi.org/10.1111/j.1467–9752.2010.00776.x

Milar, K. S. (1987). History of psychology: Cornerstone instead of capstone. *Teaching of Psychology, 14*(4), 236–238. http://dx.doi.org/10.1207/s15328023top1404_14

Morgan, B. L., & Johnson, E. J. (1997). Using a senior seminar for assessing the major. *Teaching of Psychology, 24*(3), 156–159. http://dx.doi.org/10.1207/s15328023top2403_1

National Research Council. (2003). *Bio 2010: Transforming undergraduate education for future research biologists.* Washington, DC: National Academies Press.

National Science Board. (2007). *Enhancing support of transformative research at the National Science Foundation.* Task Force on Transformative Research. http://www.nsf.gov/pubs/2007/nsb0732/nsb0732.pdf

Nauta, M. M. (2002). A career research project for undergraduate psychology students. *Teaching of Psychology, 29*(4), 288–291. http://dx.doi.org/10.1207/S15328023TOP2904_06

Nielson, M. (2012). *Reinventing discovery: The new era of networked science.* Princeton, NJ: Princeton University Press.

Nosek, B. A., & Bar-Anan, Y. (2012). Scientific utopia: I. Opening scientific communication. *Psychological Inquiry, 23*(3), 217–243. http://dx.doi.org/10.1080/1047840X.2012.692215

Nosek, B. A., Spies, J. R., & Motyl, M. (2012). Scientific utopia: II. Restructuring incentives and practices to promote truth over publishability. *Perspectives on Psychological Science*, *7*(6), 615–631. http://dx.doi .org/10.1177/1745691612459058

Obringer, J. W., & Kent, J. S. (1998). The senior biology seminar—a capstone course. *Journal of College Science Teaching*, *27*(4), 263–266.

Oh, D. M., Kim, J. M., Garcia, R. E., & Krilowicz, B. L. (2005). Valid and reliable authentic assessment of culminating student performance in the biomedical sciences. *Advances in Physiology Education*, *29*(1–4), 83–93. http://dx.doi.org/10.1152/advan.00039.2004

Olwell, R., & Delph, R. (2004). Implementing assessment and improving undergraduate writing: One department's experience. *History Teacher*, *38*(1), 21–34.

O'Rourke, K. (2007). An historical perspective on meta-analysis: Dealing quantitatively with varying study results. *Journal of the Royal Society of Medicine*, *100*(12), 579–582. http://dx.doi.org/10.1258/jrsm.100 .12.579

Orsmond, P., Merry, S., & Reiling, K. (1996). The importance of marking criteria in the use of peer assessment. *Assessment and Evaluation in Higher Education*, *21*(3), 239–250. http://dx.doi.org/10.1080/02602939602 10304

Padgett, R. D., & Kilgo, C. A. (2012). *2011 National Survey of Senior Capstone Experiences: Institutional-level data on the culminating experience*. Columbia: National Resource Center for the First-Year Experience and Students in Transition, University of South Carolina.

Parker, S. L., Jimmieson, N. L., & Amiot, C. E. (2013). Self-determination, control, and reactions to changes in workload: A work simulation. *Journal of Occupational Health Psychology*, *18*(2), 173–190. http://dx .doi.org/10.1037/a0031803

Pascual, R. (2010). Enhancing project-oriented learning by joining communities of practice and opening spaces for relatedness. *European Journal of Engineering Education*, *35*(1), 3–16. http://dx.doi.org/10.1080/0304 3790902989234

Pashler, H., & Wagenmakers, E. (2012). Editors' introduction to the special section on replicability in psychological science: A crisis of confidence? *Perspectives on Psychological Science*, *7*(6), 528–530. http:// dx.doi.org/10.1177/1745691612465253

Payne, S. L., Flynn, J., & Whitfield, J. M. (2008). Capstone business course assessment: Exploring student readiness perspectives. *Journal of Education for Business*, *83*(3), 141–146. http://dx.doi.org/10.3200/JOEB.83.3 .141–146

Peat, B. (2006). Integrating writing and research skills: Development and testing of a rubric to measure student outcomes. *Journal of Public Affairs Education*, *12*(3), 295–311.

Pergram, D. M. (2006). "What if?" Teaching research and creative-thinking skills through proposal writing. *English Journal*, *95*, 18–22.

Perlman, B., & McCann, L. I. (1999a). The most frequently listed course in the undergraduate psychology curriculum. *Teaching of Psychology*, *26*(3), 177–182.

Perlman, B. & McCann, L. I. (1999b). The structure of the psychology undergraduate curriculum. *Teaching of Psychology*, *26*(3), 171–777.

Perlman, B., & McCann, L. I. (2005). Undergraduate research experiences in psychology: A national study of courses and curricula. *Teaching of Psychology*, *32*(1), 5–14.

Persons, O. S. (1998). Factors influencing students' peer evaluation in cooperative learning. *Journal of Education for Business*, *73*(4), 225–229. http://dx.doi.org/10.1080/08832329809601635

Peterson, C. D., Anderson, L. L., & Michtom, W. D. (1996). Applications of undergraduate research proposals in general-education earth-science courses. *Journal of Geoscience Education*, *44*(2), 197–201.

Peterson, S. M., Phillips, A., Bacon, S. I., & Machunda, Z. (2011). Teaching evidence-based practice at the BSW level: An effective capstone project. *Journal of Social Work Education*, *47*(3), 509–524. http://dx.doi .org/10.5175/JSWE.2011.200900129

Pierce, P. (2004). The great Shakespeare fraud. *History Today*, *54*(5), 4–5.

Plionis, E. M., Thompson, M., & Eisenhower, C. (2005). The scholarship crash on the Internet highway: Implications for faculty-librarian collaboration. *Journal of Baccalaureate Social Work*, *11*(1), 101–114.

Posnick, M. (2014). A capstone experience: From research to performance. *CUR Quarterly*, *34*(4), 11–17.

Puca, R. M., & Schmalt, H. D. (1999). Task enjoyment: A mediator between achievement motives and performance. *Motivation and Emotion*, *23*(1), 15–29.

Pyrczak, F. (1999). *Evaluating research in academic journals: A practical guide to realistic evaluation*. Los Angeles: Pyrczak.

Ramirez, J. J., & Dickson, S. R. (2010). Promoting supportive environments for transformative research at predominantly undergraduate institutions. In K. K. Karukstis & N. H. Hensel (Eds.), *Transformative research at predominately undergraduate institutions* (pp. 13–21). Washington, DC: Council on Undergraduate Research.

Ramsden, P. (2003). *Learning to teach in higher education*. London: Routledge.

Reid, M., & Miller, W. (1997). Bridging theory and administrative practice: The role of a capstone course in P.A. programs. *International Journal of Public Administration, 20*(10), 1769–1789. http://dx.doi .org/10.1080/01900699708525274

Resner, A., Jr., (2011). Using portfolios to demonstrate theological competencies: The capstone course in the MDiv program at Hood Theological Seminary. *Teaching Theology and Religion, 14*(4), 386–388. http://dx.doi.org/10.1111/j.1467–9647.2011.00743.x

Reuse-Durham, N. (2005). Peer evaluation as an active learning technique. *Journal of Instructional Psychology, 32*(4), 338–343.

Reynolds, J., Smith, R., Moskovitz, C., & Sayle, A. (2009). BioTAP: A systematic approach to teaching scientific writing and evaluating undergraduate theses. *BioScience, 59*(10), 896–903. http://dx.doi.org/10 .1525/bio.2009.59.10.11

Rhodes, T. L., & Agre-Kippenhan, S. (2004). A multiplicity of learning: Capstones at Portland State University. *Assessment Update, 16*(1), 4–5.

Riehle, C. F., & Weiner, S. A. (2013). High-impact educational practices: An exploration of the role of information literacy. *College and Undergraduate Libraries, 20*(2), 127–143. http://dx.doi.org/10.1080/10691316.2013 .789658

Roberts, G. E., & Pavlak, T. (2002). Designing the MPA capstone course: A structured-flexibility approach. *Journal of Public Affairs Education, 8*(3), 179–191.

Rodrick, R., & Dickmeyer, L. (2002). Providing undergraduate research opportunities for communication students: A curricular approach. *Communication Education, 51*(1), 40–50. http://dx.doi.org/0.1080/036345 20216496

Roens, S., & Young, G. (2014). Undergraduate research in music. In I. Crawford, S. Orel, & J. O. Shanahan (Eds.), *Initiating and sustaining research and creative inquiry in undergraduate education: A practical guide for faculty in the arts and humanities* (pp. 69–73). Washington, DC: Council for Undergraduate Research.

Roethlisberger, F. J., Wright, H. A., Dickson, W. J., & Western Electric Company. (1939). *Management and the worker: An account of a research program conducted by the Western Electric Company, Hawthorne Works, Chicago*. Cambridge, MA: Harvard University Press.

Roscoe, L. J., & Strapp, C. M. (2009). Increasing psychology students' satisfaction with preparedness through a professional issues course. *Teaching of Psychology, 36*(1), 18–23. http://dx.doi.org/10.1080/009862808025 29426

Rowland, S. L., Lawrie, G. A., Behrendorff, J.B.Y.H., & Gillam, E.M.J. (2012). Is the undergraduate research experience (URE) always best? The power of choice in a bifurcated practical stream for a large introductory biochemistry class. *Biochemistry and Molecular Biology Education, 40*(1), 46–62. http://dx.doi.org/10.1002/bmb.20576

Rowles, C. J., Koch, D. C., Hundley, S. P., & Hamilton, S. J. (2004). Toward a model for capstone experiences: Mountaintops, magnets, and mandates. *Assessment Update, 16*(1), 1–15.

Russell, S. H. (2008). Undergraduate research opportunities: Facilitating and encouraging the transition from student to scientist. In R. Taraban & R. L. Blanton (Eds.), *Creating effective undergraduate research programs in science: The transformation from student to scientist* (pp. 53–80). New York: Teachers College Press.

Russell, S. H., Hancock, M. P., & McCullough, J. (2007). Benefits of undergraduate research experiences. *Science, 316*(5824), 548–549. http://dx.doi.org/10.1126/science.1140384

Saey, T. H. (2012). Most retractions not honest errors. *Science News, 182*(10), 13–13. http://dx.doi.org/10.1002/scin.5591821014

Sax, L. J., & Astin, A. W. (1998). Developing "civic virtue" among college students. In J. N. Gardner & G. Van der Veer (Eds.), *The senior year experience: Facilitating integration, reflection, closure, and transition* (pp. 133–150). San Francisco: Jossey-Bass.

Schachter, D. R., & Schwartz, D. (2009). The value of capstone projects to participating client agencies. *Journal of Public Affairs Education, 15*(4), 445–461.

Schermer, T., & Gray, S. (2012). *The senior capstone: Transformative experiences in the liberal arts*. New York: Teagle Foundation.

Schmid, T. J. (1993). Bringing sociology to life: The other capstone mandate. *Teaching Sociology, 21*(3), 219–222. http://dx.doi.org/10.2307 /1319013

School Spirit Study Group. (2004). Measuring school spirit: A national teaching exercise. *Teaching of Psychology, 31*(1), 18–21.

Schrecker, E. (2009). Subversives, squeaky wheels, and "special obligations": Threats to academic freedom, 1890–1960. *Social Research*, *76*(2), 513.

Schrecker, E. (2012). Academic freedom in the corporate university. *Radical Teacher*, *93*, 38–45. http://dx.doi.org/10.5406/radicalteacher.93.0038

Schroeder, M. J., Kottsick, A., Lee, J., Newell, M., Purcell, J., & Nelson, R. M. (2009). Experiential learning of electromagnetic concepts through designing, building and calibrating a broad-spectrum suite of sensors in a capstone course. *International Journal of Electrical Engineering Education*, *46*(2), 198–210. http://dx.doi.org/10.7227/IJEEE.46.2.7

Schuurman, S., Berlin, S., Langlois, J., & Guevara, J. (2012). Mission accomplished! The development of a competence-based e-portfolio assessment model. *Assessment Update*, *24*(2), 1–14.

Scott, J. T., & Orel, S. (2014). A better kind of history scaffolding: Teaching research in history studies. In I. Crawford, S. Orel, & J. O. Shanahan (Eds.), *Initiating and sustaining research and creative inquiry in undergraduate education: A practical guide for faculty in the arts and humanities* (pp. 32–41). Washington, DC: Council for Undergraduate Research.

Seo, E. H. (2013). A comparison of active and passive procrastination in relation to academic motivation. *Social Behavior & Personality: An International Journal*, *41*(5), 777–786. http://dx.doi.org/10.2224/sbp.2013.41.5.777

Seymour, E., Hunter, A.-B., Laursen, S. L., & DeAntoni, T. (2004). Establishing the benefits of research experiences for undergraduates in the sciences: First findings from a three-year study. *Science Education*, *88*(4), 493–534. http://dx.doi.org/10.1002/sce.10131

Shaffer, C. D., Alverez, C., Bailey, C., Barnard, D., Bhalla, S., Chandrasekaran, C., . . . Elgin, S.C.R. (2010). The genomics education partnership: Successful integration of research into laboratory classes at a diverse group of undergraduate institutions. *CBE—Life Sciences Education*, *9*(1), 55–69. http://dx.doi.org/10.1187/09–11–0087

Sharma, M. P. (1997). Task procrastination and its determinants. *Indian Journal of Industrial Relations*, *33*(1), 17–33. http://dx.doi.org/10.2307/27767509

Sharobeam, M. H., & Howard, K. (2002). Teaching demands versus research productivity. *Journal of College Science Teaching*, *31*(7), 436–441.

Sherohman, J. (1997). Implementing "study in depth" at St. Cloud State University. *Teaching Sociology*, *25*(2), 160–167. http://dx.doi.org/10.2307/1318661

Siegfried, J. J. (1991). The economics major: Can and should we do better than a B minus? *American Economic Review, 81*(2), 20–25.

Siegfried, J. J. (2001). Principles for a successful undergraduate economics honors program. *Journal of Economic Education, 32*(2), 169–177. http://dx.doi.org/10.1080/00220480109595182

Siegfried, J. J., Bartlett, R. C., Hansen, W. L., Kelley, A. C., McCloskey, D. N., & Tietenberg, T. H. (1991). The status and prospects of the economics major. *Journal of Economic Education, 22*(3), 197–224.

Siegfried, J. J., & Wilkinson, J. T. (1982). The economics curriculum in the United States: 1980. *American Economic Review, 72*(2), 125–138.

Sill, D., Harward, B. M., & Cooper, I. (2009). The disorienting dilemma: The senior capstone as a transformative experience. *Liberal Education, 95*(3), 50–55.

Skipper, T. L. (2012). The kids are alright: Emerging adulthood and the transition out of college. In M. S. Hunter, J. R. Keup, J. Kinzie, & H. Maietta (Eds.), *The senior year: Culminating experiences and transitions* (pp. 25–48). Columbia: National Resource Center for the First-Year Experience and Students in Transition, University of South Carolina.

Smith, W. L. (1993). The capstone course at Loras College. *Teaching Sociology, 21*(3), 250–252. http://dx.doi.org/10.2307/1319021

Spalter-Roth, R. M., Erskine, W. B., & Research Program on the Profession and the Discipline (American Sociological Association). (2003). *How does your department compare? A peer analysis from the AY 2001–2002 survey of baccalaureate and graduate programs in sociology.* Washington, DC: American Sociological Association.

Stark, J. S., Lowther, M. A., Ryan, M. P., & Genthon, M. (1988). Faculty reflect on course planning. *Research in Higher Education, 29*(3), 219–240. http://dx.doi.org/10.1007/BF00992924

Starke, M. C. (1985). A research practicum: Undergraduates as assistants in psychological research. *Teaching of Psychology, 12*(3), 158–160. doi:10.1207/s15328023top1203_12

Steele, J. L. (1993). The laden cart: The senior capstone course. *Teaching Sociology, 21*(3), 242–245. http://dx.doi.org/10.2307/1319019

Stephens, R. P., Jones, K. W., & Barrow, M. V. (2011). The book project: Engaging history majors in undergraduate research. *History Teacher, 45*(1), 65–80.

Stoloff, M., McCarthy, M., Keller, L., Varfolomeeva, V., Lynch, J., Makara, K., . . . Smiley, W. (2010). The undergraduate psychology major: An examination of structure and sequence. *Teaching of Psychology, 37*(1), 4–15. http://dx.doi.org/10.1080/00986280903426274

Sullivan, B., & Thomas, S. (2007). Documenting student learning outcomes through a research intensive senior capstone experience: Bring the data together to demonstrate progress. *North American Journal of Psychology, 9*, 321–330.

Sum, P. E., & Light, S. A. (2010). Assessing student learning outcomes and documenting success through a capstone course. *PS: Political Science and Politics, 43*(3), 523–531. http://dx.doi.org/10.1017/S104909651000764

Svinicki, M. D. (2004). *Learning and motivation in the postsecondary classroom.* San Francisco: Jossey-Bass/Anker.

Swift, J. (2014). The English department as the site of undergraduate research: Creating learners, training professionals. In I. Crawford, S. Orel, & J. O. Shanahan (Eds.), *Initiating and sustaining research and creative inquiry in undergraduate education: A practical guide for faculty in the arts and humanities* (pp. 32–41). Washington, DC: Council for Undergraduate Research.

Tappert, C. C., & Stix, A. (2010). The trend toward online project-oriented capstone courses. *Computers in the Schools, 27*(3–4), 200–220. http://dx.doi.org/10.1080/07380569.2010.523882

Taraban, R., & Blanton, R. L. (Eds.). (2008). *Creating effective undergraduate research programs in science: The transformation from student to scientist.* New York: Teachers College Press.

Taraban, R., & Logue, E. (2012). Academic factors that affect undergraduate research experiences. *Journal of Educational Psychology, 104*(2), 499–514. http://dx.doi.org/10.1037/a0026851

Testa, A. M. (2008). Assessment of student learning through an online, competency-based university. *Assessment Update, 20*(1), 1–2.

Thambyah, A. (2011). On the design of learning outcomes for the undergraduate engineer's final year project. *European Journal of Engineering Education, 36*(1), 35–46. http://dx.doi.org/10.1080/03043797.2010.528559

Thelin, J. R. (2011). *A history of American higher education* (2nd ed.). Baltimore, MD: Johns Hopkins University Press.

Thomas, D. R., & Hodges, I. D. (2010). *Designing and managing your research project: Core knowledge for social and health researchers.* Thousand Oaks, CA: Sage.

Tice, D. M., & Baumeister, R. F. (1997). Longitudinal study of procrastination, performance, stress, and health: The costs and benefits of dawdling. *Psychological Science, 8*(6), 454–458. http://dx.doi.org/10.1111/j.1467-9280.1997.tb00460.x

Tickles, V. C., Yadong Li, & Walters, W. L. (2013). Integrating cost engineering and project management in a junior engineering economics course and a senior capstone project design course. *College Student Journal, 47*(2), 244–263.

Tiemann, K. A. (1993). On making the center hold. *Teaching Sociology, 21*(3), 257–258. http://dx.doi.org/10.2307/1319024

Todd, R. H., & Magleby, S. P. (2005). Elements of a successful capstone course considering the needs of stakeholders. *European Journal of Engineering Education, 30*(2), 203–214. http://dx.doi.org/10.1080/0304379 0500087332

Trosset, C., Lopatto, D., & Elgin, S. (2008). Implementation and assessment of course-embedded undergraduate research experiences: Some explorations. In R. Taraban & R. L. Blanton (Eds.), *Creating effective undergraduate research programs in science: The transformation from student to scientist* (pp. 33–49). New York: Teachers College Press.

Troyer, R. J. (1993). Comments on the capstone course. *Teaching Sociology, 21*(3), 246–249. http://dx.doi.org/10.2307/1319020

Upson-Saia, K. (2013). The capstone experience for the religious studies major. *Teaching Theology and Religion, 16*(1), 3–17. http://dx.doi.org/10 .1111/teth.12001

Van Acker, L., & Bailey, J. (2011). Embedding graduate skills in capstone courses. *Asian Social Science, 7*(4), 69–76.

Vander Schee, B. A. (2011). Let them decide: Student performance and self-selection of weights distribution. *Journal of Education for Business, 86*(6), 352–356. http://dx.doi.org/10.1080/08832323.2010.540047

Wagenaar, T. C. (1991). Goals for the discipline? *Teaching Sociology, 19*(1), 92–95. http://dx.doi.org/10.2307/1317582

Wagenaar, T. C. (1993). The capstone course. *Teaching Sociology, 21*(3), 209–214. http://dx.doi.org/10.2307/1319011

Wagenaar, T. C. (2002). Outcomes assessment in sociology: Prevalence and impact. *Teaching Sociology, 30*(4), 403–413. http://dx.doi.org/10.2307 /3211501

Wallace, R. C. (1988). A capstone course in applied sociology. *Teaching Sociology, 16*(1), 34–40. http://dx.doi.org/10.2307/1317689

Wang, X., & Hurley, S. (2012). Assessment as a scholarly activity? Faculty perceptions of and willingness to engage in student learning assessment. *Journal of General Education, 61*(1), 1–15. http://dx.doi .org/10.1353/jge.2012.0005

Wattendorf, J. M. (1993). The sociology capstone course in a professional school. *Teaching Sociology, 21*(3), 229–232. http://dx.doi.org/10.2307/1319016

Webber, K. L. (2012). The use of learner-centered assessment in US colleges and universities. *Research in Higher Education, 53*(2), 201–228.

Webber-Bauer, K., & Bennett, J. S. (2003). Evaluation of the undergraduate research program at the University of Delaware: A multifaceted design. In R. Taraban & R. L. Blanton (Eds.), *Creating effective undergraduate research programs in science* (pp. 81–111). New York: Teachers College Press.

Weimer, M. (2002). *Learner-centered teaching: Five key changes to practice.* San Francisco: Jossey-Bass.

Weis, R. (2004). Using an undergraduate human-service practicum to promote unified psychology. *Teaching of Psychology, 31*(1), 43–46.

Weiss, G. L., Crosbey, J. R., Habel, S. K., Hanson, C. M., & Larsen, C. (2002). Improving the assessment of student learning: Advancing a research agenda in sociology. *Teaching Sociology, 30*(1), 63–79.

Withers, G., & Detweiler-Bedell, J. (2010). Using transformative research to enrich science curricula and enhance experiential learning. In K. K. Karukstis & N. H. Hensel (Eds.), *Transformative research at predominately undergraduate institutions* (pp. 35–46). Washington, DC: Council on Undergraduate Research.

Woodard, R. J. (2011). K. Anders Ericsson's theory of deliberate practice for expert performance in the senior capstone course. *Teaching Theology and Religion, 14*(4), 382–383. http://dx.doi.org/10.1111/j.1467–9647.2011.00741.x

Wright, B. D. (2005). The way to a faculty member's head is through the discipline. *Assessment Update, 17*(3), 1–2.

NAME INDEX

A

Agre-Kippenhan, S., 170, 175–177
Albertine, S., 104, 105
Allard, S. W., 105
Amiot, C. E., 82
Andersen, H., 213n1
Anderson, L., 154
Anderson, L. L., 74–75
Angelo, T. A., 184
Arnett, J. J., 150
Astin, A. W., 191, 192
Atchison, P., 22–23, 24, 25
Atkinson, D., 46
Auchincloss, L., 96
Ault, R. L., x
Awosoga, O., 65

B

Badger, K., 151, 152–153
Badre, A. N., 142
Bailey, J., 109
Bailey, R., 171
Banta, T., 213n1
Bar-Anan, Y., 94

Barnicoat, L. R., 2, 3
Barrow, M. V., 4–5, 43, 73, 107, 138, 160
Barry, B. E., 76, 121, 128, 207n5
Bauer, K. W., 6, 62, 69
Baumeister, R. F., 149
Behrendorff, J.B.Y.H., 62, 97
Bell-Hanson, J., 46–47
Bennett, J. S., 6, 62, 69, 70, 82, 206n4
Benton-Kupper, J., 171, 178
Berheide, C. W., 168, 170, 183, 184, 189, 190
Berkson, J., 45–46, 121
Berlin, S., 120
Biggs, T., 212n1
Blanton, R. L., 65, 206n2
Blattner, N. H., 177–178
Bos, A. L., 93, 113–114, 126
Bowman, J. S., 126
Boysen, G. A., x
Bradshaw, A. C., 157
Breitmeyer, J. E., xii, 2, 6, 32–33, 40, 114
Breuning, M., 46, 182, 183–184
Briggs, C. L., 139
Brinthaupt, T. M., 140

Bromwich, D., 169
Brooks, R., 171, 178
Brown, G., 213n1
Brown, J. N., 43, 45, 46
Brownell, J. E., 62, 64, 66, 67, 110
Bull, J., 213n1
Bullock, D., 76, 121, 207n5
Burnette, J. M., III, 76, 80, 207n5
Burns, D., 209n1
Busher, M., 8, 146, 189

C

Campbell, D. A., 105, 180–181
Campbell, H., 76
Carlson, J., 178
Carlson, J. L., 111, 121, 124, 125, 131, 139–140, 147
Carlson, M., 120
Carrick, C., 68
Carter, J. L., 4
Catalano, G. D., 107–108
Catau, J. C., 178
Catchings, B., 168, 170, 175, 183
Cavanagh, S. T., 66
Chamely-Wilk, D., 65
Cheesman, I., 205n1

Cheesman, K., 205n1
Chickering, A.W., 150, 212n1
Chin, J., 168
Choi, C. C., 73, 121–122, 162, 212n5
Choi, I., 141–142
Christ, W. G., 47, 170
Clinkenbeard, P. R., 158, 159
Clinton, H. R., 211n5, 212n2 (chap. 7)
Cohn, R. L., 111, 121, 139–140
Cooper, H., 74
Cooper, I., 12, 45, 47–48
Corley, C. R., 46, 64, 65, 97–98, 102
Corsaro, W. A., 142
Cortes, B. S., 170
Covington, M. V., 147
Crawford, I., 46, 47, 63, 66
Crosbey, J. R., 168
Cross, K. P., 184
Cummings, R., 169, 213n1
Curry, R., 184
Cuseo, J. B., 30–32, 35, 41
Cutucache, C. E., 99

D

Davies, P., 153
Davis, J. C., 64, 65–66, 67, 206n3
Davis, N. J., 18, 19–20
Day, M. D., 111, 125, 140, 144–145, 147
DeAntoni, T., 6–7, 64
Dei, S. O., 65
Delph, R., 132
Detweiler-Bedell, J., 211n5
Dickinson, J., 4, 26–27
Dickmeyer, L., 64, 79, 134
Dickson, S. R., 80
Dickson, W. J., 148
Dougherty, J. U., 158, 181
Drnevich, V. P., 76, 121, 207n5
Durant, R. R., 172–173
Durel, R. J., 20–22, 163
Durso, F. T., 157–158

E

Eder, D. J., 178–179
Eichenberger, R., 209n1
Eisenbach, R., 184

Eisenhower, C., 155
Elgin, S., 97
Elrod, S., 67
Erskine, W. B., 183

F

Fanelli, D., 91–92
Fernald, C. D., 157
Fernald, P., 121
Fernandez, N. P., 178
Ferrare, J. J., 109
Fletcher, R. B., 213n1
Flint, W., 25–26
Flood, L., 139
Flores, J., 122
Flynn, J., 146–147
Franchetti, M., 128, 133
Frank, M. C., 102
Frazier, C. L., 177–178
Freedman, S. M., 82
French, D., 205n1
Frey, B. S., 209n1
Frey, R. L., 209n1
Funder, D., 98–99

G

Galle, J., 178
Galle, J. K., 178
Galvan, J. L., 73
Gamson, Z., 212n1
Garcia, R. E., 75
Gardner, J. N., 4, 191
Gardner, P., 172
Garfield, J. A., 2
Garfinkel, H., 3
Genthon, M., 104
Gillam, E.M.J., 62, 97
Gnanapragasam, N., 174, 175
Goldstein, G., 121
Golich, V., 184
Gorman, M. F., 105
Grahe, J. E., xii, xiv, xv, xvii, 7–8, 13, 15, 25, 33, 37, 40, 42, 43–44, 45, 48, 50, 51, 52, 53, 55, 56–57, 76, 92, 98–99, 102, 116, 119, 123, 124, 125, 130, 135, 144, 178, 182, 184–185, 192
Gray, S., x, xi, xii, xiii, 7, 11, 34, 37, 40, 42, 49, 52, 54,

55–56, 57, 58, 87, 93, 113, 118, 124, 134, 135, 185, 186, 204n6
Gregerman, S. R., 77
Griffith, D. A., 209n1
Gruenther, K., 171
Guevara, J., 120
Guillaume, E., 98–99

H

Habel, S. K., 168
Hagen, B., 65
Halabi, A. K., 33, 45, 107
Hamilton, S. J., 170
Hancock, M. P., 67
Hansen, W. L., 139–140
Hanson, C. M., 168
Harrison, A.-L., 45–46, 121
Harrison, A. M., 78
Hartlaub, S., 145
Hartmann, D. J., 27, 46
Hartmann, J. Q., 68
Harward, B. M., 12, 45, 47–48
Hashmi, H., 171
Hathaway, D. K., 46
Hauhart, R. C., xi, xii, xiv, xv, xvii, 7–8, 13, 15, 25, 33, 37, 40, 42, 43–44, 45, 48, 50, 51, 52, 53, 55, 56–57, 73, 76, 92, 116, 119, 123, 124, 125, 130, 135, 144, 162, 178, 182, 184–185, 192, 212n5
Hay, E., 64
Haywick, D. W., 92–93
Healey, M., 45, 67, 70–71, 207n5
Hefferan, K. P., 121
Hefzy, M. S., 128
Heise, G. A., x
Henscheid, J. M., xii, 2, 3, 6, 11, 32–33, 35, 37, 40, 41, 42, 43, 44, 45, 48, 49–50, 51, 52, 53, 55, 57, 114, 115–116, 119, 124, 178, 203n3, 203n4
Hensel, N. H., 65, 77, 80, 101, 211n5
Heppner, F., 4
Herner-Patnode, L. M., 120
Heywood, N. C., 121
Hilton-Morrow, W., 64

Hitchcott, N., 209n1
Hodges, I. D., 72–73, 74, 87, 209n10
Hopkins, M., 2
Hora, M. T., 109
Howard, K., 210n2
Hummer, A., 185–186
Hundley, S. P., 170
Hunt, G. T., 47
Hunter, A.-B., 6–7, 64, 77
Hurley, S., 168, 170
Husic, D., 67

I

Ioannidis, J.P.A., 91
Irfanoglu, A., 76, 121, 207n5
Ishiyama, J., 46, 145, 182, 183–184

J

Jacobs, J. A., 169
Jenkins, A., 67, 70–71, 207n5
Jhaj, S., 111, 170, 177
Jimmieson, N. L., 82
Johari, A., 157
Johnson, E. J., 182
Johnson, G. F., 33, 45, 107
Johnson, R. L., 171
Johnston, P., 213n1
Jones, K. N., 92–93
Jones, K. W., 4–5, 43, 73, 85, 107, 112–113, 114, 115, 119, 124, 125, 129, 132–133, 138, 144, 146, 159–161, 163, 212n3 (chap. 7)
Juma, N. M., 141

K

Karukstis, K. K., 65, 77, 80, 93, 101, 211n5
Kaufman, M., 47
Kellett, P., 65
Kelly, M., 183
Kenny, R. W., 62
Kent, J. S., 45
Keogh, K., 125, 159
Kerrigan, S., 111, 170, 177
Kilgo, C. A., xii, xiv, xvii, 7, 11, 33–34, 37, 40, 41–42, 43,

44, 45, 51–52, 53–54, 55, 87, 116, 123, 165, 178, 202n1 (chap. 2), 203n4, 203n5
Kim, J. M., 75, 212n6
Kindelan, N., 47, 77
King, P. M., 150
Kinzie, J., 11, 67
Kitchener, K. S., 150
Klein, S., 64
Klos, N. Y., 46
Klunk, B. E., 183
Koch, D. C., 170
Kochen, M., 142
Kottsick, A., 76
Krathwohl, D., 154
Krilowicz, B. L., 75
Kuh, G. D., 90, 123, 212n1

L

Lambright, K. T., 105, 180–181
Landrum, R. E., 73
Laney, M. A., 171
Langford, J., 64, 66
Langlois, J., 120
Larsen, C., 168
Laursen, S. L., 6–7, 64, 77
Lawrie, G. A., 62, 97
Lee, H.-J., 120
Lee, K., 141–142
Lee, M. A., 76
Lee, N., 202n1 (chap. 3)
Levia, D. F. Jr., 121, 207n5
Levine, A., 2, 41
Levy, P., 72
Li, L. Y., 155
Light, S. A., 188–189
Lightfoot, T., 64, 66, 77
Lipson, C., 120
Locks, A. M., 77
Logue, E., 66, 68, 69–70
Lopatto, D., 9782
Lowther, M. A., 104
Lucas, C., 2

M

Maddux, C. D., 169, 213n1
Magleby, S. P., 105–106, 108–109, 174, 211–212n1, 212n3 (chap. 6)

Maki, P., 213n1
Malinauskas, M. J., 47
Mancha, R., 79, 86, 144
Masiello, L., 120
Mastrangeli, J., 139
Matthews, V. H., 178
McCann, L. I., 43, 63, 76, 181–182
McCorkendale, S. C., 171
McCormick, M., 211n5
McCullough, J., 67
McDaniels, P.E.W., 188
McGaw, D, 111
McGoldrick, K., 43, 45, 112, 119
McGuinness, C., 171
McKinney, K., 8, 111, 125, 140, 144–145, 146, 147, 189
McNair, T. B., 104, 105
McNary-Zak, B., 66
Menius, K., 122
Mercer, J. L., xii, 2, 6, 32–33, 40, 114
Merkel, C. A., 62
Merry, S., 152
Metz, T., 169
Meyer, L. H., 213n1
Michtom, W. D., 74–75
Milar, K. S., 181
Miller, W., 45
Moore, R. C., 170
Morgan, B. L., 182
Moskovitz, C., 120, 121
Motyl, M., 94
Multhaup, K. S., x

N

Nauta, M. M., 189–190
Nielson, M., 95, 102
Nosek, B. A., 94, 210n3

O

Obringer, J. W., 45
Oh, D. M., 75, 78
O'Hara, S., 4–5, 43, 73, 107, 138
Olwell, R., 132
Orel, S., 46, 47, 64, 66
O'Rourke, K., 74
Orsmond, P., 152

P

Padgett, R. D., xii, xiv, xvii, 7, 11, 33–34, 37, 40, 41–42, 43, 44, 45, 51–52, 53–54, 55, 87, 116, 123, 165, 178, 202n1 (chap. 2), 203n4, 203n5
Parfitt, M. K., 158, 181
Parker, S. L., 82
Pascual, R., 158
Pashler, H., 91
Pavlak, T., 127, 129, 131, 163
Payne, S. L., 146–147
Peat, B., 187
Pegg, S., 43
Pendlebury, M., 213n1
Pergram, D. M., 75
Perlman, B., 43, 63, 76, 181–182
Perry, A. L., 172
Persons, O. S., 153
Peters, R. T., 66
Peterson, C. D., 74–75
Phillips, J. S., 82
Pierce, P., 209n1
Plionis, E. M., 155
Plucker, C., 171
Posnick, M., 46, 161
Pourazady, M., 128
Przyborski, S., 71
Puca, R. M., 82
Pyrczak, F., 189

Q

Quarmby, K. A., 66
Quiring, S. M., 121, 207n5

R

Ramirez, J. J., 80
Ramsden, P., 212n1
Ramsey, D. D., 111, 121, 139–140
Rees, M., 213n1
Reid, M., 45
Reifman, A., 98
Reiling, K., 152
Reisser, L., 150
Resner, A., Jr., 120
Reuse-Durham, N., 152

Reynolds, J., 120, 121, 209n10
Rhodes, T. L., 170, 175–177
Richmond, A., 169, 213n1
Riehle, C. F., 155
Ritter, M. E., 121
Roberts, G. E., 127, 129, 131, 163
Rodrick, R., 64, 79, 134
Roens, S., 46, 47, 66, 77
Roethlisberger, F. J., 148
Roscoe, L. J., 134, 190
Rowland, S. L., 62, 63, 81, 97, 208n7
Rowles, C. J., 170, 173, 178, 213n2
Rudmann, J., 98–99
Russell, S. H., 67, 68–69, 82
Ryan, M. P., 104

S

Saey, T. H., 92
Saigo, R. H., 4
Sand, A., 64
Sandifer-Stech, D. M., 64, 65–66, 67, 206n3
Sax, L. J., 191, 192
Saxe, R., 102
Sayle, A., 120, 121
Schachter, D. R., 105
Schermer, T., x, xi, xii, xiii, 7, 11, 34, 37, 40, 42, 49, 52, 54, 55–56, 57, 58, 87, 93, 113, 118, 124, 134, 135, 185, 186, 202n2 (chap. 3), 204n6
Schmalt, H.-D., 82
Schmid, T. J., 20
Schneider, M. C., 93, 113–114, 126
Schrecker, E., 169
Schroeder, M. J., 76, 207n5
Schuurman, S., 120
Schwartz, D., 105
Scott, J. T., 64, 66
Senter, M. S., 168
Seo, E. H., 148
Seymour, E., 6–7, 64, 69, 77
Shaffer, C. D., 99–100
Shanahan, J. O., 46, 47, 63, 64
Sharma, M. P., 148–149
Sharobeam, M. H., 210n2

Sherohman, J., 18
Shively, J. W., 43
Siegfried, J. J., 112, 147
Sill, D., 12, 45, 48
Skipper, T. L., 120, 150–151
Slayton, D., 171, 178
Smallman, C., 128
Smith, R., 120, 121
Smith, W. L., 24–25
Snowball, D., 64
Spalter-Roth, R., 168, 183
Spies, J. R., 94, 210n3
Staple, D., 91
Stark, J. S., 104
Starke, M. C., 123
Steele, J. L., 23–24
Stephens, R. P., 4–5, 43, 73, 107, 138, 160
Sterling, L., 125, 159
Stix, A., 45
Stoloff, M., 13, 43, 45, 63, 81
Strapp, C. M., 134, 190
Straussman, J. D., 105
Sullivan, B., 120
Sum, P. E., 188–189
Svinicki, M. D., 145, 146
Swails, N., 205–206n1
Swaner, L. E., 62, 64, 66, 67, 110
Swift, J., 66

T

Tappert, C. C., 45
Taraban, R., 65, 66, 68, 69–70, 206n2
Tatro, B. J., 76
Thambyah, A., 154, 174
Thelin, J. R., 2
Thomas, D. R., 72–73, 74, 87, 209n10
Thomas, J., 205n1
Thomas, S., 120
Thompson, M., 155
Tice, D. M., 149
Tickles, V. C., 174
Tiemann, K. A., 27
Tierney, J. F., 3
Todd, R. H., 105–106, 108–109, 174, 211n1, 212n3 (chap. 6)
Trosset, C., 97

Troyer, R. J., 24
Twitty, G., 4

U

Unwin, S., 66
Upson-Saia, K., 9, 10, 33, 45, 107,
  110, 199

V

Van Acker, L., 109
Van der Veer, G., 4, 191
Vander Schee, B. A., 156
Vandermensbrugghe, J., 155
Varallo, S., 64
Venables, A., 125, 159

W

Wagenaar, T. C., 4, 18–19, 22
Wagenmakers, E., 91
Walker, D., 4
Wallace, R. C., 147
Walters, W. L., 174
Wang, X., 168, 170
Wasmundt, S., 121
Wattendorf, J. M., 26
Webber-Bauer, K., 6, 62, 69, 70,
  82, 206n4
Webber, K. L., 213n1
Weimer, M., 212n1
Weiner, S. A., 155
Weis, R., 121
Weiss, G. L., 168
Weschler, L., 111

Wessler, S. R., 76, 80, 207n5
Whitehead, A. N., 171
Whitfield, J. M., 146–147
Widner, S. C., 68
Wilbur, W., 64
Wilkinson, J. T., 112
Wilson, J., 171
Withers, G., 211n5
Woodard, R. J., 85–86, 135
Wright, B. D., 183
Wright, H. A., 148

Y

Yadong Li, 174
Yoder, C. Y., 79, 86, 144
Young, G., 46, 47, 66, 77
Youngblut, L. H., 120

SUBJECT INDEX

A

Academic credit, 48–49
Academic freedom, 169
Acceptance, 164–165
Accountability, 169, 172, 186
Accreditation Board for
    Engineering and
    Technology (ABET), 107,
    173–174
Accreditation standards,
    107–108, 172–175
Active learning, 152, 211n5
Activities. *See* Classroom activities
Administration: of capstone
    courses, 48–52; of
    undergraduate research,
    66
Admission, universal *versus*
    selective, 111–112,
    193–194
Adult identity transition:
    capstone courses for,
    20–22, 163–165;
    motivation and, 149–151;
    undergraduate research
    experiences for, 69

Alchemy, 90–91
Allegheny College, 7; capstone
    goals of, 34, 202n2
    (chap. 3); capstone
    prerequisites at, 113;
    capstone project archiving
    at, 58; faculty mentors at,
    56
American Association of Colleges
    and Universities, 13
American Chemical Society, 63
American Political Science
    Association, 3
American Psychological
    Association (APA) style,
    57, 126
American Sociological
    Association (ASA), 4;
    study-in-depth
    recommendations of, 18,
    19, 24; style guide of, 57
American sociology. *See*
    Sociology capstone
    courses
Archival work, 97–998
Arts: assessment in, 171;
    capstones in, 12–13,

46–48, 54; undergraduate
    research in, 47, 66, 77
Assessment: accountability and,
    169, 172, 186; best-
    practice recommendations
    for, 198; capstone course
    for, 167–190; of career
    preparation capstones,
    189–190; cost *versus*
    quality issue in, 183; data
    gathering for, 177; direct,
    178–179, 182, 183,
    184–189; discipline-
    specific, 178–186;
    externally-driven, 5,
    23–24, 36, 168, 169,
    172–175; faculty
    resistance to, 168–170;
    flow of influence in
    externally-driven,
    174–175; formative, 184;
    general education,
    175–178; general
    resources on, 213n1;
    versus grading, 168;
    in-class methods of, 183;
    indirect, 179, 182, 188; of

Assessment (*continued*)
  intangible learning,
  185–186; of integrative
  capstone courses,
  181–182; internally-
  driven, 172–173,
  175–186; of internships,
  179–181; major paper
  evaluation in, 184–189;
  methods of, 179;
  movement, 168–169, 170,
  179; outside-class, 183;
  prevalence of capstone
  courses in, 6, 7; purposes
  of, 167–170; rationale for,
  170–172; suitability and
  efficacy of capstones for,
  170–172, 190; summative,
  184. *See also* Negative
  assessments; Outcomes;
  Positive assessments
Association for Psychological
  Sciences, 91
Association of American Colleges
  and Universities (AACU),
  3–4, 24, 66, 143–144
Augustana College, 7, 49, 113;
  campuswide presentations
  at, 58, 185; capstone goals
  of, 34, 202n2 (chap. 3);
  faculty mentors at, 56
Authentic research experiences,
  100–101
Authoring *versus* producing,
  70–72

B

Baccalaureate institutions:
  classroom activities in, 53;
  prevalence of capstone
  courses in, 44
Behavioral sciences research
  projects: case study type
  of, 76; program evaluation
  type of, 76. *See also*
  Psychology research
Best-practice recommendations,
  193–199
Binghamton University, 180–181
"Bio 2010: Transforming
  Undergraduate Education

for Future Research
  Biologists" (National
  Research Council), 63,
  205n1
Biology capstones: alternative
  forms of, 45–46, 121,
  208n9; peer review in,
  152; research influences
  on, 4
Biology research: benefits of,
  69–70; departmental
  considerations for, 78;
  faculty considerations for,
  80; opportunities in, 63,
  205n1, 209n10
BioTAP, 209n10
Bloom's taxonomy, 154
Book project, 73, 160
Boyer Commission on Educating
  Undergraduates in the
  Research University, 4, 62
Brigham Young University
  (BYU), 106, 108–109
Business: capstones in, 121, 128,
  146–147, 157; research
  projects in, 76

C

California State Polytechnic
  University, Pomona, 178
California State University, Los
  Angeles, 78
Campuswide presentations, 58,
  161, 185
Capstone, defined, 10, 11
Capstone conferences, 57
Capstone course(s):
  administration of, 48–52;
  alternative types of, 39,
  44–48, 179; assessment
  and, 5, 6, 7, 23–24, 36,
  167–190; best-practice
  recommendations for,
  193–199; characteristics
  of, 39–59;
  communication about, 86;
  contextual nature of, 11,
  29–30; curricular role of,
  15–38; defined, 10–11;
  design of, 103–135;
  disciplinary *versus*

interdisciplinary, 10–11;
  drivers of, 3–5, 28–29, 36,
  103–104; foundational
  research on, 5–9; goals of,
  8, 15–38; as high-impact
  practice, 66, 165;
  historical overview of,
  2–3; influential research
  leading to, 3–5;
  multidisciplinary, multi-
  institutional research on,
  40, 41–42, 58; 1980s-1990s
  era of, 2, 3–4; overview of,
  1–13; as part of integrated
  course sequence, 49;
  popularity of, 3, 13;
  recommendations for
  ideal, 191–199; teaching,
  137–165; as transition to
  adulthood, 20–22,
  150–151, 163–165;
  twenty-first-century, 3,
  5–9, 13, 42–48; types of,
  11, 39, 44–48, 179; typical
  model of, defined, 39,
  58–59; undergraduate
  research leading to,
  61–87, 89–103. *See also*
  Outcomes; Prevalence
"Capstone Course, The"
  (Teaching Sociology), 17–30
Capstone Curriculum Across
  Disciplines, 9, 202n1
Career center usage, 53
Career preparation capstones,
  46, 189–190
Career preparation goals, 21, 31,
  32, 34, 35
Carleton College, 112–113, 161
Carnegie Council on Policy
  Studies in Higher
  Education, 41
Carnegie Foundation for the
  Advancement of
  Teaching, 8, 62
Case study projects, 75–76
Cautionary warnings, 149, 197
Center for Open Science (COS),
  96, 210n3–4
Centre for Collaborative
  Learning and Teaching, 9

Challenge of Connecting Learning, The (AAC), 24

Change, in higher education, 28–29, 36, 37–38. *See also* Curricular reform and innovation

Chemistry research: departmental considerations for, 78; history of, 91; opportunities in, 63

Chicago Manual of Style, 57

Choice. *See* Intentionality; Student choice

Citations, 57, 195

Citizenship goals, 20–22, 191–192

Class size: considerations in, 115–116; equation for, 50; importance of small, 24–25, 26; research findings on, 49–51, 115–116

Classics, undergraduate research in, 66

Classroom activities: research findings on, 52–54; sequencing of, 130–133; supplemental, 53, 123–124, 132, 194

Classroom discussions, 53

Cognitive skill development: assessment of, 185–186, 189; as capstone objective, 33–34; as capstone outcome, 5, 6

Collaborative course design, 105–106

Collaborative Replications and Education Project (CREP), 98–99, 101, 210n4

Collaborative research, 95, 96–100, 128

College of Wooster, 7, 49; campuswide presentations at, 58; capstone goals of, 34, 202n2 (chap. 3); capstone prerequisites at, 113; evaluation rubrics at, 186; faculty mentors at, 55–56, 205n8

Collegiality, 94–95

Colorado College, 49

Communication discipline, undergraduate research in, 64–65

Communities of practice, 158

Community-based learning, 179–181. *See also* External partnerships; Internships

Comprehensive exams, 45, 52, 54

Conference presentations, 57, 86, 93, 156, 159, 161, 188

Consensus view, in goal setting, 18–20, 22–23; debate *versus,* 17–18, 20, 22–23, 24

Conservation biology capstone, 45–46

Contribution to field, 82, 90, 96–98

Core curriculum: for academic preparedness, 145–146; connecting capstone design to, 106–107; connecting capstone goals to, 30–35; undergraduate research in, 61–87

Costs: of alternative capstone course formats, 39; of assessment, 183; of hosting student interns, 181; of undergraduate research projects, 69, 72–77, 93. *See also* Resource allocation

Council on Social Work Education, 212n3

Council on Undergraduate Research (CUR), 46, 62, 63–64, 93

Course catalogue, 86, 117–118

Course description, 116–118, 139, 194

Course mapping exercise, 188

Creating Effective Undergraduate Research Programs in Science (Taraban and Blanton), 148, 206n2

Credit, academic, 48–49

Criminal justice capstone. *See* Saint Martin's University,

Criminal Justice/Legal Studies Senior Seminar

Critical thinking: assessment of, 185–186; goal of, 33, 34, 201n1 (chap. 2), 203n5

Crowd-sourcing science project, 99

CUR Quarterly, 93

Curricular reform and innovation: contextual limitations in, 109–110; as driver of capstone course adoption, 28–29, 36, 103; intentionality in capstone design and, 104–105; research leading to capstone courses and, 3–5. *See also* Change, in higher education

D

Dartmouth College, 3

Data-collection research projects: costs and benefits of, 76–77; disciplinary considerations in, 122–123. *See also* Research projects

Data sharing, 94–95, 96–100, 102

Delivery options, research findings on, 51–52

DePaul University, 178

Description, capstone course, 116–118, 139, 194

Design, capstone course, 103–136; adjustment of, 147; best-practice recommendations for, 193–195; collaboration in, 105–106; constraints analysis in, 211n1; curricular fit and, 106–107; drivers of, 103–104; elements and guidelines for, 118–136; factors in, 103; faculty responsibility for, 17, 37; foundational components of, 104–108; intentionality in, 104–105, 138–139;

Design, capstone course
(*continued*)
internal components of,
110–118; learning
objectives as basis for,
108–111; professional
standards and, 107–108,
123; stakeholders in, 17,
105–106, 110–111,
212n2; of structural
framework, 108–118;
student preparedness
and, 147; teaching to the
planned, 137–140, 198
*Designing and Managing Your
Research Project* (Thomas
and Hodges), 87
"Digital Resource Data Sharing
and Management"
(National Science Board),
95
Disciplinary capstone courses:
assessment of, 178–186;
defining elements of, 10,
11; open *versus* select
admission to, 111–112,
193–194; prevalence of, 5,
6, 34–35, 42–44, 178;
recommendations for
ideal, 193–199; writing
style guides for, 56–57,
126. *See also*
Project/paper-based
capstone course
Disciplinary debate and
deliberation: consensus
view *versus,* 18–20,
22–23, 24; importance of,
16, 17–18, 24; process of,
22–23; as subject of
capstone courses, 25–26
Distance education capstone
courses, 45, 51–52
Doctorate-granting universities.
See PhD-granting
universities
Durham University, 71

E

Earth science research project,
74–75

Eastern Michigan University, 132
Economics capstones: admission
to, 111, 112; alternative
forms of, 45; proficiencies
list and, 139–140; writing
requirement in, 119
Emory University, 178
Empirical data-gathering
projects, 76–77, 122–123.
See also Research projects
Empowerment. *See* Student
choice
Engagement. *See* Student
motivation and
engagement
Engineering capstones: for
accreditation assessment,
173–175; collaborative
design of, 105–106;
learning objectives in,
108–109, 154; real-world,
121, 207n5; task
sequencing of, 133;
team-based, 128
Engineering research, 95, 107
English, undergraduate research
in, 66
Enrollment size, 115–116, 194
Ethical issues: capstone design
and, 107–108; in
empirical research,
90–92, 94–95
Ethical standards, 107–108
Exhibitions, 47–48, 52, 54
Exit interviews and surveys, 184,
188
Expectations. *See* Student
expectations
External partnerships:
assessment of capstones
in, 179–181; capstone
course design and,
105–106, 108–109;
collaborative relationships
with, 105–106, 157–158;
with research or grant
proposal projects, 75; role
relationships in, 157–158,
181, 197. *See also*
Internships
Externally-mandated
assessments, 5, 23–24, 36,

168, 169, 172–175. *See also*
Assessment

F

Faculty incentives and support,
for undergraduate
research, 65, 80
Faculty instructors: design and
implementation
responsibility of, 17, 37,
110; Hawthorne effect of,
148; instructor effect of,
206n3; prevalence of, by
type, 50; role of, in
monitoring internships,
157–158; topic selection
and, 55, 56, 126–129. *See
also* Single-instructor
model
Faculty-led research, 70–72
Faculty mentors: factors related
to, 55–56, 79–80, 205n8;
negative experiences of,
93; student satisfaction
with, 9; topic selection
and, 55, 56, 126–129; in
undergraduate research,
79–80, 87. *See also*
Single-instructor model
Faculty research productivity:
integration of teaching
with, 94; literature reviews
and, 73; pressures of,
93–94, 209n2;
undergraduate research
and, 80, 93–94, 96
Faculty-student meetings, 55,
116, 133–134, 196, 205n7
Faculty-student ratio, 24–25, 26
Faculty time and workload:
assessment and, 169–170,
183; compensation and,
169–170; at large public
universities, 209n2; with
mentor role, 55–56; with
research-based capstones,
142–143; research
productivity pressures
and, 93–94, 209n2; with
research projects, 65, 74,

77, 79–80, 92, 93, 209n2, 211n5
Family-life-preparation goals, 21, 31
Family studies, undergraduate research in, 65–66
Feedback mechanisms, 142–144, 149. *See also* Assessment
Fieldwork capstones. *See* External partnerships; Internships
Final exam. *See* Comprehensive exams capstones
Financial accounting capstones, 45, 153
Florida Atlantic University, 65
Focus groups, 182
Forced participation models, 128–129
Four-year institutions. *See* Baccalaureate institutions
Fraud, 90–92, 195, 209n1

G

General education capstone courses: admission to, 111; assessment and, 175–178; defining elements of, 10–11; prevalence of, 5, 178. *See also* Interdisciplinary capstone courses; Liberal arts curricula capstone courses
Genomics Education Partnership, 99–100, 101, 102
Genomics research projects, 99–100, 207n5
Geography capstone, 121
Geological Society of America, 92–93
Gifted students. *See* Students, better/high-performing
Goals and objectives: across the liberal arts curriculum, 30–35; active choice in, 24, 25–26, 29, 30, 37–38, 104; assessment to, 23–24, 184; consensus views on, 18–20, 22–23; disciplinary debate on, 16, 17–18, 22–23, 24;

identification of, 16; institutional structure and, 23; for learning outcomes, 154; lessons learned about, in sociology, 28–30, 36–37; moral aspects of, 20–22, 25–26, 29; research overview on, 8; in sociology, 15, 16–30, 191–192; structural framework in service of, 108–110; students' long-term, 80–81; subject to change, 191–192; summary overview of, 35–38
Grade point average, 9
Grading: assessment *versus*, 168; best-practice recommendations for, 198; of final capstone project, 57–58, 186–189; of integrative capstone course, 182; of major paper, 57–58, 186–189; as motivation, 156; in peer review, 152–153; of research projects, 76; rubrics for, 143–144, 152–153, 186–189; student choice in, 156, 195
Graduate school preparation: as goal of capstone courses, 31, 35; prevalence of, 53; research projects and, 80–82
Grand Valley University School of Social Work, 120
Grant proposals, 74–75
Grinnell College, 6–7

H

Harvard University, 159
Harvey Mudd College, 6–7
Hawthorne effect, 148
High-impact practice(s): capstone courses as, 66, 165; "constrained" and "unconstrained" models of, 66; student-faculty

interaction as, 134, 135; undergraduate research as, 66–77
High-performing students. *See* Students, better/high-performing
Higher Education Encyclopedia, 3
History: literature reviews in, 73; undergraduate research opportunities in, 64–65, 97–98, 102
History and Systems of Psychology course, 45, 181–182
History capstone courses: length of, 114; portfolio, 120; preparation for, 112–113, 146; research influences on, 4–5; student motivation in, 144; task sequencing of, 132–133
History Today, 209n1
Hood Theological Seminary, 120
Hope College, 6–7, 161
Humanities, undergraduate research opportunities in, 64–65, 66
Hunter Council, 98

I

Ill-structured problems: learning outcomes and, 154; procrastination and, 148–149; student transition to, 141–142, 150
Illinois State University (ISU), 125, 140, 189–190
Incorporation, 164–165
Indiana University, 160, 178
Industry-sponsored capstones, 108–109, 157–158
Information literacy, 155
InnoCentive, 95
Inquiry-based learning model, 70–72
Institutional benefits, of undergraduate research, 73, 96, 100
Institutional culture: and capstone development,

Institutional culture (*continued*)
    36, 51, 54; and curricular
    innovation, 109–110
Institutional review board
    approval, 92, 94
Institutional size: class size and,
    50; goals and, 33;
    importance of, 25; and
    prevalence of capstone
    courses, 42–44;
    undergraduate research
    and, 207n6
Institutional type: capstone
    course size and, 116;
    classroom activities by, 53;
    goals by, 34, 201n1
    (chap. 2); importance of,
    25; and prevalence of
    capstone courses, 42–44;
    and prevalence of online
    capstones, 52; research
    overview by, 7–8
Integration goals, 30, 31–32, 33,
    34, 38; assessment of,
    181–182
Integrity in the College Curriculum
    (AAC), 3–4
Intentionality: in capstone
    design, 138–139, 193; in
    capstone goals, 24, 25–26,
    29, 30, 37–38; in
    curricular innovation,
    104–105
Interdisciplinary capstone
    courses: admission to, 111;
    assessment and, 175–178;
    choice of, 193; defining
    elements of, 10–11; goals
    of, 33; prevalence of, 5,
    178. *See also* General
    education capstone
    courses; Liberal arts
    curricula capstone courses
International Situations Project,
    98
International studies capstones,
    45, 46
Internships, 39; assessment of,
    179–181; collaborative
    design of, 105–106; costs
    of, 181; defining
    expectations for, 121, 122;

prevalence of, 45, 52, 54,
    204n6; role relationships
    in, 157–158, 181, 197;
    success factors for, 181
Interviews, 182, 184

L

Laboratory costs, 76–77
Laramie Project, The, 47
Leadership training, 53
LEAP initiative, 36, 202n2
    (chap. 2)
Learning-through-teaching
    activity, 188
Lecture-based, integrative
    courses, 45–46
Lecturing, prevalence of, 53
Legal studies capstones. *See* Saint
    Martin's University,
    Criminal Justice/Legal
    Studies Senior Seminar
Length, capstone course, 114. *See
    also* Page length
Leon, United States v., 122
Liberal arts curricula capstone
    courses: defining
    elements of, 10–11;
    eighteenth-century, 2;
    goals of, 30–35. *See also*
    General education
    capstone courses;
    Interdisciplinary capstone
    courses
Liberal Education and America's
    Promise (LEAP), 36,
    202n2 (chap. 2)
*Liberal Learning and the Sociology
    Major* (ASA), 24
Library: access, 73; support
    activities, 123–124, 155,
    196
Literature review: conceptual
    versus systematic, 72–73;
    costs and benefits of, 73;
    meta-analysis, 74; rubrics
    for grading,186–187
Location of delivery, 51–52
Long-term goals, student,
    80–81
Loras College, 24–25

M

Magnets, 173, 213n2
Major Field Aptitude Test II, 145
Major projects. *See* Exhibitions;
    Paper, major;
    Performances; Portfolios;
    Project/paper-based
    capstone course
    (discipline-specific);
    Research projects
Manhattanville College, 161
Massachusetts Institute of
    Technology (MIT), 62
MA-granting institutions:
    prevalence of capstone
    courses in, 44; research
    projects in, 207n6
Meta-analysis projects, 74
Methodology, of capstone course
    research studies, 5–9
Millikin University, 178
Modern Language Association,
    57, 126
Monmouth College, 37
Moral-political perspectives,
    20–22, 25–26, 29
Motivation. *See* Student
    motivation
Mountaintops, 173, 213n2
"Multiple Approaches to
    Transformative Research"
    (Karukstis), 211n5
Music: capstones in, 46–47, 54;
    undergraduate research
    in, 66, 77

N

National Association of Schools
    of Public Affairs and
    Administration
    (NASPAA), 172–173
National Council on
    Undergraduate Research,
    62
National Institute of Mental
    Health, 94–95
National Institutes of Health, 75
National Research Council, 63,
    66, 205n1
National Research Project, 98

National Resource Center for the
Study of the First Year
Experience and Students
in Transition, 5–6
National Science Board, 90, 95
National Science Foundation
(NSF), 66, 75; data
sharing of, 94–95;
Research Experiences for
Undergraduates (REU),
62; student learning
benefits from programs
of, 68–69
National Survey of Senior
Capstone Experiences
(NSSCE), 202n2
Natural science capstone
courses: collaborative
research in, 97; research
findings on, 6–7
Negative assessments: by faculty
mentors, 93; importance
of examining, 9–10,
12–13; of undergraduate
research opportunities, 82
Newport University, 20
"Next Step, The" (Hartmann), 27
Northern Michigan University
(NMU), 139
Northwestern University, 161
Nursing capstone course, 139

O

Oberlin College, 159
Objectives. *See* Goals and
objectives
Online appendixes
(www.osf.io/tg6fa), xv,
xviii, 9, 123, 143, 202n1,
207n5
Online capstone courses, 45,
51–52
Online discussion forums, 158
Open Science Framework (OSF)
software, 210n3–4
Open science initiatives, 96
Open source journals, 91
Oral presentations: of better
students' work, 160–161;
peer review of, 124, 135,
149, 151, 196; prevalence

of, 52, 53, 57–58; types of,
57–58
Outcomes, capstone course:
assessment of, 167–190;
research overview of, 5–9;
undergraduate research
experiences and, 61. *See
also* Assessment; Goals
and objectives; Student
learning benefits
Outcomes, undergraduate
research: critical success
factors for, 79;
impediments to
successful, 92–96; student
controlling factors in,
80–83; by type of research
experience, 70–72; by
type of research project,
72–77; variables in, 66–72
Outlet option, 127
Oxford College, Emory
University, 178

P

Pace University, 45
Pacific Lutheran University
(PLU), xiv; capstone
credit at, 49; collaborative
research at, 98; grading
rubrics of, 76; music
capstones of, 46–47;
public presentations at,
57, 208n9; research
process at, 84, 87
Pacific Sociological Association,
xiv–xv, 7, 201n1 (chap. 1)
Page length: required minimum,
39, 56, 125–126, 195,
205n9; in sociology, 25
Paper, major: archiving, 58; for
assessment, 184–186;
characteristics of, 56–57;
defining the requirements
of, 119–123, 194;
elements of, research
findings on, 54–58;
format of, 126; grading of,
57–58, 186–189; page
length of, 39, 56,
125–126, 195, 205n9;

peer review of, 53,
123–124, 135, 151–153,
196; prevalence of, 52, 53,
54; public presentation of,
57–58, 159–162; readers
of, 57; references in, 56,
195. *See also*
Project/paper-based
capstone course
(discipline-specific)
Paper-based capstone course. *See*
Project/paper-based
capstone course
Participant observation, 122
Participation, universal *versus*
selective, 111–112
Peer review: with better students,
153, 196; design
considerations for,
123–124, 135;
instructional use of, 149,
151–153, 196; of major
papers, 53, 123–124, 135,
151, 196; marking criteria
for, 152–153; of oral
presentations, 124, 135,
149, 151, 196
Peer Review, x
Peer-reviewed research, 91,
129–130, 161–162, 195
Performances: prevalence and
types of capstone, 46–47,
54, 58; as research
experiences, 77
Perspectives on Psychological Science,
91, 94
PhD-granting universities:
classroom activities in, 53;
prevalence of capstone
courses in, 44; research
projects in, 207n6
Plagiarism, 195. *See also* Fraud
Political science capstone
courses: assessment of,
183–184, 187–189;
impediments to successful
completion of, 93;
prerequisites for,
113–114, 145; research
influences on, 3
Polymath Project, 95

Portfolios: art exhibition, 47–48,
77; for better students,
159–160; defining
expectations for, 120;
prevalence of, 53; public
recognition of, 159–160;
web-based, 120, 212n3
Portland State University (PSU),
111, 175–177
Positive assessments: intrinsic
motivation and, 82–83;
research findings on, 5,
8–9
Postcollege preparation:
assessment of, 189–190;
goals of, 20–22, 30, 31, 35
Poster conference, 208n9
Practical skills improvement,
findings on, 5
Practicum-based capstone
courses. See External
partnerships; Internships
Preparation for capstones:
addressing insufficient,
within capstone course,
146–163, 197–198;
approaches to improving,
144–163; core curriculum
for, 145–146;
prerequisites and,
112–114; prevalence of
courses for, 7; problem of
insufficient, 144–145;
structural approach to,
144–145; support services
for, 155; undergraduate
research for, 68, 85–87,
89–103. See also Student
preparedness
Prerequisite courses, 112–114,
194
Presentations, 39; for assessment,
188; for better students,
159–163; conference, 57,
86, 93, 156, 159, 161, 188;
public, 57–58, 159–162,
208n9. See also
Exhibitions; Oral
presentations;
Performances
Pretesting, 146

Prevalence of capstone courses:
alternative format,
44–48; discipline based, 5,
6, 42–44, 178; by
institutional type and size,
42–44;
interdisciplinary/general
education, 5, 178;
research overview on,
5–9; in twenty-first
century, 3, 5, 13, 42–48;
by type of capstone
experiences, 44–48; by
type of final product,
52–54; typical format, 5,
8, 42–44, 48
Private institutions: capstone
course type preferred by,
7; classroom activities in,
53; goal preferences of,
34; prevalence of capstone
courses in, 43–44;
prevalence of online
capstones in, 52
Problem-solving skills: as
capstone goal, 33, 34;
with ill-structured versus
well-structured problems,
141–142, 150, 154
Procrastination, 147, 148–149,
196, 197
Producing versus authoring,
70–72
Products, capstone: assessment
of, 184, 185; design
considerations for,
119–123; prevalence and
types of, 52–54. See also
Exhibitions; Oral
presentations; Paper,
major; Performances;
Portfolios; Presentations
Professional associations:
assessment and, 172–173;
writing style guides of, 57,
126
Professional experiences, types
of, 39. See also Internships
Professional standards, 107–108,
123
Professionalism-versus-morality
debate, 25–26, 29

Proficiencies list, 139–140
Program assessment. See
Assessment
Program evaluation projects,
75–76
Project Kaleidoscope, 62
Project management: of research
projects, 86–87;
sequencing and time line
for, 130–133, 147, 149,
195–196
Project/paper-based capstone
course
(discipline-specific):
administration of, 48–52;
assessment of, 182–186;
characteristics of, 39–59;
classroom activities in,
52–54; defining elements
of, 39, 42–48, 58–59;
design of, 103–136;
faculty workload in,
142–143; major paper in,
54–58; recommendations
for ideal, 193–199;
teaching, 137–165; as
typical format, 39, 48,
58–59
Proposals, research/grant, 74–75
Psi Chi, 98, 210n4
Psychology capstone courses:
alternative forms of, 45;
assessment of, 184–185,
189–190; characteristics
of, 40; classroom activities
in, 53; data collection and
analysis in, 122–123;
faculty-student meetings
in, 55, 205n7; goals of, 8,
15, 33, 191–192; history
and systems, 181–182;
impediments to
completion of, 92;
internship, 157–158;
major papers in, 56–57,
119; overview of research
on, 7–8; peer review in,
124; student engagement
in, 144
Psychology research: across
multiple institutions, 98;
benefits of, 69–70; crisis

of confidence in, 91, 94; empirical, data collection type of, 76; opportunities in, 63; range of types of, 84

Public administration capstones, 45

Public institutions: capstone course type preferred by, 7; classroom activities in, 53; faculty time pressures at, 209n2; goal preferences of, 34; prevalence of capstone courses in, 43–44; prevalence of online capstones in, 52

Publication: of better students' work, 160–162; of fraudulent research, 91; paper standards and, 205n9; preparation for, 161–162; of research papers, 73, 84, 96, 100–101, 160, 161–162; revision of process of, 91–92, 102

Purdue University, 207n5

Q

Question framing: for ill-defined problems, 142; for research projects, 126–129, 142

R

Rational model of organizational action, 29

Reading lists, common, 53

Real-world problem-based learning, 119, 121, 157, 179. *See also* Internships

Redundancy, 107

References: minimum number of, 56, 130; policies on, 129–130, 195; type of, 57

Reinventing Discovery: The New Era of Networked Science (Nielson), 95

Religion, undergraduate research in, 66

Religion capstone courses: alternatives types of, 45; approach to, 85–86; curricular alignment of, 107; design of, 107, 110; negotiation assessments of, 10; peer review in, 135; portfolio, 120

Replicability, 90–92

Research, undergraduate. *See* Undergraduate research

Research methods courses: nonscience majors' barriers to, 64; sequencing of, 85

Research paper. *See* Paper, major

Research project capstone courses. *See* Project/paper-based capstone course

Research projects: across multiple institutions, 98–100; authoring *versus* producing, 70–72; collaborative, 95, 96–100; considerations in implementing, 78–83; that contribute to professional research, 82, 90, 96–98; costs and benefits of, 72–77; defining expectations for, 120; generic, mapping student journeys onto, 83–84; impediments to successful completion of, 92–95; project management of, 86–87; question framing for, 126–129, 142; role and design of, 61–87; scientific model for, 83–84; student learning benefits from, 66–70; student performance parameters and, 81–82; successful, defined, 80; transformative, 36, 80–83, 90, 100–101, 211n5; types

of, 72–77, 84. *See also* Undergraduate research

Research proposals, 74–75

Research resources, 73, 74, 87

Research résumé, 85, 146

Research skill development, as capstone goal, 34

Research studies, on capstone courses: foundational, 5–9; that inspired adoption and development, 3–5, 29–30; longitudinal, 206n4; multidisciplinary, multi-institutional, 40, 41–42, 58; website resources on, 9, 202n1

Research Synthesis and Meta-Analysis (Cooper), 74

Resource allocation: capstone design and, 109–110; class size and, 51; institutional change and, 36; institutional type and, 44; for undergraduate research, 78–80. *See also* Costs

Rider College, 26–27

Rite of passage, 20–22, 163–165, 197–198. *See also* Student transitions

S

Saint Martin's University: capstone course description of, 117, 118; enrollment at, 212n4; peer review at, 135; senior thesis projects of, 121; task sequencing at, 131

Saint Martin's University, Criminal Justice/Legal Studies Senior Seminar, xi–xii, xiv, 117; course description of, 117, 118; enrollment in, 212n4; minimum page length in, 130; peer review in, 135; Scholar's Day at, 162; structural framework of,

Saint Martin's University
(*continued*)
121–122; topic selection
for, 135
SBES (social, behavioral,
economic science)
research projects, 68–69
Scaffolding, of research across
the curriculum, 64–65
Scheduling, of work assignments,
130–133
School Spirit Study Group, 98
Scientific method: crisis of
confidence in research
and, 90–92; model of, as
journey map, 83–84, 131
Seattle University, 175
Second-language speakers, 155
Senior culminating experience.
See Capstone courses
Senior seminar, 2. *See also*
Capstone course
Senior thesis, 119–120, 121, 124,
186–189. *See also* Paper,
major
Sequencing: for academic
preparedness, 145–146;
of capstone course in core
curriculum, 49; of
capstone prerequisites,
112–114, 194; of research
opportunities with
capstone courses, 64,
65–66, 78, 83–85; task,
130–133, 149, 195–196
Service learning: assessment of,
180–181; in performing
arts programs, 77;
prevalence of, 53
Single-instructor model: class size
and, 116; factors in choice
of, 50–51; prevalence of,
50–51, 116; topic
selection and, 55. *See also*
Faculty instructors;
Faculty mentors
Sinkers, 65
Skill development outcomes, 5,
6, 33–34
Social action, 28, 29
Social work capstone, 152–153
Sociological perspective, 20

Sociology capstone courses:
assessment-inspired,
23–24, 184–185;
characteristics of, 40;
classroom activities in, 53;
consensus voices on,
18–20, 22–23; data
collection and analysis in,
122–123; disciplinary
debate about, 16, 17–18,
22–26; faculty-student
meetings in, 55, 205n7;
goals of, 8, 15, 16–30, 33,
191–192; impediments to
completion of, 92; lessons
learned from, 28–30,
36–37; major papers in,
56–57, 119; overview of
research on, 7–8; peer
review in, 124; principles
that support, 26–27;
research influences on, 3,
4; student engagement in,
144; student preparation
for, 146; unanswered
questions about, 27
Southeast Missouri State
University (SMSU),
177–178
Southern Illinois University
(SIU), Edwardsville,
12–13
Southern Polytechnic State
University, 178
Southwest Missouri State
University, 178
Status, and Hawthorne effect,
148
STEM (science, technology,
engineering, and math)
research projects, 68–69,
209n10
Structure: best-practice
recommendations for,
193; building the internal,
110–118; confronting
insufficient preparation
and motivation with,
144–145; design of,
108–136; learning
objectives as basis for,

108–111; specific
guidelines for, 118–136
Student choice: in evaluation,
156, 195; in final product
presentation, 156;
motivation and, 128–129,
155–156, 159, 195; in
student-instructor
meetings, 133–134, 196;
in task completion, 131;
in topic selection, 55, 56,
126–129, 155–156
Student evaluation. *See* Grading
Student expectations: aligning
course requirements and,
124–125, 140, 141–144,
194; designing a
framework for, 118–124;
general and specific, 140;
guiding, with feedback,
142–144
Student factors, for
transformative research
projects, 80–83
Student-faculty meetings: class
size and, 116; frequency
of, 55, 134, 205n7; as
high-impact practice, 133;
required *versus* optional
student-initiated,
133–134, 196
Student feedback, 142–144. *See
also* Assessment; Grading;
Peer review
Student learning benefits: factors
in, 68–72; measurement
of, 178–179; as primary
consideration in design
choices, 108–111; specific
learning outcomes and,
154; from undergraduate
research opportunities,
66–69, 72–77, 80–83, 96,
100. *See also Outcomes
headings*
Student-led research, 70–72
Student maturity level, 92,
149–151. *See also* Student
transitions
Student motivation and
engagement: approaches
to improving, 144–163,

197–198; of better
students, 158–163, 197;
extrinsic, 147–148, 158;
intrinsic, 82–83, 147–148,
158; maturity level and,
149–151; meeting
expectations and, 140;
problem of insufficient,
92, 138, 144–145; in
research projects, 73,
82–83, 96; student choice
and, 128–129, 155–156,
159, 195; using, to inspire
extra effort, 147–148
Student perceptions,
measurement of, 179, 182,
184, 188, 189–190
Student preparedness:
addressing, within
capstone course,
146–163, 197–198;
approaches to improving,
144–163; assessing,
146–147; course design
and, 147; for ill-structured
problems, 141–142, 150;
prerequisites and,
112–114, 194; problem of
insufficient, 144–145; for
research projects, 92,
113–114, 208n8; support
services for, 155, 196. *See
also* Preparation for
capstones
Student time limitations, 92
Student transitions: to adult
identity, 20–22, 69,
149–151, 163–165,
197–198; assessment of
courses geared toward,
189–190; to reflexive
thinking, 150; from
well-structured to
ill-structured problems,
141–142, 150
Students, better/high-
performing: motivating,
158–163, 197; in peer
review, 153, 196;
presentation
opportunities for,
159–163; in

undergraduate research,
70, 81–82
Study abroad programs, 45, 77
Supplemental activities, 53,
123–124, 132, 194
Surveys, student, 184, 188
Swimmers, 65
Synthesis goals, 30, 31–32, 33,
34, 164–165

T

Task sequencing, 130–133, 149,
195–196
Teachers, preservice, 120
Teaching, capstone course,
137–165; best-practice
recommendations for,
195–197; to the design
plan, 137–140, 198;
general resources on,
212n1; integration of
research time with, 94;
skill sets for, 140–141;
student expectations and,
140, 141–144
Teaching Sociology, "The Capstone
Course," 17–30
Team teaching model:
prevalence of, 50, 116; for
research projects, 87
Teamwork skills goal, 201n1
(chap. 2)
Tectonic Theatre Company, 47
Theater, undergraduate research
in, 66, 77
Theatrical production, 47
Theory *versus* application debate,
29
Time line, work completion,
130–133, 147, 149,
195–196
Topic selection: approaches to,
126–129; factors in,
55–56; faculty expertise
and, 93; faculty research,
128; student choice in, 55,
56, 126–129, 155–156;
student factors in, 81–82,
92; timing of, 129
Transformative learning
experiences: active

learning and, 211n5; from
authentic research,
100–101; definition of,
90; movement toward, 36;
student factors in, 80–83;
success factors for, 90
Transformative research:
defined, 90;
undergraduate research
and, 96–98, 101
*Transformative Research at
Predominantly
Undergraduate Research
Institutions* (Karukstis and
Hensel), 101
Transitions. *See* Student
transitions
Trinity College, 144
Typical capstone course. *See*
Project/paper-based
capstone course

U

Unconscious beliefs and
assumptions, 104
Undergraduate research: across
disciplines, 63–66; across
multiple institutions,
98–100; alumni percep-
tions of, 6; for arts majors,
47, 66, 77; authentic
experiences in, 100–101;
barriers to, 64, 65–66,
211n5; better, high-
performing students in,
70, 81–82; collaborative,
95, 96–100; that contri-
butes to professional
research, 96–98; costs and
benefits of, by project
type, 72–77; critical
success factors for, 79;
departmental considera-
tions in, 78–79; ethical
issues in empirical
research and, 90–92,
94–95; factors in positive
experiences with, 9;
factors in student benefits
from, 66–70; faculty
resource considerations

Undergraduate research
    (*continued*)
        in, 79–80; as high-impact
        practice, 66–70;
        impediments to
        successful, 92–95;
        incorporating, in the
        curriculum, 78–83;
        journals of, 160; leading
        to capstone experience,
        61–87, 89–103; as motive
        for capstone courses, 5;
        movement of, 62; range of
        opportunities for, 62–63;
        rationale for, 61, 66–70;
        research study of, 8–9;
        resource allocation issues
        for, 78–80; role of, 61–87;
        sequenced with capstones,
        64, 65–66, 78, 85–87;
        student controlling
        factors in, 80–83. *See also*
        Research projects
Undergraduate research
    opportunities (UROs):
        across disciplines, 63–66;
        across multiple institu-
        tions, 98–100; benefits of,
        66–70, 96; dimensions of,
        67, 70–72; disparity in,
        67–78; faculty-led, 70–72;
        negative experiences with,
        82; range of, 62–63;
        research-content
        emphasis, 67; research-
        process emphasis, 67;
        research-tutored, 67;
        student-audience, 67;
        student-authored, 70–72;
        student-participant, 67. *See
        also* Research projects

Undergraduate Research
    Questionnaire,
    8–9
United States v. *Leon,* 122
University catalogue, 86,
    117–118
University of Baltimore, 172
University of Delaware, 6, 69
University of Detroit, Mercy,
    185–186
University of Louisiana, Monroe,
    178
University of Missouri, Kansas
    City, 112, 115, 125
University of Nebraska, 99
University of Nevada, Reno, 161
University of Queensland, 71
University of South Carolina,
    National Resource Center,
    5–6, 7, 30
University of Wisconsin,
    Madison, 139–140

V

Valid Assessment of Learning in
    Undergraduate Education
    (VALUE), 143–144
VALUE rubrics, 143–144
Victoria University, Melbourne,
    9, 202n1
Virginia Polytechnic Institute
    (Virginia Tech): the Book
    Project of, 160; campus
    presentations of, 161;
    enrollment at, 115;
    lecture-based capstone at,
    45–46; student
    preparation at, 112, 113,
    144, 146; task sequencing
    at, 132–133

W

Washington College, 7, 113;
    capstone course
    description of, 118;
    capstone goals of, 34,
    202n2 (chap. 3); capstone
    project archiving at, 58;
    faculty mentors at, 56
Wellesley College, 6–7
Western Electric Company,
    148
Western Oregon University,
    190
Western Psychological
    Association, 7
Williams College, 2
Wooster. *See* College of Wooster
Work completion time line,
    130–133, 147, 149,
    195–196
Writing centers, 155, 196
Writing requirements, 119. *See
    also* Paper, major
Writing styles, discipline-specific,
    56–57, 126, 195
Written communication goal,
    34
Written reviews, 149
Www.capstonecurriculum.com
    .au, 9
Www.osf.io/tg6fa, xv, xviii, 9,
    123, 143, 202n1, 207n5
Www.science-writing.org,
    209n10

Y

Yale University, 112, 113, 114,
    125, 129
York College, 78

If you enjoyed this book, you may also like these:

Engaging Imagination: Helping Students Become Creative and Reflective Thinkers by Alison James and Stephen D. Brookfield ISBN: 9781118409473

Creating Significant Learning Experiences: An Integrated Approach to Designing College Courses, Revised and Updated by Jeffrey L. Buller ISBN: 9781118124253

Engaging Ideas: The Professor's Guide to Integrating Writing, Critical Thinking, and Active Learning in the Classroom, 2nd Edition by John C. Bean ISBN: 9780470532904

WILEY